A CENTURY OF CIVIL RIGHTS

A CENTURY OF
CIVIL RIGHTS

By MILTON R. KONVITZ

With a Study of STATE LAW
AGAINST DISCRIMINATION

By THEODORE LESKES

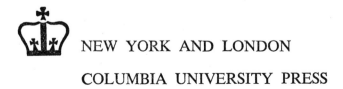

NEW YORK AND LONDON

COLUMBIA UNIVERSITY PRESS

For Mary and Florence

PREFACE

About a hundred years ago, on March 11, 1861, the congress of the Confederate States, meeting in Montgomery, Alabama, adopted a constitution that contained the following significant provisions regarding slavery:

Congress was to have no power to enact any law "denying or impairing the right of property in negro slaves." Art. I, sec. 9 (4).

Citizens of each state were to be entitled to all the privileges and immunities of citizens of the several states, and were to enjoy the right of transit and sojourn in any state of the Confederacy, "with their slaves and other property; and the right of property in said slaves shall not be thereby impaired." Art. IV, sec. 2 (1).

Fugitive slaves were not to be discharged from slavery "but shall be delivered up on claim of the party to whom such slave belongs." Art. IV, sec. 3.

Should the Confederate States acquire territory, "in all such territory, the institution of negro slavery, as it now exists in the Confederate States, shall be recognized and protected by Congress and by the territorial government; and the inhabitants of the several Confederate States and Territories shall have the right to take to such territory any slaves lawfully held by them in any of the States or Territories of the Confederate States." Art. IV, sec. 3.

What would have happened had the Confederate States won the Civil War? In all probability the entire South would be a battleground, where a war of the races would be constant and bitter, and a garrison state, in which no man, regardless of race or color, would enjoy the basic human freedoms.

About a hundred years ago, on January 1, 1863, Lincoln issued the Emancipation Proclamation, which freed the slaves in the Confederacy. Soon after the Civil War came other measures—constitutional and legislative—that sought to convert the freedmen into free men. The original liberating impulse, after a few years, was driven underground; but in our own day we have seen this impulse express itself vigorously and stridently. The pace of progress, however, in winning freedom and equality cannot today be measured by the expectations that may have been satisfactory even a generation ago. At a time when new African and Asian nations are multiplying with breathtaking speed, so that one hardly has time to learn their names, the American Negro cannot be expected to feel gratified by the fact that six years after the Supreme Court's decision that schools should be desegregated "with all deliberate speed," only 6 percent of the Negro pupils in Southern and border states attend integrated schools. At this rate it will take a hundred years to achieve integration! (Of the eleven states that were in the Confederacy, no integration has taken place in five of them after six years, and no more than one percent has been achieved in the other six.) And even this snail's pace has been won only because the National Association for the Advancement of Colored People has brought case after case, day after day, in the federal courts, while it has been fighting for its own life and rights against a program of crippling harassment in the state legislatures and courts.

The American Negro is no longer patient with the slow progress of the legal and judicial process. Many young Negroes have begun to question the legal and constitutional framework within which the NAACP has for over fifty years proceeded and for which it can show a gratifying record of success. Nor are they satisfied with the record of Congress in the field of civil rights—

no action at all from 1875 to 1957 and the enactment of only two mild measures in the last few years. These young Negroes—inspired by the successful bus boycott in the city in which the Confederate constitution was adopted—have themselves begun to act against laws and customs that are immoral and an indignity to human nature itself.

✻ About a hundred years ago, on May 16, 1865, Massachusetts enacted the first state civil rights law in this country. This act introduced the notion that the state has the affirmative duty to assure to every person, without regard to his race or color, equality of treatment in places of public accommodation or resort. In a sense, this may be the most basic right of all, for it means the right to human dignity, the right to be free from humiliation and insult, the right to refuse to wear a badge of racial inferiority at any time or place. Without this sense of human dignity, one is not fully human. At this writing, twenty-seven states have such civil rights acts, and the United Nations Universal Declaration of Human Rights affirms that the "recognition of the inherent dignity and of the equal and inalienable rights of all members of the human family is the foundation of freedom, justice and peace in the world." But this conception of civil rights is contradicted by the laws or customs based on racist superiority that obtain in the South and the border states.The student lunchroom sit-ins, started in 1958 and revived in 1960, are an attempt to break down the pattern of racial discrimination and segregation where the Negro has no hope that the state legislature will pass a civil rights act (nor any expectation that Congress will act to nationalize the concept of civil rights as a guarantee of equality of treatment in public places). The Negro's struggle for civil rights, in this sense, has far-reaching constitutional, political, and social implications.

It is against these developments that this book has been written: an attempt to analyze the constitutional aspects of a century's struggle for civil rights—or the rights of human dignity.

Chapter 4 of this book has been taken substantially from chapter 2 of my book *The Constitution and Civil Rights* (New York, Columbia University Press, 1947); otherwise this is a completely new work. Mr. Leskes is the author of chapters 6–9.

I acknowledge gratefully the assistance of the Institute for Advanced Study at Princeton and the Walter E. Meyer Research Institute of Law at New Haven.

M. R. K.

I wish to thank the Institute of Human Relations of the American Jewish Committee for assistance.

T. L.

CONTENTS

INTRODUCTION

Chapter 1

FREEDMEN OR FREE MEN?

The neo-Kantian philosopher Hermann Cohen pointed out that it was the alien, the stranger, who introduced to the ancient Hebrews—and thus to the world—the idea of humanity.[1] It was not difficult to recognize a common humanity with one's kinsman, with a member of one's own tribe or nation; but the foreigner might be of another breed, another species. It was against the natural inclination of men to see kinship in the alien, and so they had to be commanded constantly to love the alien, the stranger. This commandment in the Old Testament was probably the first acknowledgment in history of a common humanity among all men, and, at the same time, it was a recognition of man's strong disinclination to assimilate the stranger to his own kin or nation.

In later ancient civilizations the slave may have played a similar role by challenging conventional conceptions of morality. As Alfred North Whitehead has maintained, just as freedom and equality constitute presuppositions of modern political thought, so slavery was the presupposition of ancient political theory. For example, classical Hellenic and Hellenistic Roman civilizations were based on the universal assumption that a large slave population was required to perform "services which were unworthy to engage the activities of a fully civilized man. . . . A comparatively barbarous substratum had to be interwoven in the social structure, so as to sustain the civilized apex." [2] To be civilized

[1] Konvitz, *Alien,* in ENCYC. BRITANNICA (1959).
[2] WHITEHEAD, ADVENTURES OF IDEAS 13–15 (1933).

was to be a slave owner. While some masters were kind—e.g., Cicero and Pliny the Younger—a basic fact was that efficiency meant brutality.

But another fact—eventually also to become basic—was in time introduced: the dignity of human nature, "the idea of the essential rights of human beings, arising from their sheer humanity." These great ideas, started by small, gifted groups, were, however, limited by slavery, and the new principles had to take their place "among the interesting notions which have a restricted application." A whole literature arose to explain how inspiring were the new principles and how slight need be their effect "in disturbing a comfortable society." But the general ideas remained as a threat to the slave civilizations, for it was possible that at any moment "the smouldering unhappiness of mankind" might seize on these ideas as a program of social reform and quickly make changes.

The idea of human dignity and essential human rights, before it shattered slavery and the civilizations built on slavery, became embodied in special, limited applications. The general idea, while it lost "the magnificence of its generality," gained "in the force of its peculiar adaptation to the concrete circumstances of a particular age." It became "a hidden living force, haunting humanity and even appearing in specialized guise as compulsory on action by reason of its appeal to the uneasy conscience of the age." [3] It took this "hidden driving force" some two thousand years to bring slavery to an end—a period of time that moved from Plato to the Stoic lawyers, through Christianity, through the seventeenth-century England of Locke, Newton, and the Regicides, through the skeptical humanitarianism of the eighteenth century —the Age of Reason and of the Rights of Man—through the Wesleyan Methodist movement. Through these millennia Europe withdrew from slavery to serfdom, from serfdom to feudalism, from feudalism to aristocracy, from aristocracy to legal

[3] *Id.* at 18–19.

equality, from legal equality to a social order that opened careers to men of talent, whatever their class. Through all these processes slavery was maintained as a decaying institution, until the British Parliament abolished the slave trade in 1808, and purchased and emancipated all slaves in the British dominions in 1833.[4]

Reflecting on the process that led from slavery, through the idea of humanity, to the act of emancipation in 1833, Whitehead observed that the "great idea in the background of dim consciousness" was "like a phantom ocean beating upon the shores of human life in successive waves of specialization. A whole succession of such waves are as dreams slowly doing their work of sapping the base of some cliff of habit: but the seventh wave is a revolution—'And the nations echo round.' " [5]

Ideas, however, do not act as the sole forces to bring about reforms and revolutions in social relations. "A great idea," one must note, "is not to be conceived as merely waiting for enough good men to carry it into practical effect. That is a childish view of the history of ideas. The ideal in the background is promoting the gradual growth of the requisite communal customs, adequate to sustain the load of its exemplification." [6] The ideas are conscious agencies of reform, but the reforms are due to a "coincidence of senseless forces [e.g., a barbarian invasion, floods, wars, technological innovations] and spiritual. Great ideas enter into reality with evil associates and with disgusting alliances." [7] "Senseless agencies [e.g., steam power] and formulated aspirations cooperate in the work of driving mankind from its old anchorage." [8] Thus, in the change from slavery to freedom, philosophy contributed the general ideas, law the constructive ability, religion the moral energy; and—from the seventeenth century onward—technology was the greatest accessory "senseless" force which weakened the supposed necessity for slavery.[9]

---

[4] Parliament appropriated £20,000,000 as compensation to the masters, and this was done at a time of grave financial difficulties in England. *Id.* at 23.
[5] *Ibid.*   [6] *Id.* at 26.   [7] *Id.* at 21–22.
[8] *Id.* at 7.   [9] *Id.* at 32–33.

While Whitehead's statement of historical causation seems to fit the illustration he chose—the abolition of the British slave trade in 1808 and the British emancipation act of 1833—some additional considerations play a role when we look at slavery in the Southern states of the United States. A number of significant facts readily come to mind: for instance, the fact that the great idea of "the essential rights of human beings, arising from their sheer humanity," was not a part of the consciousness of Southerners, not even as a "hidden driving force," from about 1831, when the first issue of the *Liberator,* edited by William Lloyd Garrison, appeared in Boston.[10] If the idea existed in the consciousness of any Southern intellectual, he had to keep the thought to himself, or move to another part of the country. The South would not tolerate any discussion of the notion that Negroes were human beings and, therefore, entitled to the essential rights of human beings. In fact, one was free to argue the negative but not the positive side of this proposition.[11] Anyone who held to the positive side of the proposition was branded a radical and a fanatic, and was subject to prosecution under state laws or to mob violence.

A Virginia statute made it a crime to maintain, by speaking or writing, "that owners have no property in slaves," and Louisiana made it a crime to engage in conversation "having a tendency to promote discontent among free[d] colored people, or insubordination among slaves," for which the punishment was from twenty-one years imprisonment with hard labor, to death. Since legal processes "were often slow and unsatisfactory, . . .

[10] At the same time, the Nat Turner insurrection occured at Southampton, which greatly influenced the Southern mind. On the other hand, the debates on slavery in the Virginia legislature also took place in 1831–32. They were probably the last expression of public sentiment against slavery in the South. After that, the Southern press was controlled, and no one dared express abolition sentiments. See Stampp, *The Fate of the Southern Anti-Slavery Movement,* 28 J. Negro Hist. 10 (1943).

[11] Eaton, Freedom of Thought in the Old South (1940); Nye, Fettered Freedom (1949).

to provide swifter and more effective punishment, the South turned to the device of the citizen-mob, long known on the frontier as 'lynch law.' " The South was afraid of the Southerner who entertained "unsound opinions" and of the Northerner, who was likely to spread antislavery doctrine.

To silence the one and eject the other, if legal means were too slow or not justified by the case, the citizen-mob, backed by popular opinion, was the most effective instrument. . . . As Southern opinion became more completely unified, the mob technique became highly organized, taking the pattern, in most of the Southern states, of the "vigilance committee" or the "committee of safety," formed by the community for its protection.[12]

Not only did the South avoid the idea of human equality; in order to effect total suppression of this idea, it became necessary, as a means to this accomplishment, to suppress freedom of speech, press, assembly, and petition, freedom of preaching, and academic freedom. The white man himself lost the most essential liberties in the process of denying all liberties to the Negro. There were no operative bills of rights in the South for the masters or, of course, for the slaves, and even the idea of justice was greatly weakened by reversion to self-help and lynch law.

In the South, then, beginning with the 1830s, slavery was not challenged by the great idea of human dignity or "the idea of the essential rights of human beings, arising from their sheer humanity." In this respect the South excluded itself from the mainstream of Western intellectual and spiritual history.

In another way, too, the South was an exception to the general historical pattern. In other countries conscious and unconscious agencies of reform cooperated to end slavery. In the South the conscious agencies of change were ruthlessly suppressed both by law and by mobs. But more than this, the unconscious forces were not permitted to operate in ways that might weaken slavery.

[12] Nye, *op. cit. supra* note 11, at 140–42.

Despite technological advances, slavery remained economically profitable to the end. The evidence is "that the average slave holder earned a reasonably satisfactory return upon his investment in slaves." Even in the 1850s "slavery was still justifying itself economically . . . the slave was earning for his owner [in the decade before the Civil War] a substantial, though varying, surplus above the cost of maintenance." [13] Slavery in the South was not corroded from within Southern society and institutions. Slavery came to an end there not through internal evolution or internal revolution. It was brought to an end by forces that attacked, shattered, and destroyed it from the outside. There is probably no other instance in the history of the world in which this happened.

How did it happen that slavery in the South was a "peculiar institution," in such ways that what could be said about slavery in Western history generally could not be said about it as it existed and functioned in the Southern states? While obviously there can be no pretentious claims of certainty in explaining so complex a phenomenon, we shall try to suggest a probable rationale which will offer not only a key to history but also an insight into present Southern attitudes toward the problem of civil rights.

Not Slavery, but Race

Whenever in history slavery existed, it was considered basically an economic institution. As a result of war or as a consequnce of extreme poverty, anyone might become a slave. The Israelites in the Promised Land did not consider it a badge of shame that their forefathers had been slaves unto Pharaoh in Egypt. On the contrary, they were commanded to hold ever in their consciousness not only the fact that they had been led out of their bondage in Egypt, but also, and with equal importance, that before the Exodus they had been slaves. Slavery, then, like alienage, could serve as a bond to humanity in general.

[13] STAMPP, THE PECULIAR INSTITUTION 404, 408, 417 (1956).

The experience of slavery in the ancient world was so common that Plato ventured to suggest that every man has many slaves among his ancestors.[14] The poet Terence and the philosopher Epictetus had been slaves, and the father of Horace was a slave. It has been pointed out that the very word "slave" is "but Slav, and a reminder of the large numbers of the great Slav people whom the Teutons captured in war and who made up the bulk of their slave population." [15] In the broad sweep of history slavery as an institution was such that when a free man saw a slave, he could well say to himself: "There, but for the grace of God, go I." For the man (and more especially the woman or child) who was free today, might tomorrow be a slave.

In the American South slavery was regarded differently. It was not—at least in the three decades preceding the Civil War— merely a misfortune that had come to a man, not merely a useful or conventional economic arrangement; slavery was a *racial* arrangement, and it was not the misfortune but rather the proper —the only proper—estate of the Negro. If by happiness one meant being and doing that for which one was eminently fit "by nature," then the Negro slave was, by definition, happy, and the free Negro was a contradiction in terms.[16] The South fought the Civil War not merely to preserve a profitable economic arrangement; it fought to preserve the only social arrangement that was conceivably possible, in the mind of the South, between the white and Negro races. " *'The Negro question lies far deeper than the slavery question.'* This statement," Lloyd has rightly pointed out,

though voiced by a Northern minister, expressed a fundamental truth concerning the problem of the Southern Slave States which the abolitionists either failed to recognize or intentionally ignored. . . . As Calhoun pointed out in 1837, the question was much more than a "mere naked question of master and slave," for it involved an institu-

[14] THEAETATUS 175a.
[15] GREENIDGE, SLAVERY 16 (1958). See also SHERRARD, FREEDOM FROM FEAR —THE SLAVE AND HIS EMANCIPATION ch. 11 (1959).
[16] For Aristotle's thesis that it is an advantage for the slave to have a master see his POLITICS I, ch. 5.

tion which was considered "essential to the peace and existence" of the Slave States.[17]

Calhoun had held, in 1837, that the maintenance of existing relations between the races was indispensable to the peace and happiness of both races in the South.[18] The South believed and maintained that since slavery had come with the Negro, it was a question of race, which could not be solved by emancipation. On the contrary, slavery had to be continued; for, since Negroes were unfit for the state of freedom among whites, slavery was the only reasonable and workable solution of the race problem. Thus, while abolitionist sentiment was growing elsewhere in the 1830s, the South felt that slavery was good and justified; that, under the given conditions, it was a blessing to both races; that it was morally right; that it was wholly consistent with justice, reason, and Christianity. All instruments of public opinion, including the churches, held to this position unswervingly.[19] The slave in the South—unlike the slave in other parts of the world and at other periods of history—was not a challenge to the great idea of basic and inherent human rights; for the conviction of the South was that the Negro as slave "occupied such a place and fulfilled such duties as were commensurate with his capacities," and so Negro slavery was consistent with human rights.[20]

"Slavery as an economic system," Dumond wrote,

was of small account compared with slavery as a system of racial adjustment and social control. . . . Slavery was not the source of the philosophy [of the biological inequality and the racial inferiority of the Negro]. It merely enshrined it, prevented a practical demonstration of its falsity, and filled public offices and the councils of religious, educational, and political institutions with men reared in its atmosphere. . . .[21] The defense of slavery was of a social system and a system of racial adjustment, not of an economic institution.[22]

[17] LLOYD, THE SLAVERY CONTROVERSY, 1831–1860, at 224 (1939).
[18] *Id.* at 243.   [19] *Id.* at 165–66, 188, 202.   [20] *Id.* at 156–57.
[21] DUMOND, ANTISLAVERY ORIGINS OF THE CIVIL WAR IN THE U.S. 52 (1939).
[22] *Id.* at 1 n.1. See also MACY, ANTI-SLAVERY CRUSADE 13, 21, 24 (1919).

Since the issue to the South was not slavery as an economic arrangement, but something more pervasive and significant, namely, a system of race relations, it is understandable that the factors found by Whitehead to be operative in other historical epochs to dissolve slavery should not appear as effective causes in the Southern states.

Not the Slave, but the Negro

To the South, then, slavery was the tangible, social arrangement of race relations. Basic to slavery in the South—*and only in the South,* for this was not true elsewhere in the world or in history— was the firm conviction that the Negro belonged to another and an inferior species. Southerners claimed to have scientific and biblical proof for a "plurality" theory of the human race: that it was made up of distinct species that originated from different original pairs of man and woman. The Negro was not a man in the same sense in which any white individual was a man; he might even be said to be "a strong animal machine." He was sub-human not because he was a slave; he was a slave because he was subhuman.[23]

On this proposition Southerners were united, those who owned no slaves with those who did. This was the "central theme of Southern history," and this explains the Civil War, the Black Codes, opposition to Reconstruction, the politically solid South, the Jim Crow laws, and Southern resentment at "interference" in their affairs from the "outside." [24]

Equality between white man and Negro was literally unthinkable—like trying to think that $1 + 1 = 3$, or some other patently self-contradictory proposition. To be black was to be a slave.

[23] See LLOYD, *op. cit. supra* note 17, at 227, 229, 243.
[24] *Id.* at 226–27; Phillips, *The Central Theme of Southern History,* 34 AM. HIST. REV. 31 (1928). For an expression of resentment at "outside" "interference" see remarks of Senator Fulbright in 106 CONG. REC. 7186 (daily ed. April 8, 1960).

The most crucial test of this ideology was to be found when the Southerner was faced with a freedman, for here was a featherless biped, black in color, who was not a slave. The Southerner avoided the challenge of the Negro slave to the great idea of human dignity and the great idea of basic, inherent human rights by finding him either not fully human (and of course he was not, if freedom is an essential characteristic of the human being), or, if he was human, a member of an inferior species. But with the Negro who was not a slave, what manner of man was he? Was he fully human? Was he biologically and morally the equal of the white man? How should one comprehend this phenomenon?

The South had two opportunities to answer these questions: before the Civil War, when there were manumitted Negroes in the community, and after the Civil War, when all Negroes were freedmen. Let us see what image of the freed Negro the Southerner saw. First, we shall look at the freedmen after the Civil War.

Black Codes

Up to the end of the Civil War the Lincoln Administration and Congress did nothing radical on behalf of the Negro beyond the issuance of the Emancipation Proclamation in 1863. Before and during the war no blueprint respecting the future status of the freedmen was prepared. The abolitionists had assumed that once slavery had been brought to an end, the Negro would take his place as a human being who would enjoy human dignity and human rights. The abolitionists, however, saw the slavery question but not the race question in the South.

It was quite different in the Southern states. As soon as the Civil War came to an end, Southern leaders and state legislatures turned their attention to the race question. The answer to this question was formulated by them in the Black Codes which the legislatures enacted immediately after the war. These legislative enactments convey the thoughts and feelings of the white South regarding the role of the Negro freedmen in Southern communities and suggest what would have happened to the four million Negroes in the Southern and border states had not Reconstruction developed as, in part, a reaction to the Black Codes and Southern intransigence.

Although the Black Codes varied in harshness, they all aimed to withhold from the Negro the full freedom that his emancipation may have implied to him and to Northern Republicans. The code adopted in 1865 by Mississippi [25] provided that Negroes could rent or lease land only in incorporated cities or towns, "in which places the corporate authorities shall control the same"; that marriage between Negro and white shall be a felony, the penalty for which shall be life imprisonment; and a Negro was defined as one descended from a Negro to the third generation—from Negro great-grandparents—"though one ancestor in each generation may have been a white person." Another provision was that contracts for labor made with Negroes for a longer period than one month should be in writing; that if the laborer should quit the service of his employer before the end of the term of service, without good cause, he would forfeit his wages for that year up to the time of quitting; that any person might arrest and carry back such a Negro worker to his employer; and that the person who did the arresting and restoring should receive five dollars reward and ten cents per mile, to be paid by the employer and deducted from the wages of the Negro worker. It was made a criminal offense to attempt to persuade a Negro worker to leave his employer before the expiration of the contract term, or knowingly to give or sell to such Negro worker any food or clothing, or to employ him. County officers were required to report twice a year to the probate court the names of all Negro children under eighteen years of age who were orphans or who were not supported by their parents, and the clerk of the court was to apprentice the children to "some competent and suitable

[25] Miss. Black Code, Laws of Miss., 1865, at 82.

person," the former master to be preferred. A deserting apprentice
was to be arrested and punished as if he were a deserting Negro
worker.

A vagrancy law adopted by Mississippi in 1865 provided that
Negroes over eighteen years of age, "with no lawful employment
or business, or found unlawfully assembling themselves together,
either in the day or night time," would be deemed vagrants; also
to be deemed vagrants were white persons assembling with Negroes, white persons "usually associating" with Negroes "on terms
of equality," and a white man living "in adultery or fornication"
with a Negro woman. A Negro who failed or refused to pay the
poll tax was to be arrested as a vagrant and hired out to one who
would pay the tax. It was made a criminal offense for a Negro to
make "seditious speeches, insulting gestures, language, or acts,"
or to exercise "the function of a minister of the Gospel without
a license from some regularly organized church." A convicted
Negro who failed to pay the fine and costs within five days was
to be hired out by the sheriff to "any white person."

The Black Code of South Carolina [26] defined a Negro as any
person with one eighth or more "Negro blood," and provided
that the freedmen, while entitled to certain rights, were not entitled to social or political equality with white persons; that no
Negro could enter and reside in the state unless he enter into
a bond for one thousand dollars conditioned upon his good behavior; that when a misdemeanor was committed by a Negro,
any person present might arrest him and take him before a magistrate "to be dealt with as the case may require," but in the
case of a misdemeanor by a white person against a Negro, there
must be a complaint to a magistrate, who might order the arrest
of the offender. Special courts were established for the trial of
Negroes. Negro children between eighteen and twenty-one whose

---

[26] S.C. Black Code, Laws of S.C., 1865, enacted Oct. 19, Dec. 19, Dec. 21,
1865. The Black Codes are set forth in McPHERSON, POLITICAL HISTORY OF
THE U.S. DURING PERIOD OF RECONSTRUCTION 29–44 (1871; 2d ed. 1875).
Tennessee and Arkansas did not adopt codes.

parents were unable to afford them a comfortable maintenance, or who were not teaching them habits of honesty and industry, were to be bound as apprentices. No Negro was to be permitted to pursue the work of an artisan, mechanic, shopkeeper, or any other trade or employment or business—except that of "husbandry, or that of a servant under a contract of service or labor" —until he had obtained a license from the district judge. The license was to be for only one year, and was to be granted only if the judge was satisfied of the Negro's skill and fitness and of his good moral character, and upon the payment of one hundred dollars for a license to become a shopkeeper or pedlar, to be paid annually, or a ten dollar annual fee to become a mechanic or artisan or to follow any other trade.

The Black Codes were an organized attempt on the part of the Southern states to replace slavery with peonage and to make of the Negroes an inferior and subordinate economic and social caste. While slavery had been brought to an end by outside and superior force, the consequences of slavery were to be maintained and perpetuated.

The Black Codes of Mississippi and South Carolina were perhaps the most harsh, those of Virginia and North Carolina perhaps the mildest, but all gave evidence of a strong inclination to preserve the relations between the races as they were before emancipation, those of a master race to a subject race. The Negro was now to enjoy freedom without equality—a political, economic, and social monstrosity without precedent in history or logic.

A scholar writing in defense of the Black Codes asserted that this legislation,

far from embodying any spirit of defiance towards the North or any purpose to evade the conditions which the victors had imposed, was in the main a conscientious and straightforward attempt to bring some sort of order out of the social and economic chaos which a full acceptance of the results of war and emancipation involved. In its general principle it corresponded very closely to the actual facts of the situation. The freedmen were not, and in the nature of the case could not for generations be, on the same social, moral, and intellectual plane with the whites; and this fact was recognized by constituting them a separate class in the civil order. As in general principles, so in details, the legislation was faithful on the whole to the actual conditions with which it had to deal . . . the greatest fault of the southern law-makers was, not that their procedure was unwise *per se,* but that, when legislating as a conquered people, they failed adequately to consider and be guided by the prejudices of their conquerors.[27]

The defenders of the Black Codes never tried to explain how it was ever going to be possible for a race, set apart as inferior and treated as a subject people, to make the transition to full freedom and equality. The Southerners tried to preserve a social order to which they were accustomed, one that was congenial and profitable to them. At this point Northern leaders awakened to the fact that their abolitionist aim had been too narrowly conceived, that there were ends to be achieved beyond emancipation—beyond the conversion of slaves into freedmen. At this point Reconstruction came into existence.

Another defense of the Black Codes was that the freedmen were likely to become idlers under emancipation, and the important thing was to get them back to work on the plantations. How could this be accomplished? How does one learn to swim? "Throw them in the water and have them learn to swim by finding the necessity of swimming"; [28] let the freedmen learn to work by finding the necessity of working. But the same line of reasoning was not applied to other aspects of life or liberty. The Southerners did not say: "Throw them into freedom and equality and have them learn to be free and equal by finding the necessity of freedom and equality." They had a vigorous logic about work

[27] DUNNING, RECONSTRUCTION—POLITICAL AND ECONOMIC 57–59 (1907). A similar point of view was expressed by Hamilton, *Southern Legislation in Respect to Freedmen 1865–1866,* in STUDIES IN SOUTHERN HISTORY AND POLITICS 137, 156–58 (1914).
[28] Quoted by BEALE, THE CRITICAL YEAR 192 (1930).

by the Negro, but in all other matters their attitude was that life must go on as if nothing really had changed.

Essentially what had not changed was the image of the Negro in the mind of the white man in the South: it was the image of someone who might be thought of as a freedman but never as a freeman.

Freedmen before Emancipation

At the time of the Civil War there were four million slaves and 250,000 freedmen in the slave states (including the slave states that had not seceded and the District of Columbia).[29] After several hundred years of slavery, ninety-four out of every one hundred Negroes in the South were slaves. The South—at least after the early 1830s—had set itself sternly against the manumission of even individual slaves. Negro = slave—this was an equation from which few exceptions were contemplated as possible.

Macy, summarizing the tragic position of the freedmen, who were neither slave nor free, wrote that

free Negroes were banished from certain States, or were not permitted to enter them, or were allowed to remain only by choosing a white man for a guardian. It was made a crime to teach Negroes, whether slaves or freemen, to read and write. Under various pretexts free Negroes were reduced to slavery . . . they were not allowed to assemble for any purpose except under the strict surveillance of white men. Negro testimony [even that of a freed Negro] in a court of law was invalid where the rights of a white man were involved. The right of a Negro to his freedom was decided by an arbitrary court without a jury, while the disputed right of a white man to the ownership of a horse was conditioned by the safeguard of trial by jury.[30]

The laws relating to freedmen "reflected the general opinion," wrote Stampp, "that these people were an anomaly, a living denial 'that nature's God intended the African for the *status* of slavery.' "[31] He quotes the opinion of the chancellor of the South

[29] STAMPP, *op. cit. supra* note 13, at 30.
[30] MACY, *op. cit. supra* note 22, at 67–68.
[31] STAMPP, *op. cit. supra* note 13, at 215.

Carolina Court of Appeals that "a free African population is a curse to any country." [32] Freedmen in the community were such an intolerable spectacle that states enacted laws against their very presence. Virginia required the manumitted slave to leave the state within a year, unless he had "lawful permission" to remain longer. In North Carolina he had to leave within ninety days unless a superior court made an exception in his case for "meritorious service." In Tennessee after 1831, he had to leave at once for some other state, while after 1854 he had to leave for Africa. [33]

Emancipation by masters was made increasingly more difficult from year to year. A Louisiana act of 1807—and this state was one of the more liberal ones—limited manumission to slaves who were at least thirty years old and who had not been guilty of bad conduct during the previous four years; but in 1857 Louisiana entirely prohibited private emancipations, and by this act Louisiana fell in line with the other states of the Deep South. A master might, however, provide for the manumission of his slaves after his death, provided the emancipation were to take place outside the state, i.e., in a free state; but Alabama, Arkansas, Georgia, Mississippi, and South Carolina prohibited emancipation by will even when the testator directed that the act take place outside the state. [34]

Phillips summarized correctly the Southern attitude toward freedmen: they were, he said, "a third element in a system planned for two." [35]

The existence of freed Negroes, even in free states, was considered by the South a threat to slavery. The freed Negro was a potential challenge to the slave. Moreover, he might help fugitive slaves, and in case of a civil war he would be an enemy. The idea was conceived, then, to transport freedmen to Africa, and out of this motivation the American Colonization Society was

[32] *Id.* at 332.   [33] *Ibid.*   [34] *Id.* at 234.
[35] Phillips, quoted in DUMOND, *op. cit. supra* note 21, at 9.

founded in Washington in the winter of 1816–17. "In its inception the [colonization] movement was inspired by a curious
combination of humanitarianism, greed, and race prejudice." [36]
The colonizers hated the abolitionists, for the former rejected the
idea that Americans could tolerate freedmen. When the position of the colonizers became clear, abolitionists stopped supporting the movement, which then became totally dependent upon
anti-Negro elements in Connecticut, Ohio, and Pennsylvania and
upon slave owners in the South. The position of the colonizers
has been well summarized by Dumond:

> Every appeal for funds and every exposition of the Society's ob-
> jectives harped upon the depravity of the free Negroes, their hopeless
> situation, their ignorance, their misery, their lack of ability and ambi-
> tion. Over and over again we find them designated in the official organ
> of the Society as "a mildew upon our fields," "a scourge to our backs,"
> . . . "the most worthless and degraded portion of society," "greater
> nuisances than slaves," . . . "a species of population pregnant with
> future danger and present inconvenience," . . . "more noxious than
> slaves." . . .
> At no time did those who adhered to the principle of colonization
> lend their influence to the alleviation of the Negroes' distress. . . .
> Considered in all its aspects, the American Colonization Society was
> the cohesive force for all the reactionary elements in the slavery con-
> troversy.[37]

In brief, the Southern position was that there was no room in
the South for a freed Negro. A freed Negro must go to the North,
or, better yet, to Africa. So there were laws that made manumission difficult or impossible; but if by chance a slave somehow
got himself manumitted, then he was to be deported to a free
state, or he could choose to go to Africa as a colonist. The presence of the freed Negro was intolerable.

Not only was manumission made difficult or impossible, but

[36] *Id.* at 12.
[37] *Id.* at 17–19. Between 1820 and 1866 only about 12,000 freedmen left
as colonists for Africa. *Id.* at 15–16. Regarding compulsory colonization, see
GOODELL, AMERICAN SLAVE CODE 364 ff. (1853).

enslavement was made easy if not inevitable. Goodell in 1853 summarized the law as follows:

In many ways, a free colored person may be enslaved. He may be enslaved for assisting a slave, however nearly related to him, to escape into freedom. He may be enslaved for being *suspected* of being himself a runaway slave; for being thus imprisoned, and unable to pay his jail fees. He may be reenslaved, after having been emancipated, if the process were not in exact accordance with unreasonable and vexatious regulations; or if, however regularly emancipated, he presumes to remain among his friends, and amid the scenes of his childhood. He may be enslaved for incurring fines which he is unable to pay, under unjust and unequal enactments. He may be enslaved for not being able, by *white* witnesses, to prove himself free! Though a Northern man, and always before free, he may be enslaved by entering a slave State. . . . He may be enslaved, with his children after him, for being married to a slave. He may be enslaved by being unlawfully and piratically imported into a slave State, even though the kidnapper may be arrested and punished.[38]

Despite these laws, some six percent of the Negroes in the slave states were freedmen. But that these Negroes were not free is clear when one looks at the slave codes. Again to quote from Goodell's legal treatise:

Like the *slave,* the *free* colored person is held incompetent to testify against the white man! Like the slave, he is debarred, to a great extent, from the benefits of education [e.g., in Georgia a white man could be fined $500 for teaching a freed Negro to read or write], and from the right of enjoying free social worship and religious instruction! [In North Carolina, e.g., Negroes were prohibited from preaching the Gospel.] Like the slave, he is required to be passive, without exercising the right of self-defense, under the insults and assaults of the white man! Like the slave, . . . he is denied the ordinary safeguards of an impartial trial by a jury of his peers. Like the slave, he has no vote nor voice in framing the laws under which he is governed. . . . To be a "free *negro*" differs widely, it would seem, from being a free *man.*[39]

[38] GOODELL, *op. cit. supra* note 37, at 355–56.
[39] *Id.* at 357. See also STROUD, SKETCH OF THE LAWS RELATING TO SLAVERY ch. 4 (2d ed. 1856). RUSSELL, THE FREE NEGRO IN VIRGINIA, 1619–1865 (Johns Hopkins Univ. Studies in Hist. & Pol. Sci., ser. 31, no. 3, 1913).

In this connection it should be recalled that the *Dred Scott* case,[40] in 1857 involved a Negro who claimed that he was a freedman. The object of the suit was to vindicate the title of Dred Scott and his family to freedom. The Supreme Court held that Negroes, slave or free, could not sue in the courts of the United States. In the constitutional sense, said Chief Justice Taney, Negroes, even if free, were not part of the "people of the United States." Negroes, even when free, said Taney,

had for more than a century before [the Constitution was adopted] been regarded as beings of an inferior race, and altogether unfit to associate with the white race, either in social or political relations, and so far inferior that they had no rights which the white man was bound to respect, and that the Negro might justly and lawfully be reduced to slavery for his benefit.

Whether slaves or free men, Negroes were subject to the authority of white persons, "and had no rights or privileges but such as those who held the power . . . might choose to grant them."

This was the opinion not only of Taney but also of the South before the Civil War; and, except for the fact that slavery had been brought to an end, this was also the opinion of the South after the end of the war: the postbellum Negroes were to be freedmen, not freemen.

The Right to Freedom

The late Professor William L. Westermann observed that "the last criterion for determining the rigidity and harshness of any slave system is to be found in the ease and availability of its manumission procedures." [41] No matter how humanely or decently a slave must be treated according to the slave code, the slave has lost permanently his standing as a human being if he

---

WRIGHT, THE FREE NEGRO IN MARYLAND (Columbia Univ. Studies in Hist., Econ., & Pub. Law, vol. 97, 1921).

[40] Dred Scott v. Sanford, 19 How. 393 (U.S. 1857). See HOPKINS, DRED SCOTT'S CASE (1951).

[41] WESTERMANN, THE SLAVE SYSTEMS OF GREEK AND ROMAN ANTIQUITY 25 (1955).

is firmly barred from winning his freedom. Societies have provided for the humane and decent treatment of even brute animals, but this has not made the animals into men. If a society makes it difficult or almost impossible for the slave to be manumitted, it in effect says to him that it is not merely his misfortune to have lost his liberty, but that he has no liberty because it is his nature to be a slave, just as it is the nature of a horse to be a horse.

As we have seen, in the Southern states manumission was made extremely difficult, and often the law made it totally impossible. While Dutch slavery was more cruel than American slavery, in respect to manumission American slavery was perhaps the most cruel system of all. It left no hope for the slave to become a freedman and for the freedman to become a freeman.

A brief comparison of the Southern position on manumission with that found in other slave systems in history will underscore the "rigidity and harshness" of the Southern slave code.

In ancient Greece manumission was widely practiced in the fifth and fourth centuries. Westermann speaks of the "inconstancy of status and fluidity of movement from slavery to freedom which resulted from the principle and practice of manumission" in ancient Greece.[42] There were mass manumissions secured by the state and by individual actions. The slave had a manumission price, which the master was compelled to accept. Slave status in the ancient Greek world involved no racial or class antipathies.

The Greeks often set up special funds for the redemption of slaves, to which many free persons made contributions, and from which slaves could borrow and then use the money to buy their freedom. No interest was paid on the loans.[43] Once a slave won his freedom, no stigma attached to him as a freedman, and there

[42] *Id.* at 18.
[43] *Id.* at 23. Similar redemption societies existed in Jewish communities everywhere as long as slavery was a threat.

were many freedmen in Attica. At Gortyn, testimony asserting freedom was accepted over testimony of slave status.

Westermann described the over one thousand well-preserved reports of manumission on the walls of the sacred precinct at Delphi. These are very interesting. While theoretically slaves could not have money or legally make contracts, in fact they were permitted to earn money by working part-time for third parties, as well as borrow money from the special loan funds. They therefore could redeem or manumit themselves, but the form of such manumission was a fictional trust sale to the god Pythian Apollo. A typical report at Delphi was the following: "Crato, son of Mesateus . . . has sold to Pythian Apollo a female slave named Irene, Armenian by race, for three minas silver; and he has received the price in full. . . . Irene has entrusted the purchase to the god, to the end that she is free." Sometimes the slave did not have enough money to pay for total freedom; in such cases the Delphic grants provided for the freedman to carry on certain services for the former owner from two to ten years, the services becoming part payment for freedom.[44]

The discussion of Greek slavery thus far may seem strange when considered against the opinion of Aristotle, who assumed the justice of slavery for barbarians or foreigners. According to Aristotle, citizenship was limited to the leisure class. Slaves were outside the state and belonged to the household economy. The slave had only part of a soul and was, therefore, not fully a man: his whole function was to be a tool and the possession of his master. It was to his benefit to be enslaved, as well as to the benefit of his master; for a thing is benefited by fulfilling its functions. His sole argument was that all barbarians were natural slaves.

But Aristotle opened the door to his own confusion when he admitted that some Greeks were also slaves by nature. Now, how

[44] WESTERMANN, *op. cit. supra* note 41, at 35, 46; also by same author, *Between Slavery and Freedom,* 50 AM. HIST. REV. 213 (1945).

did he recognize those Greeks who were natural slaves? On this point Aristotle became quite fuzzy.[45] The fact probably is that Aristotle was himself unsure on the subject of slavery, for he manumitted his slaves by will. Had he been certain that they were slaves by nature, and that it was, therefore, to their benefit to be enslaved, he could not ever have given them their liberty.

The fact is, too, that Aristotle's views on slavery were by no means typical of the Greek and Hellenistic philosophers and dramatists. A fragment of Philemon states an opinion sharply contradictory of Aristotle's: "no one was ever made a slave by nature; but chance has enslaved a man's body"; and Alcidamus held that God had made all men free, that nature had made no man a slave.[46] After Alexander's conquests and the development and spread of Stoicism, it was not possible to hold to Aristotle's views; the idea of human dignity and of the rights inherent in human beings stood as an open challenge to those views and to the institution of slavery. Euripides openly questioned the operation of slavery, for he saw slaves who were better men than their masters, and he saw children of slaves who did not seem to be slavish by nature. The Cynics regarded slavery as an external misfortune and, therefore, a circumstance immaterial to the nature of the unfortunate man and irrelevant in our judgment of his character; and Onesicritus, a contemporary of Alexander and Aristotle, contended in favor of abolition, as a forerunner of William Lloyd Garrison.

While Roman slave law was relatively more severe than Greek slave law, there was inherent in the Roman system an ameliorating principle that in time was bound to dissolve slavery itself. The Roman jurists, looking about them, saw that slavery was common to all ancient peoples, and that even Romans, when they were war captives, were subjected to enslavement. With their

[45] Schlaifer, *Greek Theories of Slavery From Homer to Aristotle,* 47 HARV. STUDIES IN CLASSICAL PHILOLOGY 165 (1936).
[46] WESTERMANN, THE SLAVE SYSTEMS OF GREEK AND ROMAN ANTIQUITY 24, 27, 40 (1955).

generalizing, abstracting facility, they drew the broad conclusion that slavery was part of the *ius gentium* or the law of nations. But at the same time they stated it was contrary to natural law, for according to the law of nature all men were equal.[47]

In a society where such a belief prevails one should expect to find ease of manumission, and this was, in fact, generally the case in the long stretch of Roman history. For example, nearly half a million manumissions took place in Rome during a single period of thirty-two years, 81–49 B.C., or an average of sixteen thousand per year. "This will seem a reasonable number," commented Tenney Frank, "to those who recall how freely slaves were freed at Rome." [48]

At one point in Roman history, the number of testamentary manumissions by Roman citizens had become so great that it was considered a scandal and a danger, and the emperors sought ways to limit the process. Thus, for example, Augustan legislation of 2 B.C. and 4 A.D. provided that a citizen who owned from three to ten slaves could manumit one half the number of slaves he owned; one who owned eleven to thirty, could manumit one third.[49]

For the freedmen, absorption into the citizen body of Rome was a tangible possibility, since the Roman citizen body was "in a constant state of recruitment out of the former slave membership of the Roman *familiae*." [50] Westermann speaks of "the broad-minded attitude of the Romans in admitting talented slaves after their manumission into the intellectual life of the Roman community. They were accepted into its political and economic life without any manifestation of prejudice arising from their former status." [51]

Bearing in mind the two factors that have been the center of

[47] *Id.* at 57, 80. For references to the *Digest,* see *id.* at 80 n.66.

[48] Frank, *The Sacred Treasure and the Rate of Manumission,* 53 AM. J. PHILOLOGY 360, 363 (1932).

[49] WESTERMANN, THE SLAVE SYSTEMS OF GREEK AND ROMAN ANTIQUITY 89–90 (1955).

[50] *Id.* at 75.   [51] *Id.* at 79.

our interest—(1) ease, variety, and number of manumissions, and (2) acceptance of former slaves into the community of free men without discrimination—perhaps the most revealing contrast of Southern slavery is with slavery in Latin America, especially in Brazil. This contrast is more revealing than that with ancient Greek and Roman practices and attitudes, because the slave in Brazil was also the African Negro; because in both Brazil and the Southern states the masters were Christians; and because in both instances we can see the slave institutions in the New World contemporaneously, in the nineteenth century. The many common factors make the contrast extremely sharp.

Perhaps the first writer to observe this contrast was Sir Harry H. Johnston. Writing in 1910, in *The Negro in the New World*,[52] after a visit in the Southern states two years before, Johnston took the position that

on the whole the Negro had, even in slavery, a less unhappy life and far greater opportunities for bettering his position and attaining his freedom in Portuguese Brazil than he had in North America before the year 1863. . . . Slavery under the flag of Portugal (or Brazil) or of Spain was *not* a condition without hope, a life in hell, as it was for the most part . . . [in] the Southern United States.[53]

As Johnston examined slavery in Brazil, certain facts and features struck him—as they do us—as having special significance. We shall mention the more important:

1. The strongest basis for hope in the heart of the Brazilian Negro slave was the fact that "at any time *he could purchase his own freedom*." [54] The slave could by law compel his master to liberate him upon repayment of the original purchase price or a price fixed by legal process.

2. To procure money for his freedom, the slave had, for himself, Sundays and all public and Roman Catholic holidays, or 85

[52] JOHNSTON, THE NEGRO IN THE NEW WORLD (1910).
[53] *Id*. at vi, 89.   [54] *Id*. at 89. Italics in original.

out of 365 days. On these days he was allowed to work, to hire out his labor, on his own account.

3. Manumissions were so numerous that by 1872 free Negroes in central Brazil outnumbered slaves.

4. When emancipation was achieved in 1888 by an imperial decree, it made no stir; for the white people were so accustomed to living and working with free Negroes, and so accustomed to paying wages for Negro labor, that the conversion of slave labor to free labor was accomplished without difficulty.

5. Because of the manumission process, the number of slaves was progressively reduced. In 1835 there were in Brazil 2,-100,000 slaves; in 1875, only 1,470,000. After 1888, when all the remaining slaves were freed, there was no race problem.

6. Freed slaves were given all the rights and liberties of the freeborn. They had the right to vote, hold office, and enjoy the same legal protection as whites. They were admitted to all careers and trades, from the humblest to the highest, in civilian life as well as in the army, navy, and police force.

7. The priests encouraged testamentary manumission. As they sat at a master's deathbed, they encouraged him to emancipate his slaves as an act of Christian piety.

In these significant ways the humanity of the slave, of the Negro who happened to be a slave, was kept alive as a public fact. He was temporarily and accidentally a slave, permanently and essentially a man.

Manumission policies and practices and the assimilation of the freedmen into the community as citizens were undoubtedly aided by the fact that the Negro as a slave was treated as a human being and not as a mere animated tool. Johnston cited the following facts that bear out this judgment:

1. There was a public protector of slaves, who saw to it that masters treated their slaves the way they treated free workers, providing them with the same food and clothing as those en-

joyed by wage laborers. In addition, public visitors were appointed, who went to the estates three times a year to observe and report on the treatment of slaves. Priests went from estate to estate to give religious instruction to the slaves and to say Mass. On these visits they obtained information from the slaves about their treatment, and they reported abuses to the public protector.

2. The criminal law made no distinction between persons accused of crime on the basis of race or color, or whether they were free or slave, and a person who committed a crime against a slave was tried without distinction as to whether the victim was a slave or a free man.

3. The slave was looked upon as a moral being. As a consequence, the marriage of slaves was respected. The master was expected to encourage the marriage of slaves; and when the slave of one master wished to marry the slave of another master, the man's master was required to purchase the woman, at a price to be fixed by an impartial tribunal. Thus the couple were to be brought together, and their living together in a state of matrimony was made possible.[55]

Later research has not weakened Johnston's judgment on the contrast between slavery in the South and in Latin America. Writing in 1930, a scholar emphasized the following facts about Brazilian slavery: [56]

1. By 1888, as a result of voluntary manumissions, there remained only 600,000 slaves to be emancipated by governmental decree.

2. All slaves were baptized and were members of the Roman

[55] *Id.* at 96–97, 98–100, 38–47. Mention might be made of the fact that in other Latin American countries slavery came to an end before it was terminated in Brazil in 1888. In Guatemala slavery was abolished in 1824; in Mexico, in 1829; Argentina, Peru, Chile, Bolivia, and Paraguay, about 1825; Colombia, Venezuela, and Ecuador, 1840 to 1845.

[56] Williams, *Treatment of Negro Slaves in Brazilian Empire—A Comparison With the U.S.A.*, 15 J. Negro Hist. 315 (1930).

Catholic Church. Priests worked with devotion on behalf of re-captured fugitive slaves. They encouraged slaves to come to them as friends and protectors. The priests gave Negro slaves burial in consecrated ground. Master and slave were bound together in a religious fellowship. (At night before retiring it was the custom for slaves to appear before the master and say: "I beseech your blessing in the name of our Lord Jesus," and the master would answer: "The Lord Jesus Christ bless you forever.")

3. The moral integrity of the slave was respected. For example, a law of 1869 prohibited the separation of husband and wife, and of children under fifteen years of age from their parents. Another example: if a master was inhumane, the slave could have himself sold to another master, and the former owner was compelled to accept the sale and the price as binding on him.

As a result of these practices and attitudes, after emancipation Brazil faced no race problem. The country had a slave, but never a race, problem.

Donald Pierson quotes the following interesting passage from Sir Richard F. Burton, about the Negro slave in Brazil between 1869 and 1883:

He may educate himself, and he is urged to do so. He is regularly catechised, and in all large plantations there is a daily religious service. If assailed in life or limb he may defend himself against his master, or any white man. . . . He is legally married, and the chastity of his wife is defended against his owner. He has little fear of being separated from his family: the humane instincts and the religious tenets of the people are strongly opposed to this act of barbarity. He has every chance of becoming a free man: manumission is held to be a Catholic duty and priestly communities are ashamed of holding slaves.[57]

Summarizing the detailed facts concerning the ease, variety, and number of manumissions in Brazil (despite the fact that the estimates of the number of Negro slaves brought to Brazil varied

[57] Pierson, Negroes in Brazil 83 (1942).

from three to eighteen millions, in any case the number was great [58]), Pierson said:

The custom of manumission became firmly intrenched in the Brazilian mores, constituting, under certain circumstances, universally expected behavior. . . . Abolition sentiment and agitation was not limited to any one section of Brazil. . . . The Brazilian white has never at any time felt that the black or the mixed-blood offered any serious threat to his own status. No feelings of fear, distrust, apprehension, dread, resentment, or envy have been stirred up, as in our South during and following the Civil War, no sense of unwarranted aggressions or attacks.[59]

In *Slave and Citizen*,[60] Frank Tannenbaum made a detailed and dramatic comparison between Southern and Brazilian slavery. The author acknowledged the fact that his study stemmed from a seminar conducted at Columbia University by several professors, including himself and the late Professor William L. Westermann, whose work on Greek and Roman slavery we have cited. Westermann's thesis was succinctly stated by himself as follows:

In any community which has adopted slave employment as an integral part of its labor organization the harshness of the rules of control imposed upon the enslaved and the resulting bitterness which develops are largely dependent upon two factors. The first is the number and variety of the methods of liberation provided and the ease with which their procedures may be set in motion. The second factor depends upon the spontaneity of the acceptance of former slaves into some group of the free population and the lack of discrimination against these new freedmen which is manifested in the social class within which they are to be assimilated.[61]

He applied this thesis to the ancient systems of slavery which he studied. Tannenbaum applied it to his comparative study of

[58] *Id.* at 33.
[59] *Id.* at 346. See generally, FREYRE, THE MASTERS AND THE SLAVES (1946), and his NEW WORLD IN THE TROPICS (1960).
[60] TANNENBAUM, SLAVE AND CITIZEN (1947).
[61] WESTERMANN, THE SLAVE SYSTEMS OF GREEK AND ROMAN ANTIQUITY 154 (1955).

Freedmen or Free Men? **31**

the Southern and Brazilian slave systems, stating the thesis broadly as follows:

> Slavery was not merely a legal relation; it was also a moral one. It implied an ethical bias and a system of human values. . . . Wherever the law accepted the doctrine of the moral personality of the slave and made possible the gradual achievement of freedom implicit in such a doctrine, the slave system was abolished peacefully. Where the slave was denied recognition as a moral person and was therefore considered incapable of freedom, the abolition of slavery was accomplished by force—that is, by revolution.[62]

Though Westermann and Tannenbaum did not mention the thesis of Alfred North Whitehead, with which our discussion started, they implicitly accepted it as an explanation for the gradual disappearance of slavery, by peaceful means, in the societies that were permeated by the great idea of human dignity and of the rights inherent in human beings by reason only of their being human. Whitehead was not concerned with societies that stood outside the influence of this idea. In point of fact, however, the Southern states, at least after 1831, almost by conscious effort, took themselves out of the mainstream of Western intellectual and moral development by reducing the nature of the Negro to that of slave, and by making it practically impossible for a slave to win his freedom and for the freed Negro to live the life of a free man; and the South attempted to assure and perpetuate this degradation of the Negro by making it impossible for anyone in the community to keep alive the idea of human dignity and human rights. There was no equality for the Negro, and there was no civil liberty for the white.

This meant that emancipation of the slave—and of the Negro —could be brought about in the South only by force—as we have pointed out before, only by force exerted from the outside, where the idea of human dignity and human rights was alive and active as an intellectual, spiritual, moral, and social force. In Brazil, the

[62] TANNENBAUM, *op. cit. supra* note 60, at vii–viii.

idea was effective within the slave system; in the South, it was effective only as an attacking force from outside the slave system.

It was, according to Tannenbaum, the Roman Catholic
Church that carried to Latin America, and institutionalized
there, the great stream of humanistic values, transmitted from
Cicero, Seneca, Stoicism in general, and other pagan sources,
as well as the Christian fathers and canon law, which influenced
the formation of the Spanish law on slavery. These values pierced
through slavery and also flowed over it, so that slavery in Latin
America never became "the peculiar institution" that was part of
our South. In Latin America slavery was not "peculiar," it was
not outside the broad stream of Western intellectual, moral, and
spiritual history. Spanish law, custom, and tradition, when transferred to Latin America, reached out to protect the Negro slave
and "made him the beneficiary of the ancient legal heritage."
This legal heritage,

containing the legal tradition of the Spanish people and also influenced
by the Catholic doctrine of the equality of all men in the sight of God,
was biased in favor of freedom and opened the gates to manumission. . . . The law in Spanish and Portuguese America facilitated
manumission, . . . and the church ranked it among the works singu-
larly agreeable to God. A hundred social devices narrowed the gap
between bondage and liberty, encouraged the master to release his
slave, and . . . to achieve freedom on his own account.[63]

The slave could buy his own freedom and pay off the price in
installments. "In effect, slavery . . . had . . . become a contractual arrangement between the master and his bondsman."
Slavery was thus cut off from the notion that it was in any way
natural or innate or inseparable from the person or his race or
caste, and had become merely a matter of money, an amount
needed for redemption. Religion and custom provided so many
occasions for manumission that the wonder is that slavery lasted
as long as it did.

[63] *Id.* at 48, 52, 53, 54.

The Church favored manumission, as evidenced by condemnation of the slave trade by the popes in 1462, 1537, 1639, 1741, and 1839; and it favored manumission because it insisted that slave and master were equal before God, and, therefore,

the master had an obligation to protect the spiritual integrity of the slave, to teach him the Christian religion, to help him achieve the privileges of the sacraments, to guide him into living a good life, and to protect him from mortal sin. The slave had a right to become a Christian, to be baptized, and to be considered a member of the Christian community. . . . The Catholic churches in [Latin] America insisted that masters bring their slaves to church to learn the doctrine and participate in the communion. . . . As a Catholic the slave was married in the church, and the banns were regularly published. [The Church] gave the slave's family a moral and religious character unknown in other American slave systems. . . . If married by the church, they could not be separated by the master.[64]

In the Southern states, on the contrary, everything was done to place obstacles in the way of manumission. All the presumptions were in favor of the Negro being a slave: if he was a Negro, he was presumed to be a slave, and this meant that Negro = slave.

Always, we are forced to recognize the fact that "the attitude toward manumission is the crucial element in slavery." [65] To the Negro in Brazil, slavery was an open system; to the Negro in the South, slavery was a closed system. In the South, even when the door was opened a bit and a Negro escaped, he found that as a freedman he was not much better off than as a slave, for he was still, of course, a Negro. So the Negro was driven to recognize the truth that perhaps his real misfortune lay, not in the fact that he was a slave, but in the fact that he was a Negro. As a Negro, he was in no sense to think of himself as part of "the people," and he had "no rights which the white man was bound to respect"—and all this could be said of him even when he was a freedman! [66]

[64] *Id.* at 63–64.   [65] *Id.* at 69.
[66] Dred Scott v. Sanford, *supra* note 40.

As important as is the test of manumission for our judgment of a slave system, the morality or degradation of a slave system can perhaps best be tested by the attitudes of the masters toward the marriage of slaves. As we have seen, the marriage of slaves in Brazil was respected and protected; but in most of the Southern states

> there was no regard for the Negro family, no question of the right of the owner to sell his slaves separately, and no limitation upon separating husband and wife, or child from its mother. . . . The law recognized no marriage relation between slaves. . . . The demise of the sanctity of marriage had become absolute, and the Negro had lost his moral personality. Legally he was a chattel under the law, and in practice an animal to be bred for the market.[67]

This was the ultimate reduction of the Negro slave to the level of the mere beast of burden, the erasure of the last trace of recognition of him as a human being. One is tempted to go even further and say that the Negro slave was reduced to something even lower than some species of animals among which mating takes place within a social order and gives rise to "rights" that others are bound to respect.

Against the possibility of such degradation the Catholic Church in Latin America, basing itself on the canon law and church traditions, stood as a countervailing force. The Protestant churches in the South, with a tradition in which the emphasis was on grace and in which law was associated with a "rejected" covenant, accommodated themselves to prevailing secular mores, and, at least with respect to slavery and the Negro, uttered no prophetic word, no protest, no law higher than that of the state legislatures and courts. Their position for the three decades immediately preceding the Civil War was not unlike that of the Federal Council of the Dutch Reformed Churches of South Africa in mid-twentieth century, which proclaimed in 1960 that the true unity of races and of mankind is not to be found any-

[67] TANNENBAUM, *op. cit. supra* note 60, at 76, 77, 82.

where but "in Christ," in "the mystic body of Christ"—not in personal relations and in a just social order. What Reinhold Niebuhr has said of the South African Dutch Reformed churches was no less true of the sermons and publications of the Protestant churches in the South in the days of Negro slavery: "We have never witnessed such flagrant misuse of religious and theological terms to hide rather than illumine moral dilemmas, nor the use of religion as an escape for an uneasy conscience." [68]

Another countervailing force in Latin America was the Spanish-Portuguese law and tradition, which grew out of a society that had known slavery for centuries—a law and tradition to which the Catholic Church had made important contributions. But the South was largely settled by European people who brought with them no knowledge of slavery, no law and tradition with respect to it. To them slavery was not a familiar but a "peculiar" institution: "In neither tradition, policy, nor law was there room for the slave. The law did not know him and could not make provision for him when he came upon the scene. The same is true of public practice and policy. . . . He [the imported Negro] certainly was not a free man. And the [English] law did not know a slave." [69] Accordingly, without a slave tradition, without a slave law, and without a church concerned with the spiritual and moral personality of the slave,[70] the South gradually, but in the end firmly, built the institution of slavery on the premise that the Negro was a slave by nature. Since this was the case, the Western moral, spiritual, and legal inheritance was stopped short in the South at the Negro. He was by nature a slave; a few Negroes might, by accident, as it were, become freedmen; but no Negro could ever be a free man. As abolition threat-

---

[68] Niebuhr, *The Cold Comfort of a "Mystic Unity,"* 20 CHRISTIANITY AND CRISIS No. 8 (May 16, 1960).

[69] TANNENBAUM, *op. cit. supra* note 60, at 101. While England was involved in the slave trade and encouraged slavery in the colonies, the English courts refused to recognize the legality of slavery in England itself. See HOPKINS, *op. cit. supra* note 40, at 143.

[70] TANNENBAUM, *op. cit. supra* note 60, at 65.

ened slavery, the slave question became a racial question; and
when emancipation finally arrived, the South quickly, through
the Black Codes in particular, converted the former into the
latter question. The South accommodated itself to the end of
slavery by outside force and arms, but it never contemplated
an end to the race question.

Forgetting that the South never solved the slavery question—
it was solved for it by Union soldiers and arms—that section has
consistently repeated the cry of Calhoun: "We can take care of
ourselves." [71] Speaking on the Civil Rights Bill of 1960, Senator
Strom Thurmond of South Carolina told the United States Senate
that segregation in the South was a matter of public policy, law,
and custom. As such it was "open and above board," "honest."
But it may be, he said,

that we [Southerners] shall not be permitted to maintain our own style
of segregation. We southerners are a realistic people; history has made
us so. We know that this is not the first time in history that a small
people have been forced by their aggressive and numerically superior
neighbors to make certain changes in their way of life. The southern
people have had to yield once before—though it took overwhelming
force to make them yield, and in essentials of spirit and mind they
yielded nothing.

He went on to say that all attempts from the outside to make the
South change have been failures "so far as essentials and funda-
mentals have been concerned." [72] A week later Senator J. William Fulbright of Arkansas also argued in the Senate against
"outside" interference with the South. "An attempt by the North
to decree a mode of life for the South . . . can only lead to
serious trouble." [73] Calhoun before the Civil War contended that
it was "impossible" for the races "to exist together in the community . . . under any other relation than that which now
exists [i.e., the master-slave relation]. Social and political equality

[71] Quoted in *id.* at 108.
[72] 106 Cong. Rec. 6637, 6639 (daily ed. April 1, 1960).
[73] *Id.* at 7187 (daily ed. April 8, 1960).

between them is impossible. No power on earth can overcome the difficulty." [74] Slavery was overcome by military might, but "the difficulty," after a hundred years, remains—"the difficulty" of two races existing together in the community when the law, traditions, customs, practices, and ideas all have cooperated to establish the image of the Negro as that of one who by nature is fit for no status but that of slave, or, at the most, freedman.

It is only against the background of the Southern conviction of the "difference" of the Negro—not merely in color, but in moral and spiritual dignity—that the history of civil rights legislation and the continuing controversy over it can be understood and evaluated. For the South never attacked the problem of slavery—it attacked the abolitionists instead.[75] For the South never attacked the problem of race—it attacked the Reconstructionists instead. For the South now does not attack the problem of racial segregation and racial disfranchisement—it attacks the North and the civil rights movement instead.

[74] Quoted in TANNENBAUM, *op. cit. supra* note 60, at 109.
[75] See ELKINS, SLAVERY 207 (1959). This book follows in part the thesis of Tannenbaum and re-enforces it with interesting insights.

FEDERAL CIVIL RIGHTS LEGISLATION

Chapter 2

CIVIL WAR AMENDMENTS AND
CIVIL RIGHTS LEGISLATION

In July, 1862, Lincoln discussed with his cabinet the draft of a proclamation that would emancipate the Negro from slavery; but he was advised not to issue it until after a notable military victory. Following the successful battle of Antietam, Lincoln, on September 22, 1862, issued a preliminary proclamation, which stated that on the following January 1, 1863, all persons held as slaves in states that would then be in rebellion would be then and forever free, and that the executive department and the military and naval authorities would recognize and maintain the freedom of such persons, and that the President would, on that day, declare the states that were then in rebellion.

From this preliminary proclamation it was clear that Lincoln desired to put the Confederate States on notice that he intended to free their Negro slaves exactly one hundred days later, and that he would not extend his effort at emancipation to reach the slaves in loyal states—a state that would rejoin the Union would not have its slaves freed. He was also warning the Union slave states—Delaware, Kentucky, Maryland, West Virginia,[1] and Missouri—not to go over to the side of the enemy.

[1] For the sake of convenience, we mention here among the loyal slave states West Virginia, although it was not yet a state at this time. West Virginia was admitted conditionally on December 31, 1862. It was proclaimed a separate state on April 20, 1863, and admission was to be gained sixty days later. Its constitution as submitted to Congress provided for gradual abolition of slavery. Lincoln justified setting up the state as a war measure. Regarding Tennessee, see note 3 *infra*.

On January 1, 1863, Lincoln issued what has come to be known as the Emancipation Proclamation.[2] In this document he designated by name [3] the ten states that were then in rebellion —Alabama, Arkansas, Florida, Georgia, Louisiana, Mississippi, North Carolina, South Carolina, Texas, and Virginia—and declared that all persons held as slaves in those states were free. He stated that the executive department, including the military and naval departments, would recognize and maintain the freedom of these persons; he enjoined the freedmen to abstain from violence, "unless in necessary self-defense"; and he recommended to them that "in all cases when allowed, they labor faithfully for reasonable wages." He also declared that they would be received into the armed forces. Lincoln stated that he was issuing the proclamation as "an act of justice, warranted by the Constitution upon military necessity" (he was acting by virtue of the power vested in him as Commander in Chief of the Army and Navy) [4] "and as a fit and necessary war measure for suppressing" the rebellion in the named states.

Lincoln's action was not received with favor in all quarters in the Union states. The slave states in the Union [5] had obvious reason to feel uneasy. Northern Democrats, having voted against Lincoln for the presidency, were not ready to accept the idea that the war was being fought to free the slaves. Thus, seven days after the issuance of the proclamation, the legislature of Lincoln's own loyal and free state of Illinois adopted a resolution [6] condemning Lincoln's act "as unwarrantable in military as in civil law," as "a gigantic usurpation, at once converting the war, professedly commenced by the administration, for the vindication of the authority of the Constitution, into the crusade for

[2] 12 Stat. 1268–69 (1863).

[3] Tennessee was not mentioned although it was one of the eleven original Confederate states. Tennessee was occupied by federal troops in 1862, with Andrew Johnson as military governor.

[4] U.S. CONST. art. II, § 2.

[5] Slavery was abolished in the District of Columbia by an act of Congress of April 16, 1861.

[6] Ill. State Leg., Jan. 7, 1863.

the sudden, unconditional and violent liberation" of Negro slaves. The resolution stated that the freeing of the Negro slaves in the Confederate States was "a result which would not only be a total subversion of the Federal Union but a revolution in the social organization of the Southern States, the immediate and remote, the present and far-reaching consequences of which to both races cannot be contemplated without the most dismal foreboding of horror and dismay."

Lee surrendered to Grant at Appomattox Court House on April 9, 1865. Less than a month before this event, Congress had passed an act to establish the Freedmen's Bureau, that was to be in existence for the remainder of the war and one year thereafter. The act provided for the appointment of a commissioner who was to be head of the bureau, and of assistant commissioners in the Southern states. The bureau was to have charge of the freedmen and to provide for their needs, including the assignment to each freedman of forty acres of abandoned or confiscated land for a term of three years, with an option to purchase the land within that period.

When Congress met at the end of 1865, the Republican majority excluded the members-elect from the Southern states and set up the Joint Committee of Fifteen on Reconstruction. This was the beginning of Reconstruction. Shortly before, Mississippi had adopted its postbellum Black Code, which clearly pointed the direction in which the South was going to move unless stopped from the outside. It looked as if the Southern position in Congress might even be strengthened unless radical measures were undertaken, for now Negroes were to count as whole persons and not as three fifths of their number in the congressional apportionment process as provided in the Constitution (Art. I, Sec. 2), and this would mean an additional million and a half persons and additional Democratic members for the South in the House of Representatives.

A new Freedmen's Bureau Bill was passed by Congress early

in 1866. This bill extended the life of the bureau and enlarged its powers. The bureau was to construct schools for Negro children. The bill provided that it should be the duty of the President, acting through the bureau, to extend protection and jurisdiction over all cases affecting Negroes discriminated against in their "civil rights or immunities" in the Southern states, "in consequence of any State or local law, ordinance, police or other regulation, custom, or prejudice." The term "civil rights" was defined in the bill as being

any of the civil rights or immunities belonging to white persons, including the right to make and enforce contracts, to sue, be parties, and give evidence, to inherit, purchase, lease, sell, hold and convey real and personal property, and to have full and equal benefit of all laws and proceedings for the security of person and estate, including the constitutional right of bearing arms.

The law was to apply when civil rights or immunities were refused or denied to Negroes or any other persons on account of race, color, or previous condition of slavery or involuntary servitude, or when such persons were subject to different punishments or penalties than were prescribed for white persons committing like offenses.

The bill provided that any person who, "acting under color of any State or local law, ordinance, police, or other regulation or custom," shall in any Southern state subject, or cause to be subjected, any Negro, on account of race, color, or previous condition of slavery or involuntary servitude, or for any other cause, to the deprivation of "any civil right secured to white persons," or to any other or different punishment than those to which white persons were subject for the same offenses, shall be guilty of a misdemeanor. It was to be the duty of the Freedmen's Bureau to take jurisdiction of all offenses committed against the provisions of the bill. The jurisdiction was to cease whenever the discriminations ceased or whenever a state had been fully restored in all of its constitutional relations to the United States.[7]

President Johnson vetoed the bill.[8] In his message to Congress, Johnson contended that the measure was "not warranted by the Constitution"; that it failed to define "civil rights and immunities"; that trials under this bill were to take place without juries and under military authority and procedures, without normal constitutional safeguards and guaranties and without supervision by the federal courts. The rebellion, he said, was at an end, and therefore the measure was inconsistent with the actual conditions of the country and with the Constitution. Now that the Thirteenth Amendment had been ratified, he said, the powers originally vested in the Freedmen's Bureau appeared to be ample to meet the ends for which it was established. Johnson specifically objected to the provision for the construction of schools for Negro children, for this was a departure from past practice, when education was left to the states, local communities, private associations, and private individuals. Nor was it within the competence of the United States government to provide homes out of public money. It could not do this for indigent white persons, and so it could not do it for the Negro race. Since the rebellion was over, said Johnson, the Negro freedmen must look to themselves for sustenance and support. Furthermore, the costs to be incurred would be great, and the time had come for the federal government to practice, "not merely customary economy, but, as far as possible, severe retrenchment."

Johnson argued, too, that the Negro was not in need of the protection promised by the bill, for the South would need his labor, and competition for it would assure him a fair wage: "The laws that regulate supply and demand will maintain their force, and the wages of the laborer will be regulated thereby." Besides, he would have the liberty to change his place of residence and

[7] For the bill, see MCPHERSON, POLITICAL HISTORY OF THE UNITED STATES DURING PERIOD OF RECONSTRUCTION 72 (1871; 2d ed. 1875).

[8] For the veto message see MCPHERSON at 68.

go to places where his labor would be esteemed and properly rewarded.

In complete disregard of the Black Codes, Johnson stated that the four million freedmen could "protect and take care of themselves." It was only simple justice to the Negroes, he said,

to believe that they will distinguish themselves by their industry and thrift, and soon show the world that in a condition of freedom they are self-sustaining, capable of selecting their own employment and their own places of abode, of insisting for themselves on a proper remuneration, and of establishing and maintaining their own asylums and schools. It is earnestly hoped that, instead of wasting away, they will, by their own efforts, establish for themselves a condition of respectability and prosperity. It is certain that they can attain to that condition only through their own merits and exertions.

The veto message was concluded with an appeal to Congress to readmit the Southern states at once, for any measure affecting them should not be enacted in the absence or exclusion of their elected representatives.[9]

Not being able to repass the bill over the veto,[10] Congress, on July 16, 1866, passed the second Freedmen's Bureau Act (which was also vetoed but was passed over the veto).[11] This act continued the life of the bureau for two years, and provided that the bureau should have supervision and care of the freedmen "to enable them to become self-supporting citizens of the United States, and to aid them in making the freedom conferred . . . available to them and beneficial to the Republic." It provided that the bureau should have the power to sell land and buildings

[9] In response to this plea, on the very next day following the veto message the House of Representatives, by vote of 109 to 40, resolved that no representatives of the Southern states shall be admitted "until Congress shall have declared such State entitled to such representation." Ten days later the Senate, by 29 to 18 votes, passed a similar resolution. McPherson, *op. cit. supra* note 7, at 72.

[10] The vetoed bill was not re-enacted—the vote was 30 to 18, two votes less than the required two thirds.

[11] This act may be found in 1 Fleming, Documentary History of Reconstruction 321 (1906).

formerly held under color of title by the Confederate states and use the proceeds for the education of the freedmen; and that when the bureau ceased to exist, the remaining funds should be distributed among the former Confederate states in proportion to their population for educational purposes, if such states had made provision "for the education of their citizens without distinction of color." Until the states had been restored in their constitutional relations to the United States government and the ordinary course of judicial proceedings resumed, there would be secured in these states

the right to make and enforce contracts, to sue, be parties, and give evidence, to inherit, purchase, lease, sell, hold, and convey real and personal property, and to have full and equal benefit of all laws and proceedings concerning personal liberty, personal security, and the acquisition, enjoyment, and disposition of estate, real and personal, including the constitutional right to bear arms, . . . without respect to race or color, or previous condition of slavery.

Military protection and jurisdiction were to extend "over all cases and questions concerning the free enjoyment of such immunities and rights," and no penalty or punishment was to be imposed or permitted because of race or color, or previous condition of slavery other than that applicable to white persons for the same offense.[12]

This act, partly responsive to the criticism of Johnson, avoided use of the term "civil rights" but instead spoke of "personal liberty, personal security," and the "free enjoyment" of "immunities and rights." [13]

In order to complete the work of emancipation started by

[12] For a general treatment of the Freedmen's Bureau, see PEIRCE, THE FREEDMEN'S BUREAU (State Univ. of Iowa Studies in Sociology, Econ., Pol., & Hist., vol. III, no. 1, 1904).

[13] On July 6, 1868, an act to extend the life of the bureau for still another year was passed over Johnson's veto. There was subsequent legislation affecting the bureau (see PEIRCE, *op. cit. supra* note 12, at 71 ff.). The life of the bureau ended in the summer of 1872 (*id.* at 74). For veto of the second Freedmen's Bureau Bill see McPHERSON, *op. cit. supra* note 7, at 147.

Lincoln's proclamation of January 1, 1863, Congress, two years later, proposed the Thirteenth Amendment, which provides simply that:

Neither slavery nor involuntary servitude, except as a punishment for crime whereof the party shall have been duly convicted, shall exist within the United States, or any place subject to their jurisdiction.

Congress shall have power to enforce this article by appropriate legislation.

Ratification, completed December 6, 1865, meant the ending of slavery throughout the United States and the assurance that it would be beyond the reach of any state in the future.

The Civil Rights Act of 1866

Although Congress had omitted the term "civil rights" in the bill of July 16, 1866, it had by no means dropped the notion or the term altogether. Indeed, some four months before passage of the second Freedmen's Bureau Act, Congress passed (on March 13, 1866) an act entitled: "An Act to Protect All Persons in the United States in Their Civil Rights, and Furnish the Means of Their Vindication." [14]

The act was, in its intentions, one of the most far-reaching in congressional history. It declared all persons born in the United States to be citizens of the United States, and that all citizens, "of every race and color, without regard to any previous condition of slavery or involuntary servitude," shall have the same right in every state and territory "as is enjoyed by white citizens," to sue, be parties, give evidence; to inherit, purchase, lease, sell, hold, and convey real and personal property; "and to full and equal benefit of all laws and proceedings for the security of person and property"; and to be subject to "like punishment, pains, and penalties, and to none other, any law, statute, ordinance, regulation, or custom to the contrary notwithstanding."

[14] 14 Stat. 39 (1866). MCPHERSON, *op. cit. supra* note 7, at 78.

The act made it a criminal offense for any person, acting "under color of any law, statute, ordinance, regulation, or custom," to subject or cause to be subjected any inhabitant to the deprivation of any right secured or protected by the act, or to different punishment, pains or penalties, by reason of color or race. It gave federal courts jurisdiction to try all crimes and offenses committed against the act. Federal officers were given the right to proceed against all persons violating the act, and were directed to afford "protection to all persons in their constitutional rights of equality before the law, without distinction of race or color, or previous condition of slavery or involuntary servitude."

President Johnson vetoed the bill,[15] but the Senate repassed it by vote of 33 to 15, and the House of Representatives by vote of 122 to 41; so the bill became law on April 9, 1866.

Johnson objected to the bill because it declared all native-born persons (including, he pointed out, Chinese on the Pacific coast, "the people called Gipsies," Negroes, and Indians who were taxed) citizens of the United States (though not of the individual states), at a time when eleven of the thirty-six states were not represented in Congress. Was it sound policy, Johnson asked, under these conditions to make all these colored peoples citizens? "Four millions of them have just emerged from slavery into freedom. Can it be reasonably supposed that they possess the requisite qualifications to entitle them to all the privileges and immunities of citizens of the United States?" He asked whether it was necessary to declare them citizens in order to secure them "in the enjoyment of the civil rights" enumerated in the bill. Those rights were, he said, already secured to all aliens in the United States, and it might be assumed they were already secured to the Negroes as well.

Johnson argued that the naturalization laws required aliens to demonstrate their fitness to receive citizenship, but there was no

---

[15] The veto message is in MCPHERSON at 74.

such requirement of Negroes under the bill. So the bill, "in effect, proposes a discrimination against large numbers of intelligent, worthy, and patriotic foreigners." The Negro was, he said, less informed about our principles of government than was the foreigner.

Furthermore, hitherto all the rights enumerated in the bill had been considered within the province of state authority and jurisdiction, and now the bill proposed to wipe out all race distinctions in the enjoyment of these rights. If Congress could do this, then it might also proceed next to legalize interracial marriages, despite state laws against miscegenation. No, said Johnson, all these rights pertain to "the internal police and economy of the respective States." If the principle of the bill were admitted, then Congress could legislate against racial discrimination with regard to voting, office-holding, jury service, and similar rights.

Johnson also objected to the provision in the act making it a criminal offense for anyone, acting "under color of any law, statute, ordinance, regulation, or custom," to deprive any other person of any right secured or protected by the act, or to subject him to a different punishment, by reason of race or color. This might subject a state judge or other state official to criminal charges for carrying out his duties under state laws. This went too far, said Johnson, for the only remedy contemplated by the Constitution was, in case of conflict between the Constitution and state law, to declare the former the supreme law of the land.

Johnson attacked the act as "another step, or rather stride, towards centralization, and the concentration of all legislative powers in the national Government." To this he would not be a party. The details of the act, he said, were fraught with evil.

The white race and the black race of the South have hitherto lived together under the relation of master and slave—capital owning labor. Now, suddenly, that relation is changed, and, as to ownership, capital and labor are divorced. They stand now each master of itself. In this new relation, one being necessary to the other, there will be a new adjustment, which both are deeply interested in making harmonious. Each has equal power in settling the terms, and, if left to the laws that regulate capital and labor, it is confidently believed that they will satisfactorily work out the problem. Capital, it is true, has more intelligence, but labor is never so ignorant as not to understand its own interests, not to know its own value, and not to see that capital must pay that value.

This bill frustrates this adjustment. It intervenes between capital and labor, and attempts to settle questions of political economy through the agency of numerous officials, whose interest it will be to foment discord between the two races.

The Fourteenth Amendment

Although President Johnson's veto message failed to convince Congress, it had the effect of stimulating the national legislators to prepare a constitutional amendment that would remove all or most of the President's constitutional objections to the act. Two months after the Civil Rights Act became law, the Senate passed the Fourteenth Amendment, on June 8, 1866, and a few days later (June 13) the amendment was passed by the House. Ratification was completed on July 9, 1868.[16] Before Reconstruction governments took over the states of the South, the amendment was rejected in late 1866 and early 1867 by all the Southern states but Tennessee. The action rejecting the amendment by the legislatures of the ten states is summarized in the following table.[17]

[16] See historical note in THE CONSTITUTION OF THE UNITED STATES—ANALYSIS AND INTERPRETATION 45, prepared by CORWIN (1953).

[17] See 105 CONG. REC. at A 1062 (daily ed. app. Feb. 12, 1959); also McPHERSON, *op. cit. supra* note 7, at 194. Three slave, though not Confederate, states also rejected the amendment early in 1867: Delaware, Kentucky, and Maryland. New Jersey, Ohio, and Oregon at first ratified and then "withdrew," in 1868, their ratifications. According to McPHERSON, at 194, California, Iowa, and Nebraska failed to act on the amendment; but later Iowa and Nebraska ratified and California rejected the amendment. *Id.* at 353.

State	House	Senate	Date
Texas	70 to 5	21 to 1	Oct. 13, 1866
Georgia	147 to 2	38 to 0	Nov. 9, 1866
Florida	49 to 0	20 to 0	Dec. 3, 1866
Alabama	66 to 8	28 to 3	Dec. 7, 1866
North Carolina	93 to 10	45 to 1	Dec. 13, 1866
Arkansas	68 to 2	24 to 1	Dec. 17, 1866
South Carolina	95 to 1	rejected	Dec. 20, 1866
Virginia	74 to 1	27 to 0	Jan. 9, 1867
Mississippi	88 to 0	27 to 0	Jan. 25, 1867
Louisiana	unanimous	unanimous	Feb. 5, 1867

Following these actions, Congress passed the first Reconstruction Act on March 2, 1867.[18] It made readmission of representatives from the Southern states to Congress conditional upon each of these states holding a constitutional convention of delegates elected by all citizens without regard to race or color, except those disfranchised for participation in the rebellion; on each adopting a constitution with a suffrage provision in similar terms; on ratification of the new state constitution by persons enjoying the suffrage as thus defined; and on ratification of the Fourteenth Amendment by the new state legislature. The reconstructed state legislatures all ratified the amendment as shown in the following table.[19]

State	House	Senate	Date
Arkansas	56 to 0	23 to 0	April 6, 1868
Florida	23 to 6	10 to 3	June 8, 1868
North Carolina	82 to 19	34 to 2	July 2, 1868
South Carolina	108 to 12	23 to 5	July 9, 1868
Louisiana	ratified	22 to 11	July 9, 1868
Alabama	94 to 3	33 to 0	July 13, 1868
Georgia	89 to 71	ratified	July 21, 1868
Virginia	126 to 6	34 to 4	Oct. 7, 1869
Mississippi	87 to 6	23 to 2	Jan. 7, 1870
Texas	ratified	ratified	Feb. 18, 1870

[18] Act is in McPherson, *op. cit. supra* note 7, at 191.
[19] 105 Cong. Rec. at A 1063 (daily ed. app. Feb. 12, 1959). McPherson,

Because of this history of the ratification process, there is still the feeling in some quarters, especially in the South, that the Fourteenth Amendment was placed in the Constitution through unconstitutional and indefensible practices. In 1868, when the amendment was declared, by joint resolution of Congress, to be a part of the Constitution,[20] there were thirty-seven states in the Union. Ratification by twenty-eight states was required. Even if all Northern and border states voted solidly to ratify the amendment—which was not, in fact, the case [21]—ratification by at least one of the Southern states was essential for adoption of the amendment. It has been contended that the Reconstruction Act of March 2, 1867, was unconstitutional, that the representatives of the Southern states had been locked out of Congress for several sessions without constitutional warrant, that the Fourteenth Amendment—and the Fifteenth as well—had been adopted by an illegally constituted Congress, that these amendments had been rejected by the duly constituted legislatures in the Southern states and had been ratified subsequently under coercion by illegally constituted, usurping state legislatures.

Southern resentment against the Fourteenth Amendment revived again after the school desegregation decision of the Supreme Court in 1954.[22] To go into the details of the attack would cover many pages. It will suffice here to relate two incidents that typify the nature of the opposition.

Maryland, a slave border state, rejected the amendment early in 1867. The vote in the state senate was 13 nays and 4 yeas; in the house, 45 nays and 12 yeas—a decisive defeat of the resolution to ratify. At the legislative session in the spring of 1955, a proposal in the state senate formally to approve the amendment

---

op. cit. supra note 7, at 352–53. There are some minor discrepancies between these two reports.

[20] The joint resolution was adopted July 21, 1868.

[21] See note 17 *supra*.

[22] See, *e.g.,* David Lawrence in U.S. News & World Report, Sept. 27, 1957, pp. 139–40; his syndicated column in newspapers for Oct. 16, 1957, and Feb. 18, 1959.

was rejected. The vote was 13 yeas and 12 nays (15 votes in favor were required). There was no debate. "But, though unvoiced, the old opposition on the old ground figured in the action." [23]

Early in 1957 the Georgia senate went further. It adopted a resolution that declared the Fourteenth and Fifteenth Amendments null and void. It stated that the Thirty-ninth, Fortieth, and Forty-first Congresses which introduced and adopted the amendments had been illegally constituted, and stated that "the continued recognition of the Fourteenth and Fifteenth Amendments as valid parts of the Constitution of the United States is incompatible with the present day position of the United States as the world's champion of constitutional government." [24]

A fair reading of the record of history leads to the conclusion that had the Reconstruction Act of March 2, 1867, not been adopted, the Fourteenth and Fifteenth Amendments would not today be in the Constitution, and the Southern states—and the other former slave states—would still have Black Codes in operation. Although the Civil War was the bloodiest in our history, its only accomplishment without the Reconstruction Act would have been the ending of slavery in its most technical and narrowly economic sense. Everything else would have been the same as before, or worse.

In vetoing the first Reconstruction Act,[25] President Johnson clearly stated that the Southern states, unless subject to congressional reconstruction, would not grant citizenship, suffrage, and legal equality to the freedmen. The new rule imposed in these states, he said, was intended

solely as a means of coercing the people into the adoption of principles and measures to which it is known that they are opposed, and upon which they have an undeniable right to exercise their own judgment. . . . The purpose and object of the bill . . . is to change the entire structure and character of the [ten] State governments and to

[23] Krock, N.Y. Times, April 7, 1955, editorial page.
[24] N.Y. Times, Feb. 9, 1957, p. 21.
[25] Veto message of March 2, 1867, in McPHERSON, *op. cit. supra* note 7, at 166. The bill was passed over the veto on the same day, March 2, 1867.

compel them by force to the adoption of organic laws and regulations which they are unwilling to accept if left to themselves. The negroes have not asked for the privilege of voting. . . . This bill not only thrusts it into their hands, but compels them, as well as the whites, to use it in a particular way. If they do not form a constitution with prescribed articles in it [granting suffrage to the Negro] and afterwards elect a legislature which will act upon certain measures [the Fourteenth Amendment] in a prescribed way, neither blacks nor whites can be relieved from the slavery which the bill imposes upon them. . . . The Federal Government has no jurisdiction, authority, or power to regulate such subjects [as citizenship and voting rights] for any State. To force the right of suffrage out of the hands of the white people and into the hands of the negroes is an arbitrary violation of this principle.

Johnson spoke of the "slavery" that the Reconstruction Act would impose on the population of ten states: the measure reduced them, he said, "to the most abject and degrading slavery." He had not, however, a word to say about the fact that these states, by adopting the Black Codes, by refusing to grant citizenship and suffrage, even to some Negroes, if only as a moral token, and by rejecting the Fourteenth Amendment had manifested a determination not to change the status of the freed Negroes beyond the compulsion of the Thirteenth Amendment.[26]

By the original Constitution (Art. I, Sec. 2), the apportionment of representatives among the states was determined by adding to the number of free persons three fifths of the slaves. Now, under the Thirteenth Amendment, Negroes in the ten states were to be counted as free persons, so that the number of members in the House of Representatives from these states would be increased and the political power of these states would be enhanced; yet they were unwilling to admit these persons, now free, to citizenship and suffrage, by state legislation, act of Congress, or constitutional amendment.

Despite the action of the senate of Maryland and of Georgia

[26] It should be noted that Delaware, Kentucky, and Mississippi rejected the amendment in 1865, and that the amendment was ratified by Alabama, Florida, and South Carolina with provisos affecting the political and civil rights of the Negro. DuBois, BLACK RECONSTRUCTION 329 (1935); CORWIN, *op. cit. supra* note 16, at 44.

and the arguments by or on behalf of Southerners regarding the constitutional status of the Fourteenth and Fifteenth Amendments —which may or may not have been conceived and begotten in constitutional sin—were they not in the Constitution today, the United States would have inherited the same whirlwind that shakes and devastates the Union of South Africa. But one must add the tragic observation that this is not the view that pervades the South, which still agrees with and repeats the arguments of Andrew Johnson.

As we have noted, two months after passing the Civil Rights Act of 1866, granting citizenship to the Negro, Congress passed the Fourteenth Amendment and submitted it to the states for ratification. In view of the existence of the Civil Rights Act, what was the need of the amendment? The answer is that, although the act was upheld by the federal circuit court in two cases in 1866 and 1867,[27] its constitutionality was in doubt. At any rate, it was thought safer to place the substance of the act beyond the reach of the Supreme Court (which had not been reconstructed—some members of the Court who had participated in the Dred Scott [28] decision were still on the bench; and on the central question of citizenship of the freed Negro, the case might still have been considered a binding precedent), and also beyond the reach of a later Congress.

The most important provision in the amendment is Section 1, which reads as follows:

All persons born or naturalized in the United States and subject to the jurisdiction thereof, are citizens of the United States and of the State wherein they reside. No State shall make or enforce any law which shall abridge the privileges or immunities of citizens of the United States; nor shall any State deprive any person of life, liberty, or property, without due process of law; nor deny to any person within its jurisdiction the equal protection of the laws.

[27] United States v. Rhodes, 27 Fed. Cas. 785 (No. 16,151) (C.C. Ky. 1866); *In re* Turner, 24 Fed. Cas. 337 (No. 14,247) (C.C. Md. 1867).
[28] Dred Scott v. Sanford, 19 How. 393 (U.S. 1857). Justice Nelson was on the bench to 1872, Justice Grier to 1870, and Justice Wayne to 1867; all wrote concurring opinions in the case.

The Fifteenth Amendment was passed by Congress in February, 1869, and was ratified a year later.[29] It provided that

the right of citizens of the United States to vote shall not be denied or abridged by the United States or by any State on account of race, color, or previous condition of servitude.

Each of the two amendments provided that Congress shall have the power to enforce the articles by appropriate legislation.

The Civil Rights Act of 1870

Several months after ratification of the Fifteenth Amendment had been completed, Congress enacted a new Civil Rights Act,[30] "to enforce the right of citizens of the United States to vote in the several States of this Union, and for other purposes." The act dealt with voting rights and with civil rights.

It declared that all citizens of the United States who are otherwise entitled to vote in any election in any state, municipality, or other territorial subdivision, shall be "entitled and allowed" to vote without distinction of race, color, or previous condition of servitude, "any constitution, law, custom, usage, or regulation of any State or Territory, or by or under its authority, to the contrary notwithstanding."

If any act should be required as a prerequisite for voting under the authority of a state, it would be the duty of officials to give to all citizens "the same and equal opportunity to perform such prerequisite, and to become qualified to vote, without distinction of race, color, or previous condition of servitude." Violation of this

[29] McPHERSON, *op. cit. supra* note 7, at 399, 488, and 545; also at 557–62. Four slave states that were not subject to the Reconstruction Acts rejected the amendment: Delaware, Kentucky, Maryland, and Tennessee. In Tennessee the votes on the ratification resolution in the state house of representatives were 12 yeas and 57 nays; the senate did not vote on it. In Delaware, in the senate the votes were 2 yeas and 7 nays, in the house, no yeas and 19 nays. In Maryland, in the senate there were no yeas and 25 nays, in the house, no yeas and 87 nays. The vote in Kentucky was, in the senate 6 yeas and 27 nays, in the house 5 yeas and 80 nays.

[30] 18 Stat. 140 (1870). McPHERSON, *op. cit. supra* note 7, at 547. This was the so-called First Enforcement Act.

provision was made a misdemeanor, and subjected the offender also to the payment of $500 damages to the aggrieved party.

If a person, otherwise qualified to vote, offered to fulfill the prerequisites, but was kept from qualifying by the wrongful act or omission of the official in charge, his offer to perform was to be deemed a performance, and he would be entitled to vote by presenting an affidavit to the officer whose duty it was to receive and count the votes. A refusal to permit voting under these circumstances was made a misdemeanor and also subjected the election official to the payment of $500 damages to the aggrieved party.

Any interference with an attempt to qualify to vote was made a criminal offense and subjected the offender to a suit for damages.

If any person should interfere with the right to vote guaranteed by the Fifteenth Amendment, "by means of bribery, threats, or threats of depriving such person of employment or occupation, or of ejecting such person from rented house, lands, or other property, or by threats of refusing to renew leases or contracts for labor, or by threats of violence to himself or family," he would be guilty of a misdemeanor.

An anti–Ku Klux Klan provision stated that if two or more persons banded or conspired together, or went in disguise upon the public highway or upon the premises of another, with intent to violate any of the provisions of the act, or to injure, oppress, threaten, or intimidate any citizen with intent to prevent or hinder his free exercise or enjoyment of any right or privilege granted or secured to him by the Constitution or laws of the United States or because of his having exercised the same, those persons would be guilty of felony.

Federal courts were given exclusive jurisdiction of all cases, criminal and civil, arising under the act.

Federal circuit courts were given power to designate commissioners "to afford a speedy and convenient means for the arrest and examination of persons charged with a violation of this act."

The President was authorized to use such part of the armed forces as would be necessary "to aid in the execution of judicial process issued under this act."

All persons were to have the same right in every state to make and enforce contracts, to sue, be parties, give evidence, and to the full and equal benefit of all law proceedings for the security of person and property as was enjoyed by white persons, and should be subject to like punishment, licenses, and exactions of every kind, and none other, "any law, statute, ordinance, regulation, or custom to the contrary notwithstanding."

Any person who, "under color of any law, statute, ordinance, regulation or custom," subjected or caused to be subjected any person to the deprivation of any right secured or protected by this act, or to different punishment or pains, by reason of his color or race, would be guilty of a misdemeanor.

The Civil Rights Act of 1866 was re-enacted.

It was made a crime for any person to prevent a qualified voter "from freely exercising the right of suffrage" by "force, threat, menace, intimidation, bribery, reward, or offer, or promise thereof," or by such means to induce any voter to refuse to exercise such right. The same provision applied to voting registration for an election for Congress.

The act passed the Senate on May 25, 1870, by a vote of 48 yeas and 11 nays. It is notable that of the negative votes, six were from the senators of the loyal but former slave states of Delaware, Maryland, and Kentucky. The senators from the "reconstructed" states, except one senator from Virginia, voted for the measure.[31] In the House of Representatives the vote was 133 yeas and 58 nays, with the division along partisan as well as sectional lines.[32]

---

[31] One senator from Virginia, John W. Johnston, admitted early in 1870, voted nay. Senator Fowler of Tennessee also voted against the bill, as did three senators from California, New Jersey, and Ohio. McPherson, *op. cit. supra* note 7, at 550 and 507.

[32] *Id.* at 550 and 507–8. The Southern and border negative votes were as

The Civil Rights Acts of 1871

Congress was not satisfied with its enactments; it seemed to have a passion for turning out statutes that would assure to the Negro full and equal rights. Never before in the history of any people was there such an obsessive concern with the establishment of fundamental rights for a minority which, until then, had had no rights at all. Congress was intent on not merely passing laws giving rights to the Negro but on the vindication and enforcement of these rights against the former masters of slaves in sixteen states.

On February 28, 1871, Congress passed yet another act,[33] to protect the Negro in his voting rights. It was a long, detailed statute. Its more significant provisions were the following.

It made it a crime for any person, by force, threat, menace, intimidation, or other unlawful means, to prevent or hinder any person, having a lawful right to register to vote, from exercising such right.

In cities having 20,000 or more inhabitants, two persons, prior to an election for Congress, could request a federal circuit court judge to appoint commissioners to guard and scrutinize the process of registration or an election. The judge was to appoint two commissioners (known as election supervisors) for each voting precinct. The commissioners were to belong to different political parties. They were to attend the registration and voting places and have broad powers to assure "the truth or fairness" of the process. The United States marshal and his special deputies were required to keep the peace at registration and polling places and protect the election supervisors.

The federal judge was to designate a chief election supervisor from among the commissioners named by him.

All votes in a congressional election were to be by written or printed ballot.

---

follows: Alabama 1, Arkansas 1, Delaware 1, Kentucky 7, Maryland 4, Missouri 2, North Carolina 1, Tennessee 1, Texas 1, and Virginia 3.
[33] Second Enforcement Act. 2 FLEMING, *op. cit. supra* note 11, at 112.

Several months later—on April 20, 1871—Congress enacted an act which contained the following provisions.[34]

Any person who, "under color of any law, statute, ordinance, custom, or usage of any State," subjected any person to the deprivation of any rights, privileges, or immunities secured by the Constitution would be liable to the party injured in the federal courts.

If two or more persons (*a*) conspired to oppose by force the authority of the federal government, or by force, intimidation, or threat prevent, hinder or delay the execution of any law of the United States; or (*b*) went in disguise on the highway or on the premises of another person for the purpose of depriving any person or class of persons of equal protection of the laws or of equal privileges or immunities under the law; or (*c*) conspired for the purpose of impeding, hindering, obstructing, or defeating the due course of justice with intent to deny to any United States citizen due and equal protection of the laws; or (*d*) by force, intimidation, or threat tried to prevent any United States citizen, lawfully entitled to vote, from supporting the election of a presidential elector or a candidate for Congress, those persons would be guilty of a high crime, and in addition, subject to an action for damages in the federal courts.

In case insurrection, domestic violence, unlawful combination, or conspiracy were to so obstruct or hinder execution of the laws of the state and of the United States as to deprive any portion or class of any of the rights, privileges, or immunities or protection named in the Constitution and secured by this act, and the constituted authorities of the state should be unable, or should fail or refuse to protect the people in such rights, then the state would be deemed to have denied equal protection, and the President must take measures necessary for the suppression of the violence, combination, or conspiracy.

[34] 17 Stat. 13 (1871), the so-called Ku Klux Act or Third Enforcement Act. 2 FLEMING, *op. cit. supra* note 11, at 123.

When a combination was so numerous and powerful as to defy the state authorities and the federal authorities within the state, "or when the constituted [state] authorities are in complicity with, or shall connive at the unlawful purposes of, such powerful and armed combinations," and when conviction of the offenders and the preservation of public safety had become impracticable, an insurrection should be deemed to have taken place, and the President might then suspend the writ of habeas corpus.

The Civil Rights Act of 1875

One of the broadest civil rights acts adopted by Congress was entitled "An Act to Protect All Citizens in Their Civil and Legal Rights." It was passed on March 1, 1875.[35] The preamble or "whereas" clause with which the act opened is notable for its echo of some phrases in the Declaration of Independence. It read:

Whereas, it is essential to just government we recognize the equality of all men before the law, and hold that it is the duty of government in its dealings with the people to mete out equal and exact justice to all of whatever nationality, race, color, or persuasion, religious or political; and it being the appropriate object of legislation to enact great fundamental principles into law . . .

This was followed by a brief first section, providing:

That all persons within the jurisdiction of the United States shall be entitled to the full and equal enjoyment of the accommodations, advantages, facilities, and privileges of inns, public conveyances on land or water, theaters, and other places of public amusement; subject only to the conditions and limitations established by law and applicable alike to citizens of every race and color, regardless of any previous condition of servitude.

Then the act further provided that any person who violated the foregoing section

by denying to any citizen except for reasons by law applicable to citizens of every race and color, and regardless of any previous condition

[35] 18 Stat. 335 (1875). 2 FLEMING, *op. cit. supra* note 11, at 295.

of servitude, the full enjoyment of any of the accommodations, advantages, or privileges in said section enumerated, or by aiding or inciting such denial

would be liable to criminal and civil penalties in the federal courts. It also said, however, that the aggrieved person might elect to seek his common law remedy or that provided by state statute in the state courts.

Section 4 provided that no citizen, otherwise qualified, would be disqualified for service on a grand or petit jury, in any federal or state court, on account of race, color, or previous condition of servitude.

The Object of the Reconstruction Acts

The Civil Rights Act of 1875 was the last congressional enactment to protect the Negro in his civil or political rights until eighty-two years later Congress adopted the Civil Rights Act of 1957, followed three years later by the Civil Rights Act of 1960.

What, in brief, did the Reconstruction statutes attempt to accomplish? As these statutes are reviewed—looking at the statutes themselves and without considering the legislative intent as expressed by members of Congress in hearings and discussions— it is clear that Congress sought to wipe out every racial distinction that had any form of legal support, whether that support came from legislation, regulation, custom, or judicial decision, and whether the racial discrimination was the result of governmental action or inaction. Congress proceeded on the assumption that not only had slavery as an economic institution come to an end, but that all the incidents and badges of slavery must also be wiped out. Congress sought to transform the image of the Negro, first from a slave to a freedman and then from a freedman to a freeman. The law was to become totally color-blind. The Negro was to enjoy the "full" and "equal" benefit of all laws and other governmental acts for his personal security, personal liberty, security of property, personal dignity, and "equal" justice. From the civil and political standpoint, no racial distinctions were to be recognized or tolerated in governmental or public acts.

Congress proceeded on the assumption that if left to their own devices, if they could act as independent sovereignties, the Southern states would place the Negro in a separate, inferior caste, where he would be kept by a rule of superior political, economic, and social force. Using as an excuse the relatively low literacy and educational level of the Negro population (itself the product of slavery), the Negro would be deprived of educational opportunities, and thus the image of the Negro as an ignorant, noneducable being would be perpetuated. From slavery the Negro would be moved up a rung to peonage, and there he would remain. This is what the philosophy of states' rights or federalism would mean in practice. Congress, therefore, acted to nationalize civil and political rights, to make the federal government the guarantor and protector of these rights as against state action, and also as against private action, where the state failed, neglected, or refused to protect these rights adequately.

Congress nationalized citizenship, the right to vote without racial discrimination, the right to jury service without racial discrimination; the right to sue, be sued, and give evidence in courts of law in all cases, and not only where another Negro was involved; the right to own or lease property; the right to make and enforce contracts; the right to be protected by law in personal and property relations; the right to accommodations in places of public resort: in all respects the Negro was to enjoy the "full and equal" benefit of all laws, decisions, regulations, and customs; in all public relations the Negro was to enjoy equality of treatment and dignity. Where these ends could not be achieved through state or local courts, the federal courts were to have jurisdiction, including the right to supervise the registration and voting processes.

To achieve these purposes, Congress enacted the Reconstruction acts, the civil rights acts, and the enforcement acts, and secured the ratification of the three Civil War amendments to the Constitution.

From the standpoint of human rights, this program, legislative and constitutional, remains a monument to faith in human equality. The history of these legal strivings to wipe out the incidents and badges of slavery, as well as its roots, and to bring the four million freed Negroes into full membership in the human family, where they could enjoy and suffer the condition of being human equally with white persons, belongs among the noblest pages of the history of mankind. Certainly the Northern, Republican legislators had partisan and economic motives and sought power. This only means that they were not angels; it does not mean they were not men. Those men who signed the Declaration of Independence were also moved by economic incentives and the urge to win power; but these facts do not limit the truth of their assertions or the justice of their acts. "Great ideas enter into reality with evil associates and with disgusting alliances," Alfred North Whitehead has said; but the greatness of the ideas endures.

What Remains of the Civil War and Reconstruction Enactments

The three amendments to the Constitution remain. Their intended reach and depth have been circumscribed by Congress and the Supreme Court, but they endure. Had they not been adopted and ratified during Reconstruction, it is doubtful if they ever would have been added to the Constitution, especially the Fourteenth and the Fifteenth Amendments; yet it is very difficult to form a mental picture of our political and social orders without them. Would the Negro ever have been granted citizenship? Would freedom of speech, press, and religion ever have won constitutional protection against restriction by the states? [36] Would property rights be protected against invasion by the states? These and

---

[36] Barron v. Baltimore, 7 Pet. 243, 8 L. Ed. 672 (U.S. 1833). *Cf.* CROSSKEY, POLITICS AND THE CONSTITUTION ch. 30 (1953).

many more questions may be asked. Perhaps the Supreme Court would have invented some legal fictions or constitutional myths to achieve some of the ends that have been achieved under the amendments, but one may have serious doubts if personal, as distinguished from property, rights would have been won through such devices. The Negro has benefited from these amendments, but the gains for others have been infinitely greater, with respect to both personal liberties and property rights.

While the constitutional amendments remain—despite Southern attacks on the ratification of the Fourteenth and Fifteenth Amendments—very little is left of the legislative enactments. Congressional repeal and Supreme Court decisions have crushed most of the statutes.

Of the forty-nine sections of the enforcement acts, all but seven were repealed by a single act of Congress in 1894.[37] The adoption of the Criminal Code of 1909 reduced the civil rights and suffrage enactments to eight sections in Chapter 3, devoted to "offenses against the elective franchise and civil rights of citizens." [38]

What remains of the Reconstruction legislation in the current United States Code can be summarized as follows.

Of civil remedies:

42 U.S.C. § 1981: All persons shall have the same right in every state to make and enforce contracts, to sue, be parties, give evidence, "and to the full and equal benefit" of all laws "for the security of persons and property as is enjoyed by white citizens," and shall be subject to "like punishment, pains, penalties, taxes, licenses, and exactions of every kind, and to no other." (Derived from the act of May 31, 1870.)

42 U.S.C. § 1982: All citizens shall have the same right in every state as is enjoyed by white citizens to inherit, purchase,

[37] 28 Stat. 36 (1894). See also Davis, *The Federal Enforcement Acts,* in STUDIES IN SOUTHERN HISTORY AND POLITICS 205, 228 (1914).
[38] 35 Stat. 1088, 1153 (1909).

sell, lease, and hold real and personal property. (Derived from the act of April 9, 1866.)

42 U.S.C. § 1983: "Every person who, under color of any statute, ordinance, regulation, custom or usage, of any State or Territory, subjects, or causes to be subjected, any citizen of the United States or other person within the jurisdiction thereof to the deprivation of any rights, privileges, or immunities secured by the Constitution and laws, shall be liable to the party injured in an action at law, suit in equity, or other proper proceeding for redress." (Derived from the act of April 20, 1871.)

42 U.S.C. § 1985: If two or more persons conspire to prevent an officer of the United States from performing his duties; or to intimidate a witness, party, or juror; or to impede, obstruct, or defeat the due course of justice, "with intent to deny to any citizen the equal protection of the laws, or to injure him or his property for lawfully enforcing, or attempting to enforce, the right of any person, or class of persons, to the equal protection of the laws," the person injured or whose rights have been deprived may have an action for damages against the conspirators. If two or more persons conspire or go in disguise for the purpose of depriving any person of the equal protection of the laws, or of equal privileges and immunities under the laws, or for the purpose of preventing or hindering state authorities from giving or securing to all persons in the state equal protection of the laws; or if two or more persons conspire to prevent by force, intimidation, or threat any citizen entitled to vote from giving his support in favor of a person in a presidential or congressional election, the person injured or whose rights or privileges have been deprived may have an action for damages against the conspirators. (Derived from the act of April 20, 1871.)

42 U.S.C. § 1986: Every person who, with knowledge that any of the wrongs conspired to be done and mentioned in the preceding section and having power to prevent the wrongs, neglects or

refuses to prevent them or to aid in preventing them shall be liable to the injured party for damages. (Derived from the act of April 20, 1871.)

Of criminal actions:

18 U.S.C. § 241: "If two or more persons conspire to injure, oppress, threaten, or intimidate any citizen in the free exercise or enjoyment of any right or privilege secured to him by the Constitution or laws of the United States, or because of his having so exercised the same," or if two or more persons go in disguise with intent to prevent or hinder a citizen's free exercise or enjoyment of any right or privilege secured to him by the Constitution or laws of the United States, they shall be fined not more than $5,000 or imprisoned not more than ten years, or both. (Derived from the act of May 31, 1870.)

18 U.S.C. § 242: "Whoever, under color of any law, statute, ordinance, regulation, or custom, wilfully subjects any inhabitant . . . to the deprivation of any rights, privileges, or immunities secured or protected by the Constitution or laws of the United States, or to different punishments, pains, or penalties, on account of such an inhabitant being an alien, or by reason of his color, or race, than are prescribed for the punishment of citizens, shall be fined not more than $1,000 or imprisoned not more than one year, or both." (Derived from the act of April 9, 1866.)

18 U.S.C. § 243: No citizen otherwise qualified shall be disqualified for service on a grand or petit jury in any federal or state court on account of race, color, or previous condition of servitude; and the officer guilty of such discrimination shall be fined not more than $5,000. (Derived from the act of March 1, 1875.)

This is all that remains as the legislative inheritance from Reconstruction. But even these provisions are not to be taken at face value. Judicial construction has circumscribed the generality of meaning we might be inclined to read into such phrases as "any right or privilege of a citizen of the United States," or "equal privileges and immunities under the law," or "rights, privileges, or immunities secured or protected by the Constitution or laws of the United States." These were ideas of high generality, like the ideas embodied in the Civil War amendments to the Constitution, and they were intended to guide the "reconstructed" American society toward new forms of relations and new moral, political, social, and economic institutions. They were hints at higher notions of humanity. They were intended to make clear that, instead of slavery, freedom and equality would be the basic presuppositions of American society in the future. These broad generalities—flowing from the belief of Congress, as expressed in the preamble to the Civil Rights Act of 1875, that it was "the appropriate object of legislation to enact great fundamental principles into law"—were intended as a condemnation of slavery and as an expression of the idea that all human beings—or all American citizens—have essential rights that flow from their sheer humanity—or sheer American citizenship. But these ideas were soon cut down, by judicial interpretation, to fit the social structure as it then existed. American society, the society of the white people, was left undisturbed, comfortable, entrenched, as if nothing, really, had happened from secession to surrender. The constitutional and legislative phrase "privileges and immunities" became practically meaningless, "equality" became "separate but equal," and segregation became the means by which the social system—to borrow from Whitehead—was inoculated against full infection of the new principles of freedom and equality for all men: the broad ideas then took their place "among the interesting notions which have a restricted application."

Reconstruction—and the cause of Negro equality—was abandoned in the compromise of 1877;[39] but the idea of equality, extricated from its associates and alliances (good and evil, honorable and disgusting), remained as a force for reform, haunting

[39] See WOODWARD, REUNION AND REACTION (rev. ed. 1956).

and troubling the conscience, and ready for union with tangible
and material forces to seize opportunities and bring about
changes. The first change finally came in 1954 in the Supreme
Court, and other changes followed in the civil rights acts of Congress adopted in 1957 and 1960.

Recommendations of the President's Committee on Civil Rights

While this is not the place to trace in full detail the history of civil
rights developments from the end of Reconstruction to the present
day, in the chain of events, however, some of the legislative proposals of President Truman's Committee on Civil Rights must
receive mention.

The report of the President's committee, made in 1947,[40] contained recommendations the importance of which was emphasized by subsequent developments. Those which follow were
especially notable, as we shall see.

First, the reorganization of the Civil Rights Section of the Department of Justice, to elevate it to the status of a full division. It
should receive a substantial increase in appropriation and staff,
to enable it to engage in more extensive research and to act more
effectively to prevent civil rights violations.

Second, the establishment of a permanent Commission on Civil
Rights in the Executive Office of the President, preferably by act
of Congress.

Third, the enactment of new legislation to supplement 18
U.S.C. § 241, which would impose the same liability on one person as is now imposed by that statute on two or more conspirators.[41]

Fourth, the amendment of 18 U.S.C. § 242 to increase the

---

[40] PRESIDENT'S COMM. ON CIVIL RIGHTS, TO SECURE THESE RIGHTS (1947).
The committee was established at the end of 1946 by Executive Order 9808,
with Chas. E. Wilson as chairman. Robt. K. Carr was executive director.

[41] The committee report refers to 18 U.S.C. § 51, which is now 18 U.S.C.
§ 241.

penalties from a fine of $1,000 and a prison term of one year to a fine of $5,000 and a prison term of ten years, thus bringing its penalty provisions into line with those in 18 U.S.C. § 241.[42]

Fifth, the enactment of a new statute to supplement 18 U.S.C. § 242, specifically directed against police brutality and related crimes. The act should enumerate such rights as the right not to be deprived of property by a public officer except by due process of law. The right to be free from personal injury inflicted by a public officer; the right to engage in a lawful activity without interference by a public officer; the right to be free from discriminatory law enforcement resulting from either active or passive conduct by a police officer.[43]

Sixth, the enactment of a federal antilynching act. The act should define lynching broadly. It should cover participation of public officers in a lynching, or their failure to use proper measures to protect an accused person against mob violence. It should be an offense for public officers to fail or refuse to make proper efforts to arrest members of lynch mobs and to bring them to justice. It should cover action by public officers or private persons against an accused person meting out on him private vengeance because of his race, color, creed, or religion.

Seventh, the enactment of a federal statute protecting the right of qualified persons to participate in federal primaries and elections against interference by public officers and private persons. This act would apply to federal elections and to primaries that are an integral part of the federal electoral process, or that affect or determine the result of a federal election.

Eighth, the enactment of a federal statute protecting the right to qualify for or participate in federal or state primaries or elections against discriminatory action by state officers based on race

[42] The committee report refers to 18 U.S.C. § 52, which is now 18 U.S.C. § 242.

[43] This proposal was made in the light of the decision of the Supreme Court in Screws v. United States, 325 U.S. 91 (1945), considered in KONVITZ, THE CONSTITUTION AND CIVIL RIGHTS (1947).

or color or on some other unreasonable classification of persons for voting purposes. This statute would apply to both federal and state elections and primaries but would be limited to protection of the right to vote against discriminatory interferences based on race, color, or other unreasonable classification.

The above are some of the recommendations made by the committee. We have selected those which, in one way or another, have a bearing on the legislation adopted by Congress in 1957 and 1960. In the light of developments in our courts and in the light of the lunch counter sit-ins in 1960, we should call attention to the following general recommendation of the committee:

In general: The elimination of segregation, based on race, color, creed, or national origin, from American life. The separate but equal doctrine has failed in three important respects. First, it is inconsistent with the fundamental equalitarianism of the American way of life in that it marks groups with the brand of inferior status. Secondly, where it has been followed, the results have been separate and unequal facilities for minority peoples. Finally, it has kept people apart despite incontrovertible evidence that an environment favorable to civil rights is fostered whenever groups are permitted to live and work together. There is no adequate defense of segregation.

The Civil Rights Act of 1957

Many civil rights bills were introduced in Congress before and after the release of the report of President Truman's Committee on Civil Rights, but there was no enactment until September 9, 1957, when President Eisenhower signed the Civil Rights Act of 1957.

Prior to the adoption of this act, Congress—and the nation—seemed to be frustrated by the Southern threat of a filibuster in the Senate and by the informal coalition of conservative Republicans and Southern Democrats, which defeated civil rights proposals year after year. But in 1957 circumstances conspired to break this paralyzing pattern.

For one thing, the Republican leadership had become aware

of the fact that Negro voters, discouraged by the tight hold that Southerners seemed to have on the Democratic Party, had shifted substantially to Eisenhower in 1952 and 1956, and the Republican Party sought to win over the Negro vote for the whole party. At the same time, the Democratic Party leadership became aware that rule by the Dixiecrats had cost the party a considerable number of liberal and Negro votes. Both parties, therefore, stood to gain, as they saw it, by taking a strong position in favor of civil rights. The decision of the Supreme Court in 1954 against school segregation and the Southern resistance to the Court's mandate to desegregate the public schools "with all deliberate speed" also stimulated interest and concern; for the Southern efforts at nullification of the decision implied a threat to the Constitution, to one of the branches of the government, and to the rule of law. Finally, the Negroes in Africa were winning national independence and were rapidly filling places in the United Nations, in international blocs and conferences, and were playing a role in the East-West conflict.

In June, 1956, the House of Representatives passed a civil rights bill by vote of 279 to 126.[44] This was in the closing days of the Eighty-fourth Congress. When the Eighty-fifth Congress convened on January 3, 1957, Senator Clinton Anderson at once offered a motion that the Senate adopt new rules. The purpose of the motion was to eliminate Rule 22, under which debate on any matter before the Senate can be limited (cloture) by the affirmative vote of 64 senators, except that a motion to change the rule was not subject to any limitation whatsoever. Rule 22 has been aptly referred to as "the grave-digger" of all civil rights bills, for under it filibustering senators have had an effectual veto over any proposal to change the Senate rules. Senator Anderson contended that the Senate of each new Congress could, by majority vote, adopt new rules.

In 1917 and in 1953 similar motions had been introduced at

[44] H.R. 627.

opening sessions of Congress, but at no time in the history of the Senate had there been a vote on this question of whether or not the rules of the Senate must continue from one Congress to another.

Opponents of the motion did not permit a direct vote on the issue in 1957. Senator Lyndon B. Johnson moved to table the motion, and this move was carried by a vote of 55 to 38. Although Johnson's action preserved Rule 22, Vice President Nixon, presiding, stated his parliamentary opinion that "the right of a majority of the Senate at the beginning of a new Congress to adopt its own rules . . . cannot be restricted or limited by rules adopted by the Senate in previous Congresses." [45] Under the circumstances, however, this ruling did not have binding force, and Rule 22 was preserved.

Senator Johnson then warned that a filibuster would probably fail because of strong Republican determination to pass a civil rights bill. The Southern senators, after a long caucus, agreed not to filibuster if they could succeed in amending the administration bill [46] in two respects, which will be considered later, but with regard to which—with the help of Democrats from the Northwest, where there is no Negro vote—they were ultimately successful. On August 7, 1957, the Senate passed the amended bill by vote of 72 to 18.[47] Up to this point 122 hours of debate had been devoted to the bill in the Senate.

The bill then went to a conference between the House [48] and the Senate, where new compromises were reached. On August 29, 1957, the Senate passed the bill by a vote of 60 to 15, after

[45] 7 NAIRO Reporter No. 5 (Feb. 1957).

[46] S. 83 (Dirksen) and H.R. 1151 (Keating).

[47] The bill that was passed was H.R. 6127, which was the bill that had passed the House, with modifications. The only non-Southerner to vote against the bill in the Senate was Wayne Morse, who called the bill a sham. The other seventeen votes against the bill were by the senators from Alabama, Arkansas, Georgia, Louisiana, Mississippi, North Carolina, South Carolina, and Virginia, and by one senator (Holland) from Florida.

[48] The bill, H.R. 6127, had previously passed the House, by vote of 286 to 126, on June 18, 1957.

Senator Strom Thurmond of South Carolina surrendered the floor which he had held for over twenty-four hours.[49] As we have noted, the bill was approved by President Eisenhower on September 9, 1957, thereby making it the first civil rights statute enacted by Congress since 1875.[50]

The act was acceptable to liberals only as the "minimum meaningful" measure that was politically feasible at the time. Its chief significance was to be found in the consoling fact that it restored civil rights as a legitimate subject for congressional action after a lapse of over eighty years; and its adoption marked the first reduction of strength of the Southern bloc since the 1877 compromise.

The Civil Rights Act of 1957,[51] to "provide means of further securing and protecting the civil rights of persons within the jurisdiction of the United States," established a Commission on Civil Rights, consisting of six members, no more than three of whom may belong to the same party. The commission was authorized to have a full-time staff. While it might not accept the services of uncompensated personnel, it could set up advisory committees in the states. All federal agencies were required to cooperate with the commission. It might conduct hearings and might issue subpoenas for the attendance of witnesses and production of written or other matter.

The commission was charged with the duty to investigate written and sworn allegations that certain citizens were being deprived of "their right to vote and have that vote counted" by reason of their color, race, religion, or national origin; to study and collect information "concerning legal developments constituting a denial of equal protection of the laws under the Constitution"; and to "appraise the laws and policies of the Federal Govern-

[49] Senator Thurmond's act was spoken of as a one-man demonstration, not a filibuster. His was the longest delaying action by a single member in the history of the Senate.
[50] For 1949 proposals in Congress, see 1 EMERSON & HABER, POLITICAL AND CIVIL RIGHTS IN THE UNITED STATES 125–32 (2d ed. 1958).
[51] 71 Stat. 634 (1957) (in titles 42 and 28 U.S.C.).

ment with respect to equal protection of the laws under the Constitution."

The commission was required to submit its final report not later than two years from the date of the enactment (i.e., not later than September 9, 1959) and was to go out of existence sixty days later.

The act provided for an additional assistant attorney general. (It did not state that he would be in charge of civil rights work in the Department of Justice, but this was implied.)

The act amended existing legislation to make clear that federal district courts could hear actions brought under federal civil rights statutes. It repealed one of the few remaining Reconstruction sections, 42 U.S.C. § 1993, providing that the President could use federal troops to enforce certain civil rights statutes— a law that had not been used for over eighty years.[52]

A separate part of the act provides "means of further securing and protecting the right to vote." It provides that no person, "whether acting under color of law or otherwise"—i.e., no public official or private individual—shall intimidate, coerce or threaten another person for the purpose of interfering with the latter's right to vote for any federal office at any general, special, or primary election.

The Attorney General is given the power to institute an action for an injunction to prevent interference with the right to vote, and the federal district courts are given power to hear such cases without regard to the question of whether there had been an exhaustion of administrative or other remedies.

A person cited for contempt under the act may have counsel appointed for him by the court if he cannot afford to engage private counsel.

[52] President Eisenhower's use of federal troops in Little Rock, Arkansas, following the opening of school there on September 23, 1957, was based on the Constitution and on 10 U.S.C. §§ 332, 333. See opinion of Attorney General Herbert Brownell, Jr., to the President, dated November 7, 1957, in 41 OPS. ATT'Y GEN. No. 67.

The act provides that in criminal contempt cases [53] arising under the act the fine shall not exceed $1,000 and imprisonment shall not exceed a term of six months. In such cases the judge, in his discretion, may try the accused with or without a jury; but if there is a trial without a jury, the fine may not be more than $300, and imprisonment may not be in excess of a term of forty-five days. Should the punishment exceed these limits, the accused shall be entitled to a trial *de novo* before a jury.

Finally, the act defines the qualifications of federal jurors. Any citizen over twenty-one years of age who has resided for a year within the judicial district is competent to serve as a grand or petit juror unless he has been convicted in a state or federal court of record of a crime punishable by imprisonment for more than one year and his civil rights have not been restored; is unable to read, write, speak, and understand the English language; or is incapable, by reason of mental or physical infirmities, to render efficient jury service.

The act omitted from the original bill a provision that would have added to 42 U.S.C. § 1985 (dealing with conspiracy to interfere with civil rights) a paragraph giving power to the Attorney General to institute proceedings for an injunction to prevent the harm threatened by the conspiracy (the existing legislation gave the injured party the right to sue for damages). The Senate vote to omit this provision for injunctive relief was 52 to 38. To many people this action meant the removal of the most important part of the bill.

The Southerners wished to go further and provide for jury trials in all criminal contempt cases, knowing that Southern juries are not likely to bring in verdicts of guilty in civil rights cases. They succeeded in this effort in the Senate by a vote of 51 to 42.

[53] Criminal contempt is punishment for past defiance of the court's order; civil contempt is punishment in order to bring about compliance by the defendant with the court's order—as soon as he complies, he is restored to his liberty. The act makes no change in the law respecting civil contempt, nor in cases of contempt committed in the presence of the court.

The Department of Justice objected to this sweeping and dangerous innovation in federal procedure,[54] and so the bill, as finally
enacted, limited the right to a trial by jury to cases arising under
the act.

Substantively, the act could hardly be described as a victory
for civil rights. The best that one can say for it was said by the
late Senator Richard L. Neuberger, who characterized the act
as "a step in the proper direction, however limited and modest
that step might be." [55] The act satisfied no one, for it was too
little for the liberals and too much for the Southerners.

Report of the Commission on Civil Rights

In compliance with the provisions of the Civil Rights Act of 1957,
the Commission on Civil Rights submitted its report to the President and Congress on September 9, 1959.[56] While there appeared to be no disagreement in the bi-partisan commission along
party lines, there was disagreement along geographical lines—
three Northern against three Southern members.[57] The report—
a document of 668 pages—contained fourteen recommendations
for federal action against racial discrimination in voting, education, and housing. We shall summarize only those recommendations that proved to have a bearing on the civil rights act later
adopted by Congress.

First, in investigating complaints of denial of the right to vote
by reason of race or color, the commission found obstructions
in its way in Alabama and Louisiana, where state officials, interpreting state law, took the position that they had no right to

[54] See text of memorandum in N.Y. Times, Aug. 8, 1957.

[55] N.Y. Times, Aug. 11, 1957.

[56] U.S. COMM'N ON CIVIL RIGHTS, REPORT (1959). An abridgment of the report was also published, under the title WITH LIBERTY AND JUSTICE FOR ALL
(1959).

[57] The Northern members were John A. Hannah, chairman, of Michigan; the
Reverend Theodore M. Hesburgh, of Indiana; and Geo. G. Johnson, of Wash-
ington, D.C. The Southern members were John S. Battle, of Virginia; Doyle
E. Carlton, of Florida; and Robt. G. Storey, of Texas.

permit federal officers to examine voting or registration records. In Alabama, during the course of the investigation by the commission, the legislature passed an act permitting state officials to destroy the records of persons to whom registration was denied.

The commission, therefore, recommended that there should be an act of Congress requiring that all state registration and voting records be public records and that they must be preserved for five years, during which time they should be subject to public inspection, provided that all care must be taken to preserve the secrecy of the ballot.

Second, the commission found that in Alabama some boards of registrars frequently did not function as boards to register Negro applicants on scheduled dates. In some instances, several members of such boards resigned their posts so that there would not be a majority required for approval of registration; and state officials responsible for appointing registrars repeatedly delayed filling vacancies created by these resignations. Resort to these and other devices made it impossible for Negro citizens to register. The commission found that the Civil Rights Act of 1957 was insufficient to meet the conditions, and accordingly it recommended that 42 U.S.C. § 1971 should be amended by adding a provision that no state officer shall act in such manner as to deprive an individual of the opportunity to register or vote for any federal office at any general or primary election.

Third, the commission found that in Southern states a substantial number of Negroes were being denied the right to vote through discriminatory application and administration of state registration laws. Where no registration board was in existence or where there was none capable of functioning lawfully, those already registered were predominantly white persons. When the United States Attorney General brought an action to compel registration of qualified Negroes who had complained to the commission, under the procedure provided by the 1957 act, the court had to dismiss the complaint because there were no regis-

trars to be sued. When new registrars were appointed, they refused to serve. "In short," said the commission report, "no one
had yet been registered through the civil remedies of the 1957
act." The report went on:

The delays inherent in litigation, and the real possibility that in the
end litigation will prove fruitless because the registrars have resigned
make necessary further remedial action by Congress if many qualified
citizens are not to be denied their constitutional right to vote. . . .
Some method must be found by which a Federal officer is empowered
to register voters for Federal elections who are qualified under State
registration laws but are unable to register.[58]

The commission, therefore, recommended that upon receipt
by the President of sworn affidavits that the affiants have unsuccessfully attempted to register, though qualified to do so, and
that they have been denied the right to register because of race,
color, religion, or national origin, the President shall refer the
affidavits to the commission (assuming that its life is extended
by Congress), which shall investigate the allegations. If the commission then certifies to the President that the affidavits are well
founded, he shall designate a temporary registrar in the area
from which the complaints came. The temporary registrar shall
then administer the state registration laws and issue registration
certificates to all qualified persons, which will entitle them to
vote for candidates for federal office in any primary or general
election. The temporary registrar will hold office until the President has determined that his services in the area are no longer
necessary.[59]

The echo from the Reconstruction enforcement acts can be
clearly heard in this recommendation. After more than eighty
years the problem was the same and the remedy the same.

[58] U.S. COMM'N ON CIVIL RIGHTS, REPORT 140, 141 (1959).

[59] Mr. Battle, former governor of Virginia, dissented from this recommendation on the ground that present laws were sufficient and that the appointment
of federal registrars would place in the hands of the federal government a
vital part of the election process "so jealously guarded and carefully reserved
to the States by the Founding Fathers." U.S. COMM'N ON CIVIL RIGHTS, REPORT
142 (1959).

Fourth, the three Northern commission members recommended in addition a constitutional amendment, which read:

The right of citizens of the United States to vote shall not be denied or abridged by the United States or by any State or by any person for any cause except inability to meet State age or length-of-residence requirements uniformly applied to all persons within the State, or legal confinement at the time of registration or election. This right to vote shall include the right to register or otherwise qualify to vote, and to have one's vote counted.

The Congress shall have the power to enforce this article by appropriate legislation.[60]

The commission—or at least the three Northern members— found, on the basis of extensive investigations, hearings, and studies, that the Southern states used their complex voting laws —including tests of literacy, "interpretation," and education— to deny arbitrarily the right to vote, through discriminatory application and administration of these state laws. The report stated that "the difficulty of proving discrimination in any particular case is considerable. It appears to be impossible to enforce an impartial administration of the literacy tests now in force in some States, for, when there is a will to discriminate, these tests provide the way." [61] The aim of the constitutional amendment would have been to prohibit all complex voting requirements and to remove the need of further federal intervention. Only nineteen states require proof of literacy, for the "march of education has almost eliminated illiteracy," and there is no excuse for whatever illiteracy remains. "Ratification of the proposed amendment would . . . provide an additional incentive for its total elimination." [62] In addition, today, much information about candidates and issues comes over the radio and television, which are so common as to inform illiterate and literate alike.

Running through the discussion of voting in the report is the shock of recognition that, after nearly a century and even with

[60] *Id.* at 144–45.   [61] *Id.* at 143.   [62] *Id.* at 144.

the Fourteenth and Fifteenth Amendments in the Constitution, there should still be a need for another constitutional amendment as "a reaffirmation of our faith in the principles upon which this Nation was founded." [63]

Fifth, turning to the problem of school desegregation, the commission found that desegregation by court order was notably more difficult than desegregation by voluntary action "wherein the method and timing have been locally determined." The commission recommended that Congress authorize the commission to act as a clearinghouse of information on school desegregation to states and local communities, and as an advisory and conciliation agency to assist local school boards to meet the constitutional requirement of desegregated schools and the local conditions.[64]

Sixth, the Northern members of the commission recommended that institutions of higher learning that practice racial discrimination in their admission policies should be denied federal grants. (The Southern members objected that this would mean "a program of economic coercion as either a substitute for or a supplement to the direct enforcement of the law through the orderly processes of justice as administered by the courts.") [65]

The commission also made recommendations relating to housing, but the details of these need not be stated here.[66] However, their statement of the interrelations among education, voting, and housing deserves emphasis:

Slavery, discrimination, and second-class citizenship have demoralized a considerable portion of those suffering from these injustices, and the consequent demoralization is then seen by others as a reason for continuing the very conditions that caused the demoralization.

The fundamental interrelationships among the subjects of voting, education, and housing make it impossible for the problem to be solved by the improvement of any one factor alone. If the right to vote is secured, but there is not equal opportunity in education and housing,

[63] *Ibid.*   [64] *Id.* at 326.   [65] *Id.* at 328–29.   [66] See *id.* at 534 ff.

the value of that right will be discounted by apathy and ignorance. If compulsory discrimination is ended in public education but children continue to be brought up in slums and restricted areas of racial concentration, the conditions for good education and good citizenship will still not obtain.

If decent housing is made available to nonwhites on equal terms but their education and habits of citizenship are not raised, new neighborhoods will degenerate into slums. . . .

At its worst, the problem involves a massive demoralization of a considerable part of the nonwhite population. This is the legacy of generations of slavery, discrimination, and second-class citizenship. Through the vote, education, better housing, and other improving standards of living, American Negroes have made massive strides up from slavery. But many of them . . . are still being denied equal opportunity to develop their full potential as human beings.[67]

The Civil Rights Act of 1960

On May 6, 1960, President Eisenhower signed the Civil Rights Act of 1960. A civil rights bill had passed the House of Representatives on March 24, 1959, by vote of 311 to 109. Of those who voted against the bill, 94 were Democrats and 15 were Republicans. Of the Democratic votes against the bill, all but 2 were from the South or border states.[68] Of the 15 Republican negative votes, 5 were from the South. On April 8, 1960, the Senate passed a version of the bill that amended the House measure in sixteen provisions. The Senate vote was 71 to 18, with all of the negative votes coming from the South.[69] On April 21, 1960, the House passed the Senate bill by vote of 288 to 95. The negative votes were from 87 Southerners, 1 Northern Democrat and 7 Northern Republicans.[70] The intransigent op-

[67] *Id.* at 545–46, 548. H.R. 8385, Mutual Security Appropriation Bill, 86th Cong., 1st Sess. (1959), extended the life of the Civil Rights Commission for two years to Nov. 9, 1961.
[68] One was from Indiana and one from Oklahoma. Of the 94 votes against the bill, 90 were from the original eleven Confederate states, one was from Missouri, and one from Kentucky. N.Y. Times, March 25, 1960.
[69] N.Y. Times, April 9, 1960. 106 CONG. REC. 7267 (daily ed. April 8, 1960).
[70] N.Y. Times, April 22, 1960.

position from the South was manifested not only in the votes but also in the debates and the filibuster.[71]

Soon after the Eighty-sixth Congress convened in January, 1959, and it became apparent that a major part of the session would be taken up with controversy over civil rights bills, liberal senators tried to persuade the Senate to change its rules so as to destroy the filibuster; but these efforts failed.[72] On January 12, 1959, however, the Senate adopted a measure that changed the rules in three respects: (1) Two thirds of the senators present and voting might cut off debate (or force cloture). The old rule required two thirds of the full membership of the Senate. (2) Cloture might be imposed on debate relating to change of rules by two thirds of the senators present and voting. The old rule made it impossible to cut off debate on changing the rules. (3) The rules now provide that the Senate shall henceforth "continue [these rules] from one Congress to the next Congress" unless they are changed in accordance with the rules, including the new two-thirds requirement.

Although Southern senators did not filibuster against these changes in the rules, most of them voted against the changes.[73] On February 29, 1960, however, they began a filibuster against civil rights measures, which the Senate tried to meet by round-the-clock sessions. The filibuster broke all Senate records for continuous sessions.[74] Eight weeks were consumed by the filibuster and other tactics before a final vote was taken. The eighteen Southerners were unable to win a single vote from the border senators or from the Republican ranks; yet the measure

[71] Note should be made of the fact that while Southern members of Congress opposed civil rights bills, in the final House vote nine Southerners voted for the bill, and in the Senate there were votes for the bill from senators from Delaware, Kentucky, Maryland, Missouri, Tennessee, Texas, and West Virginia.

[72] Senator Douglas led the fight to change the rules. His motion lost by 60 to 36. See N.Y. Times, Jan. 10, 1959.

[73] The vote was 72 to 22. A few liberal senators voted against the changes on the ground that they were meaningless and a sham. N.Y. Times, Jan. 13, 1959.

[74] N.Y. Times, March 6, 1960. The filibuster broke the records of 1915 and 1954.

finally enacted could scarcely be described as a strong statute. At almost every point it showed evidence of compromise.

The substance of the Civil Rights Act of 1960 is as follows.

It was made a federal crime for a person, by threats or force, to obstruct, impede, or interfere with the exercise of rights or the performance of duties under a decree or order of a federal court.

It was made a federal crime for a person to move from one state to another to avoid prosecution under state law for having attempted to destroy or damage, by fire or explosive, any church or synagogue or any other building, or if he flee in order to avoid giving testimony in a case relating to such an offense. It was also made a federal crime to transport explosives in interstate commerce with knowledge or intent that they would be used to commit such an offense.

Election officers are required to preserve for twenty-two months all registration, poll tax payment, and other records that are prerequisite to voting in any primary, special, or general election for federal office. Violation of this duty, or destruction, concealment, or mutilation of records by any person, was made a federal crime. Such records are to be made available to the Attorney General or his representative upon written demand. Unless ordered by a federal court, the Department of Justice shall not disclose any record or paper except to Congress, a congressional committee, governmental agencies, or a court or grand jury. Federal courts were given power to compel production of such records or papers.

Where children of members of the Armed Forces cannot get free public education because the public schools have been shut down by state or local action, the federal government is to provide suitable free public education for them.

The law relating to voting, 42 U.S.C. § 1971, was amended so that when the Attorney General institutes an injunctive procedure to restrain deprivations of the right to vote by reason of race or color, and the court finds that there has been such deprivation, the court may go into the question whether the deprivation was pursuant to a pattern or practice. If the court finds such a pattern or practice, any Negro within the affected area shall, for one year and until the pattern or practice has ceased, be entitled to an order declaring him entitled to vote upon proof that he is qualified under state law and that, since such finding by the court, he has been deprived of his right under color of law. The applicant shall then be entitled to vote. The refusal by an election official to permit him to vote shall be contempt of court. An application for an order under this law shall be heard within ten days.

The court may appoint voting referees to receive applications, take evidence, and report findings to the court. The applicant's statements under oath shall be prima facie evidence as to his age, residence, and prior efforts to register or vote. If proof of literacy or an understanding of other subjects is required by state law, the applicant's answers shall be included in the referee's report to the court.

When the court has received the report, it shall have the Attorney General transmit a copy to the state attorney general and to each party to the proceedings, together with an order to show cause within ten days why an order should not be entered in accordance with the report. Exceptions as to matters of fact in the report may be filed, as may also a memorandum on matters of law, and the issues raised shall be determined by the court, or, if due and speedy administration of justice requires, they may be referred to the voting referee.

If an application is filed but undetermined by the time of the election, the court shall issue an order authorizing the applicant to vote provisionally—provided that the applicant is qualified to vote under state law—and the ballot shall be impounded pending determination.

If a state official is charged with deprivation of the right to register or vote, and if prior to the institution of proceedings he has resigned and no successor has been named, the proceeding may be instituted against the state.

On the day the statute was enacted, the Attorney General, William P. Rogers, made a formal statement in which he spoke of the act as having "historic significance" and said, further, that the act "makes clear that all branches of the Federal Government firmly support the proposition that the Fourteenth and Fifteenth Amendments of the Constitution are not to be considered mere promises but must become realities for all citizens in all areas of the country." [75] Had this statement been made of the Reconstruction enforcement acts, it would have had a true ring; but coming as it did three generations later, following the passage of a statute that offers little when set against the grand promises of the constitutional amendments, the statement exaggerates the result. The statute, for all that, is not a mere nullity; it does, as other parts of the Attorney General's statement made clear, enhance the citizen's right to vote by prohibiting the destruction of records for twenty-two months, by nullifying the effect of the resignation of election officials, and by providing for the appointment of voting referees. The act relieves the citizen who has been deprived of the suffrage of some of the burden by shifting it to the Attorney General, who will have the duty to proceed to vindicate the right to vote where the pattern of racial discrimination obtains. In the future much will depend upon the character of the Attorney General and his sense of dedication to fundamental rights and privileges, and on the good faith with which Congress will vote adequate appropriations for the Department of Justice to permit the Attorney General to engage the staff that will be needed to keep up with Southern ingenuity in inventing devices to void the Constitution and the laws adopted under its provisions. For some years to come the new law will be challenged in the courts, and in the meantime the act will not

[75] N.Y. Times, April 22, 1960.

have much bite. As in the case of the school desegregation decree, so, too, in the case of the new act, progress will be seen where citizens and state and local officials voluntarily proceed to end discriminatory practices step by step. For the rest, many and long delaying tactics can be foreseen, the inadequacies of the 1960 act will be disclosed, the struggle for civil rights in Congress and in the courts will continue, and the need to reexamine and adopt more of the Reconstruction enforcement processes will be urged even by Americans who in the past have thought of themselves as liberal moderates.

On the day the bill passed the Senate, the Republican Minority Leader, Senator Dirksen, said that enactment of the bill demonstrated that the Senate was "capable of moderation and of avoiding the extremes. . . . What we have now wrought is a moderate bill. . . . I salute the tolerance of the U.S. Senate." [76] But one might ask whether fundamental constitutional liberties and guarantees ought to be the subjects of "moderate" bills. The right to vote or to other civil rights is not the same thing as an income tax rate, over which reasonable minds might differ, and with respect to which legislative horse-trading might not be a bad thing. Why should basic human rights become subject to compromises? Horse-trading "is no way to enforce constitutional rights; they were not intended to be checked and blocked." [77]

A more just judgment was expressed by Senator Paul Douglas in his comments to the Senate as the bill was about to be passed:

Mr. President, the bill which the Senate is about to pass sets up an elaborate obstacle course which the disenfranchised Negro in the South must successfully run before he will be permitted to vote at all. At every strategic point there are high technical walls which he must scale, and along the course there are numerous cunningly devised legal pitfalls into which he may fall. The delays and the discouragements

[76] 106 CONG. REC. 7263 (daily ed. April 8, 1960).
[77] BLACK, THE PEOPLE AND THE COURT 132 (1960). For a list of some of the parliamentary steps followed in connection with the bill, see memorandum of Senator Johnson in 106 CONG. REC. 7267 (daily ed. April 8, 1960).

have been multiplied so . . . that the bill would permit only a very few additional Negroes to vote.

The precise nature of these unnecessary hurdles, pitfalls, and water jumps which have been constructed by the framers of the bill . . . will be revealed to the country in the months and years ahead. . . . [The bill] is grossly inadequate to right the great wrongs which are now practiced. . . . Ninety years after the 15th amendment and ninety-three years after the 14th, this is not a good day for the American tradition of equal opportunity.

He ended his remarks by saying that the senators from the North and West will soon renew their drive "for a more meaningful and robust proposal." [78]

Another supporter of a "meaningful" civil rights bill remarked that after eight weeks of debate, "the surprising thing is . . . that it took so long to accomplish so little." The real losers, he said, were not those who had tried for a strong bill, but the Negroes of the South. For this was "a watered-down bill that has been so further diluted that it will wash right out of [the Senate] Chamber and hardly will be noticed in the mainstream of American life." He promised that there will be another bill in the next Congress and still another in the one after that.[79]

[78] *Id.* at 7261–62 (daily ed. April 8, 1960).
[79] Senator McNamara of Michigan, in *id.* at 7190 (daily ed. April 8, 1960).

Chapter 3

THE CIVIL RIGHTS ACT OF 1875

As stated in the Preface, our central—though not exclusive—interest in this book is the right to equality in the enjoyment of accommodations in places of public resort. For an understanding of this right, detailed consideration of the Civil Rights Act of 1875 [1] is indispensable, and so we must return to this statute that was mentioned only briefly in the previous chapter.

The act proceeded on the notion, stated in the preamble, that it was an appropriate object of legislation "to enact great fundamental principles into law." The principles enacted were: (1) that all persons shall be entitled to the full and equal enjoyment of the accommodations and privileges of inns, public conveyances, theaters, and other places of public amusement, subject only to the legal limitations that are applicable alike to all citizens of every race and color, and regardless of any previous condition of servitude; (2) that no citizen shall be disqualified for jury service in a federal or state court on account of race, color, or previous condition of servitude; (3) that the foregoing rights may be vindicated by civil and criminal penalties in the federal courts.

There is a general impression that during Reconstruction it was a simple and easy matter to push through Congress legislation favorable to the Negro, for, it is assumed, Congress was "packed" with Northern radicals and with Negro and pro-Negro senators and congressmen. The facts are quite different. Only

[1] 18 Stat. 335 (1875). See 2 FLEMING, DOCUMENTARY HISTORY OF RECONSTRUCTION 295 (1906).

two Negroes were senators. Hiram R. Revels, who had attended Knox College in Illinois and was a schoolteacher and Methodist minister, was elected senator from Mississippi in 1870 to fill the seat vacated by Jefferson Davis. The other Negro elected to the Senate, also from Mississippi, was Blanche K. Bruce, who had attended Oberlin College and was also a teacher. He was elected in 1874. In the House of Representatives, three Negroes were elected to the Forty-first Congress in 1869; in the Forty-second Congress, there were five Negro congressmen; in the Forty-third and Forty-fourth, there were seven. In the judgment of James G. Blaine, who knew most of them, the Negro members of Congress were not ignorant men but "studious, earnest, ambitious men, whose public conduct . . . would be honorable to any race." [2]

As to the impression that Congress during Reconstruction was a pushover for pro-Negro legislation, a brief review of the legislative history of the 1875 act should dispel this illusion.

It took five years for this civil rights bill to go through Congress, from its introduction by Senator Charles Sumner of Massachusetts on May 13, 1870, to its enactment on March 1, 1875. During these five years the measure was subject to all the delaying tactics that the rules of procedure permitted. It would take many pages to trace the history of the bill in detail; we shall mention only the highlights.

As introduced by Senator Sumner, the bill provided for equal rights in "railroads, steamboats, public conveyances, hotels, licensed theatres, houses of public entertainment, common schools, and institutions of learning authorized by law, church institutions, and cemetery associations incorporated by national or state authority; also on juries in courts, national and state." [3] The bill was reported adversely by the Senate Judiciary Committee three months later.[4] The identical bill was reintroduced by Sumner at

[2] FRANKLIN, FROM SLAVERY TO FREEDOM 315–17 (1947).

[3] CONG. GLOBE, 41st Cong., 2d Sess. 3434 (1870).

[4] *Id.* at 5314.

the next session, with the identical fate.[5] In the first session of
the next Congress, Sumner again introduced the bill, but this
time the Judiciary Committee did not even report it.[6]

In the second session of the Forty-second Congress, Sumner
offered his bill as an amendment to an amnesty bill that had been
passed by the House. After his amendment had been amended,
it passed by a vote of 29 to 28, but then the amnesty bill with
the civil rights amendment was defeated.[7]

The House passed a second amnesty bill. When it was brought
up in the Senate, Sumner unsuccessfully tried to substitute for
it his civil rights bill. Then he moved his bill as an amendment
to the amnesty bill, and the vote on this move was a tie. The
Vice President broke the tie by voting for the amendment. But
again the amnesty bill with the Sumner amendment failed to
pass.[8] Later in the same session the Sumner bill itself came up for
consideration. Against the wishes of the sponsor, the bill was
amended to leave out references to schools and juries, and in
this form it passed the Senate.[9]

Now it was up to the House to take action on an identical
bill, but its opponents resorted to all sorts of dilatory tactics.
An attempt to suspend the rules, so that the bill could be brought
up, failed to win the necessary two-thirds vote, though it won
majority support. All efforts to bring up the bill in the House,
after it passed the Senate, failed during this session.[10] In the next
session the House considered the bill by amending it to add an
amnesty proposal, but again the bill, with the amendment, was
lost.[11]

When the Forty-third Congress convened in December, 1873,
Senator Sumner once more introduced his bill, including a prohibition against school segregation. The bill was referred to the

[5] CONG. GLOBE, 41st Cong., 3d Sess. 619, 1263 (1871).
[6] CONG. GLOBE, 42d Cong., 1st Sess. 832 (1872).
[7] CONG. GLOBE, 42d Cong., 2d Sess. 237, 240, 435, 453, 919, 929 (1872).
[8] *Id.* at 3181, 3268, 3270.   [9] *Id.* at 3734, 3736, 3738.
[10] *Id.* at 1117, 1956, 2074; 3383; 3932, 4321–22.
[11] CONG. GLOBE, 42d Cong., 3d Sess. 2110–11 (1873).

Judiciary Committee, which reported it favorably some five months later—ironically, a month after Sumner's death. After an all-night session, the bill was passed May 22, 1874, but only after moves to amend it were beaten.[12]

In the House, attempts to bring up the bill, after the Senate had passed it, failed during the entire first session of the Forty-third Congress. Efforts to suspend the rules were unsuccessful. The House Judiciary Committee, however, introduced its own bill, which on coming up for consideration brought threats of a filibuster. The bill went back to the committee and was not again brought up at that session.[13]

In the second session of the Forty-third Congress, unsuccessful attempts were made in the House to call up the Sumner bill, as it had passed the Senate, with a ban on segregated schools. Then attempts were made to bring up the bill reported by the House Judiciary Committee; but opponents resorted to dilatory devices. One House session lasted for forty-six continuous hours, taken up with motions to adjourn. This time, however, the House rules were amended, and the bill was brought up for consideration. There were three days of debate, and finally the House passed the bill, but without mention of schools. The Senate concurred; and thus was the Civil Rights Act of 1875—originally of 1870—finally enacted.[14]

This brief summary of a very complex legislative history shows how tortuous and rocky has been the path of development of civil rights policies in the United States, starting with Reconstruction. Every step proposed in favor of a nationalization of American citizenship, of national privileges and immunities, of a national concept of basic human rights has been fought over with bitterness and hate.

In view of the great importance of the issue of equal rights to public accommodations, a basic human right and our main in-

[12] 2 Cong. Rec. 2, 12, 3053, 3451, 4176 (43d Cong., 1st Sess., 1873).
[13] *Id.* at 4242, 4439, 4691, 5162; 97–98, 318, 337–38, 458.
[14] 3 Cong. Rec. 704, 938, 1010; 116, 786–828, 890–902, 938 (1875).

terest here, a further consideration of certain aspects of the debates in Congress over the Civil Rights Act of 1875 will be revealing and instructive.

In reporting the Sumner bill with amendments from the House Judiciary Committee, Congressman Butler of Massachusetts said that the bill would not affect social relations—such relations must always be voluntary. Riding in a public car, he said, does not bring about the social equality of the passengers or make associates of them. There were white men with whom he would not associate who have, nonetheless, the right to ride in public cars; and this was true, too, of theaters and public amusements—the persons found there do not make up social gatherings. This was equally true, said Butler, of inns. Men are entitled to equal accommodations in inns when they pay for them, without regard to whether they are rich or poor, learned or ignorant. There is no association in meeting a man at an inn. One is not obliged to speak to him. So, too, when men are together in a railway dining room. To all such places, Butler said, he would apply the rule of the common law that required equal treatment.

Sharply, Butler told the House:

There is not a white man at the South that would not associate with the Negro . . . if the Negro were his servant. He would eat with him, suckle from her, play with her or him as children, be together with them in every way, provided they were slaves. There never has been an objection to such an association. But the moment you elevate this black man to citizenship from a slave, then immediately he becomes offensive.[15]

A Negro member of the House, John Lynch of Mississippi, made a strong argument for the bill. Social equality, he said, does not exist among white men who share public facilities. Why, then, assume that the bill would bring about social equality between the races? The Negro does not ask for social rights, but he does ask for "protection in the enjoyment of *public* rights."

[15] *Id.* at 939–40.

He asks for rights "which should be or are accorded to every citizen alike." Under the system of race relations familiar to members of Congress, he said,

a white woman of questionable social standing, yea, I may say, of an admitted immoral character, can go to any public place or upon any public conveyance and be the recipient of the same treatment, the same courtesy, and the same respect that is usually accorded the most refined and virtuous; but let an intelligent, modest, refined colored lady present herself and ask that the same privileges be accorded to her that have just been accorded to her social inferior of the white race, and in nine cases out of ten, except in certain portions of the country, she will not only be refused, but insulted for making the request.

Speaking out of his own experiences, Lynch said:

Think of it for a moment; here am I, a member of your honorable body, representing one of the largest and wealthiest districts in the State of Mississippi, and possibly in the South; a district composed of persons of different races, religions, and nationalities; and yet, when I leave my home to come to the capital of the nation, to take part in the deliberations of the House and to participate with you in making laws for the government of this great Republic, in coming through . . . Kentucky and Tennessee, if I come by the way of Louisville or Chattanooga, I am treated, not as an American citizen, but as a brute. Forced to occupy a filthy smoking-car both night and day, with drunkards, gamblers, and criminals; and for what? Not that I am unable or unwilling to pay my way; not that I am obnoxious in my personal appearance or disrespectful in my conduct, but simply because I happen to be of a darker complexion. . . .

Mr. Speaker, if this unjust discrimination is to be longer tolerated by the American people, . . . then I can only say with sorrow and regret that our boasted civilization is a fraud; our republican institutions a failure; our social system a disgrace; and our religion a complete hypocrisy.

Turning to a consideration of the school clause (omitted from the bill as enacted), Lynch said that separate schools by reason of race, enforced by law, were as wrong as would be separate schools by reason of religion, if enforced by law. "The duty of the law-maker is to know no race, no color, no religion, no nationality, except to prevent distinctions on any of these grounds, so far as the law is concerned." Negroes in wanting passage of the bill, he said,

do not admit that their children can be better educated in white than in colored schools; nor that white teachers because they are white are better qualified to teach than colored ones. But they recognize the fact that the [racial] distinction when made and tolerated by law is an unjust and odious proscription; that you make their color a ground of objection, and consequently a crime [when they cross the color bar]. This is what we most earnestly protest against.

He ended his argument with a plea for passage of the bill, so that the "Negro question" might at long last be removed from politics.[16]

Congressman Whitehead of Virginia, after using some patently racist language, accused proponents of the bill of stirring up bad blood. What was the cause of the Civil War? he asked, and proceeded to answer: "The continual picking at that subject of slavery—a continual irritation of sections with that question—a continual interfering with other people's business, disturbing the country time and again." The war was over, but, he went on, "We [Southerners] did not come back very repentant for anything we had done." And now "you have turned right around and commenced that same picking, and not having the slave to pick at, you pick at the free Negro." [17]

He was answered by Congressman Cain, a Negro: "I have been surprised at his [Whitehead's] attempt to ridicule and cast a slur upon a race of men whose labor has enabled him and his for two hundred years to feed, and drink, and thrive, and fatten." It is the Southerners, like Whitehead, who stir up strife, for they have refused, he said, to acquiesce in the amendments to the Constitution and the laws of Congress and to recognize the rights of Negroes. They have sought to nullify all enactments and to re-enslave the Negro.

[16] *Id.* at 944–45.   [17] *Id.* at 954.

Addressing himself to the widespread segregation practices in the South and to the bill before the House, Cain said that he regretted to hear so much talk of "social equality." This was the opposition's "bugaboo," he said.

O, if you put colored men upon an equality before the law they will want social equality! I do not believe a word of it. Do you suppose I would introduce into my family a class of white people I see in this country? Do you suppose for one moment I would do it? No, sir; for there are men who have positions upon this floor, and for whom I have respect, but of whom I should be careful how I introduced them into my family.

Cain said that he was willing to see the school provision dropped, "for the sake of peace in the republican ranks, if for nothing else—not as a matter of principle." [18]

Whitehead asked Congressman Harris of Massachusetts if he favored a law that would force a white man and a Negro to sit at the same table in a hotel. Harris answered that in Massachusetts they did not force all classes of white men to sit at the same table or sleep in the same bed. All that he wanted was that black and white men receive common hospitality in public places. He went on to point out that Southerners were not really prejudiced against the Negro race, for when the Negroes were slaves there was no feeling against their riding in the same carriage and railroad cars or stopping at the same hotels. The prejudice was against the Negro's freedom. Now that the Negro was free, there was prejudice—because of his freedom. [19]

Congressman J. H. Rainey of South Carolina, a Negro, considered the question whether the act was aimed at achieving "social equality" of the races. He observed that white persons who frequent places of public accommodation could not possibly expect or want to find there such equality, for "suspicious characters" often occupy first-class seats in amusement places, persons of questionable repute are at home in restaurants and inns; yet none of these are considered the "social equals" of other

[18] *Id.* at 957. [19] *Id.* at 958.

guests. What is social equality? It consists, said Rainey, "in congeniality of feeling, a reciprocity of sentiment, and mutual social recognition among men, which is graded according to desire and taste, and not by any known or possible law."

He spoke of the ever-present fear that the sharing of public facilities might lead to intermarriage, which would affect the superiority of white blood. But should not, he asked, "this much talked of superiority" be "sufficient security and safeguard of itself to defy all assaults, intrusions, or intrigues"? He added with biting sarcasm:

If the future may be judged by the results of the past, it will require much effort upon the part of the colored race to preserve the purity of their own households from the intrusions of those who have hitherto violated and are now violating with ruthless impunity those precious and inestimable rights which should be the undisturbed heritage of all good society. . . .

I venture to assert to my white fellow-citizens that we, the colored people, are not in quest of social equality. For one I do not ask to be introduced into your family circles if you are not yet disposed to receive me there. Among my own race we have as much respectability, intelligence, virtue, and refinement [as are] possible to expect from any class circumstanced as we have been.[20]

Another Congressman stated that the legislation would not accomplish its purpose. "Was it legislation," he asked, "that made Frederick Douglass so great . . . ? No, it was the power of his great intellect and the quality of his personal appearance." Rainey at once countered by asking: "Did the talent and good conduct of . . . Douglass enable him to sit at the same table on the Potomac boat with his fellow-members of the San Domingo Commission?"[21]

Congressman E. R. Hoar said that proponents of the bill were not concerned with social equality. What was wanted and needed was equality of opportunity; equality of privileges regarding any matter that the law regulates and determines. Social equality and

[20] *Id.* at 960.   [21] *Id.* at 979.

personal tastes would take care of themselves without law.[22] Another member of the House contended that in so far as common carriers and inns were concerned, the bill simply gave to Negroes what the common law has always given to others.[23] Williams of Wisconsin said: "We ride with them in sleeping-cars if they perform menial service there; but if they pay their fares and take their seats like orderly, refined gentlemen, then we say we will spurn them from our presence." [24] Phillips of Kansas said that the question was "whether we can have a class to look down upon; whether we can have, not slavery, but a degraded class of poor, unprotected, ignorant people." [25]

Regarding the school provisions, much was said that anticipated Little Rock and other events that followed the decision of the Supreme Court in *Brown v. Topeka* [26] about eighty years later. A few examples will suffice.[27]

The school provision, said Phelps of New Jersey, would close the schools. The white people have money for private education, but the Negroes do not and would have to go without any education at all.

Another Congressman cited the following statistics to show that segregated schools had worked against the Negro: according to the 1870 census, one fifth of the white population was in schools, while only one Negro out of twenty-seven attended. While only one twelfth of the whites were illiterate, one half of the Negroes were.

The Southern hatred of integrated schools, a number of Congressmen observed, would be far greater than their love of education. Since public schools had not won firm roots in the South, passage of the bill would break up the schools there. On the other hand, a Congressman pointed out that wherever school integration had been tried in the South, it had worked successfully.

Whitehead of Virginia said:

[22] *Id.* at 979.   [23] *Id.* at 998.   [24] *Id.* at 1003.
[25] *Id.* at 1003.   [26] Brown v. Topeka, 347 U.S. 483 (1954).
[27] 3 CONG. REC. 954, 979, 981, 999, 1003 (1875).

We are not going to have any bayonets down our way; you may as well understand that. I know that this bill is intended to stir up blood to mix the two races in the schools, so that the children may first get to fighting and then the parents, and then instantly there will be a call for bayonets. But you will be mistaken in your expectation.

Some of the Negro members of Congress made it possible for proponents of the bill to vote to delete the school provision, for they indicated that they felt more strongly about the other provisions and would be willing to drop school integration in order to get the bill passed.[28] The experience in Mississippi may have been in the minds of the Negro members of Congress, for in that state the legislation that replaced the Black Code assured merged schools; yet, as a congressman pointed out, there was no integration in the schools there because the people voluntarily chose segregated schools—no white boy, he stated, had applied to a Negro school or college, and no Negro had applied to a white institution.[29]

The House omitted the school provision by vote of 128 to 48, but passed the bill by vote of 162 to 99.[30]

Ironically, the Supreme Court, eight years after the Civil Rights Act was passed, struck out as unconstitutional the provisions regarding public conveyances,[31] inns, theaters, and places of public amusement; but nearly eighty years after Congress had dropped the provision for integration of schools, the Court held that, under the Constitution and without the aid of congressional legislation, segregation in the schools was unconstitutional; and six years after the school desegregation decision—eighty-five years after Congress had concerned itself for the last time with the question—the student lunch counter demonstrations revived the issues over racial equality in places of public accommoda-

[28] *Id.* at 981; 957–58.   [29] *Id.* at 998.   [30] *Id.* at 1010–11.
[31] Decisions of the courts have made federal legislation to outlaw Jim Crow in public conveyances unnecessary. See Lyons v. Illinois Greyhound Lines, 192 F.2d 533 (1951); Browder v. Gayle, 142 F. Supp. 707 (M.D. Ala. 1956), *aff'd*, 352 U.S. 903 (1956).

tion. By their bold but simple acts, the students in the South thus compel a re-examination of the decision of the Court in the *Civil Rights Cases* of 1883,[32] to a consideration of which we now turn.

[32] Civil Rights Cases, 109 U.S. 3 (1883).

tion. By their bold but simple acts, the students in the South thus compel a reconsideration of the decision of the Court in the Civil Rights Cases of 1883," in a consideration ... now

Chapter 4

THE CIVIL RIGHTS CASES OF 1883

About eight years after the adoption of the 1875 Civil Rights Act, the Supreme Court was called upon to pass on the constitutionality of the statute. The Court considered together seven cases: two were indictments for denying to Negroes accommodations and privileges of an inn or a hotel; two cases were actions for denying to individuals privileges and accommodations of a theater; one action was for refusing a Negro a seat in the dress circle in a San Francisco theater; one was for denying to a person full enjoyment of accommodations in the New York Grand Opera House; and the last was an action to recover the statutory penalty from a railway company because of the refusal of the conductor to allow the complainant's wife to ride in the ladies' car because she was a Negro.

The decision and opinions in the *Civil Rights Cases* [1] are of such far-reaching importance that a full analysis of them is necessary. The civil rights legislation adopted by Congress in the years 1866 to 1875 created a new concept of equality: that in the absence of slavery, no man should be subject to the incidents of slavery; that where the reality or substance of slavery is gone, its visible form or appearance should not be seen. The legislation was probably the first attempt in the history of mankind to destroy the branches of slavery after its root had been demolished. What did the Supreme Court do with this legislation?

It is to be noted at the outset that up to 1883 the Supreme Court had declared only two acts of Congress unconstitutional,

[1] 109 U.S. 3 (1883).

in *Marbury v. Madison* (1803) [2] and in the *Dred Scott* case (1857).[3] In 1883, in the *Civil Rights Cases,* it added a third instance. In the history of the people of the United States the *Civil Rights Cases* have played almost as tragic a role as has *Dred Scott.*

Mr. Justice Bradley wrote the opinion for the majority of the Court. In it he stated that the purpose of the 1875 law was to declare that in the enjoyment of accommodations and privileges of inns, public conveyances, theaters, and other places of public accommodation, no distinction shall be made between citizens of different races or color, or between those who have and those who have not been slaves. How was this found unconstitutional?

Constitutionality under the Fourteenth Amendment

The first section of the Fourteenth Amendment, said Bradley, is prohibitory upon *states* only; *state action* of a particular character is prohibited; but the invasion of rights by an *individual* is not covered by the amendment. The legislative power of Congress is only to nullify state action which violates the prohibition. While Congress may adopt legislation to meet the exigency of state action adverse to the rights of citizens as secured by the amendment, such "legislation cannot properly cover the whole domain of rights appertaining to life, liberty and property, defining them and providing for their vindication." Congress is authorized by the amendment to adopt only corrective, not general, legislation; it may counteract only state action.

Said Bradley further, "If this legislation is appropriate for enforcing the prohibition of the amendment, it is difficult to see where it is to stop. Why may not Congress with equal show of authority enact a code of laws for the enforcement and vindication of all rights of life, liberty, and property?" The statute, he continued, is repugnant to the Tenth Amendment, which reserves

[2] 1 Cranch 137 (U.S. 1803).   [3] 19 How. 393 (U.S. 1857).

to the people and the states the powers not delegated to the United States. In other words, laws for the "enforcement and vindication of all rights of life, liberty, and property" are within the province of the states exclusively.

The Court held that the 1866 and 1870 civil rights acts were to be distinguished from the objectionable 1875 act, for the earlier laws were limitations on the states only. They were corrective in character, intended to counteract and furnish redress against state laws and proceedings, and against customs having the force of law; the penal part of the laws referred to state action only.

As to the civil rights guaranteed by the Constitution, the Court held that the wrongful acts of an individual, unsupported by state authority in the shape of laws, customs, judicial, or executive proceedings, are "simply a private wrong, or a crime of that individual"; the person wronged must look for vindication or redress to the laws of the state.

The case is different, said Bradley, from the situation in which Congress is clothed with direct and plenary powers of legislation over a whole subject, accompanied by express or implied denial of such power to the states as, for example, in the regulation of foreign or interstate commerce, or commerce with Indian tribes, or the coinage of money, or the establishment of post offices and post roads, or declaring war.

In these cases Congress has power to pass laws for regulating the subjects specified in every detail, and the conduct and transactions of individuals in respect thereof. But where a subject is not submitted to the general legislative power of Congress, but is only submitted thereto for the purpose of rendering effective some prohibition against particular state legislation or state action in reference to that subject, the power given is limited to its object, and any legislation by Congress in the matter must necessarily be corrective in its character, adapted to counteract and redress the operation of such prohibited state laws or proceedings of state officers.

Here the legislation, said Bradley, was not corrective but primary and direct.

Up to this point the Court had discussed the question presented by the act on the assumption that a right to enjoy equal accommodations and privileges in all inns, public conveyances, and places of public amusement is one of the essential rights of the citizen with which no state can interfere. The Court construed the law as unconstitutional because it was intended not as a restraint on state action but only on individual action. The Court said, therefore, that it was unnecessary to go further and examine the act's initial assumption.

Congress has plenary power as to territories and the District of Columbia; the cases considered, however, arose within the states. Therefore, the constitutionality of the act as limited to territories and the District of Columbia was not presented; nor did the cases present the question of the power of Congress under the commerce clause to pass laws regulating rights in public conveyances passing from state to state.

Constitutionality under the Thirteenth Amendment

Under the Thirteenth Amendment primary and direct legislation may be enacted by Congress, as the amendment is not a limitation on state action only. It was argued on behalf of the Negroes that Congress has the power to pass all laws necessary and proper for abolishing all badges and incidents of slavery in the United States, and that under this power the law in question was constitutional, for a denial of equal accommodations and privileges is, in itself, a subjection to a species of servitude within the meaning of the Thirteenth Amendment. Assuming that Congress has the power to outlaw badges and incidents of servitude, the question was, then, whether, under the Thirteenth Amendment, denial to a person of admission to the accommoda-

tions and privileges of an inn, a public conveyance, or a theater
subjects that person to any form of servitude, or tends to fasten
upon him any badge of slavery.

Is there any similarity, asked the Court, between servitudes
outlawed by the amendment and a denial by the owner of an inn,
a public conveyance, or a theater of its accommodations and
privileges to an individual, even though the denial be founded
on the race or color of that individual? Bradley asked: "Where
does any slavery or servitude, or badge of either, arise from
such an act of denial? . . . What has it to do with the question
of slavery?"

While it was true that when slavery prevailed proprietors of
inns and public conveyances were forbidden by the Slave Codes
of the states to receive persons of the African race, the purpose,
said the Court, was to prevent escapes from the control of masters; it "was no part of the servitude itself."

Does slavery have any inseparable incidents? Yes, said the
Court, and named the following: compulsory work; restraints of
movements; disability to hold property; disability to make contracts; disability to have standing in court; disability to act as a
witness against a white person; severer punishments; "and such
like burdens and incapacities." The 1866 Civil Rights Act,
passed under the Thirteenth Amendment and before the adoption of the Fourteenth, undertook to wipe out these incidents
of slavery, "constituting its substance and visible form." This
legislation—certainly since its re-enactment under the Fourteenth
Amendment—is constitutional, said the Court; and the following are fundamental rights which are the essence of civil freedom: right to make and enforce contracts; right to sue; right to
be parties; right to give evidence; right to inherit property; right
to purchase, sell, lease, and convey property. These rights, according to the Court, constitute the essential distinction between
freedom and slavery.

Altogether different is the 1875 act, said the Court, for this law covers "social rights of men and races in the community."

The Thirteenth Amendment has not outlawed race, class, or color distinctions, although they may be outlawed by the Fourteenth Amendment when created by state actions.

Can the act of a mere individual, the owner of the inn, the public conveyance or place of amusement, refusing the accommodation, be justly regarded as imposing any badge of slavery or servitude upon the applicant, or only as inflicting an ordinary civil injury, properly cognizable by the laws of the state, and presumably subject to redress by those laws until the contrary appears?

Such an act of refusal, said the Court, has nothing to do with slavery or involuntary servitude.

It would be running the slavery argument into the ground to make it apply to every act of discrimination which a person may see fit to make as to the guests he will entertain, or as to the people he will take into his coach or cab or car, or admit to his concert or theatre, deal with in other matters of intercourse or business.

However, the Court did say that if state laws themselves were to make any unjust discrimination, Congress would have the power under the Fourteenth Amendment to afford a remedy.

In slavery days there were thousands of free Negroes who enjoyed all the essential rights of life, liberty, and property, the same as white citizens;

yet no one, at that time, thought that it was any invasion of his personal status as a freeman because he was not admitted to all the privileges enjoyed by white citizens, or because he was subjected to discriminations in the enjoyment of accommodations in inns, public conveyances and places of amusement. Mere discriminations on account of race or color were not regarded as badges of slavery. If, since that time, the enjoyment of equal rights in all these respects has become established by constitutional enactment, it is not by force of the Thirteenth Amendment (which merely abolishes slavery), but by force of the Fourteenth and Fifteenth Amendments.

Dissent by Mr. Justice Harlan

The Court was not unanimous in its opinion, but Mr. Justice Harlan was the lone disenter. His forty-page opinion deserves a high place among the writings of American statesmen marking progress in the development of democratic thought. We shall give here a close analysis of his statement.

He opened his dissent with the remark that the opinion for the majority of the Court proceeded upon grounds

entirely too narrow and artificial. I cannot resist the conclusion that the substance and spirit of the recent amendments of the Constitution have been sacrificed by a subtle and ingenious verbal criticism. Constitutional provisions, adopted in the interest of liberty, and for the purpose of securing, through national legislation, if need be, rights inhering in a state of freedom, and belonging to American citizenship, have been so construed as to defeat the ends the people desired to accomplish, and which they supposed they had accomplished by changes in their fundamental law.

The purpose of Section 1 of the 1875 act was to prevent *race* discrimination in respect of accommodations and facilities of inns, public conveyances, and places of public amusement, said Harlan; and Section 2 merely provided a penalty against anyone's denying, or aiding or inciting a denial, to a citizen of that equality of right given by Section 1.

Harlan called attention to the well-established principle that in doubtful cases the question of the constitutionality of legislation should be decided in the affirmative. There must be a clear and strong conviction of the incompatibility of the Constitution with the legislative act for the latter to be declared void: the case must be a clear one.

Harlan interestingly contrasted the decision of the majority under the amendments with three Supreme Court precedents involving the rights of masters over their slaves.

The first was *Prigg v. Pennsylvania.*[4] In Section 2 of Article

[4] 16 Pet. 539 (U.S. 1842).

IV of the Constitution it was provided that "no person held to service or labor in one state, under the laws thereof, escaping into another, shall, in consequence of any law or regulation therein, be discharged from such service or labor, but shall be delivered up on claim of the party to whom such service or labor may be due." Under the authority of this clause Congress in 1793 passed a Fugitive Slave Law, establishing a mode for the recovery of fugitive slaves and prescribing a penalty against the person who should obstruct or hinder the master in recovering the fugitive slave.

Pennsylvania argued that the obligation to surrender fugitive slaves rested upon the states, subject to the restriction that they should not pass laws liberating such fugitives; that the Constitution did not take from the states the right to determine the status of all persons within their jurisdiction; that it was for the state in which the alleged fugitive was found to determine whether he was in fact a freedman or a fugitive slave; that the only power of the federal government was, by judicial instrumentality, to restrain and correct, but not to prevent or forbid, in the absence of hostile state action. Pennsylvania argued, in other words, that the 1793 law was unconstitutional, for Article IV of the Constitution was intended *as a restraint only on state legislative action, but not on individual action; while the act passed by Congress was directed against individuals.*

The Court turned a deaf ear to such suggestions and held that Congress was authorized by the Constitution to adopt primary legislation to enforce the master's right. It held that the clause of the Constitution conferring a right should not be so construed as to make the right a shadowy one, or to leave citizens without remedial power adequate for its protection, when another construction of the clause would enforce and protect the right granted. Congress is not restricted to legislation for the execution of its expressly granted powers, or for the protection of such means as are necessary and proper, or appropriate, to attain the proposed ends. Since the right of the master to have his slave delivered to him was guaranteed by the Constitution, the fair implication was that the national government was clothed with appropriate authority and functions to enforce that right. The Court said: "It would be a strange anomaly and forced construction to suppose that the national government meant to rely for the due fulfilment of its own proper duties, and the rights which it intended to secure, upon state legislation, and not upon that of the Union." And the 1793 act was upheld as constitutional.

The second case was *Ableman v. Booth.*[5] The provisions of the Fugitive Slave Act of 1850 were greatly amplified over those of previous legislation. The act placed at the disposal of the master seeking to recover his fugitive slave substantially the whole power of the nation: "Congress omitted from it [the act] nothing which the utmost ingenuity could suggest as essential to the successful enforcement of the master's claim to recover his fugitive slave." The Court held the act to be "in all of its provisions fully authorized by the Constitution of the United States."

The third precedent cited by Harlan was *Dred Scott v. Sanford.*[6] The case was instituted by Scott, who claimed to be a citizen of Missouri. The defendant was a citizen of another state. The object of the case was to assert the title of Scott and his family to freedom. The defendant pleaded in abatement that Scott, being a Negro whose ancestors were brought into this country and sold as slaves, was not a citizen. The only issue, according to the Court, was whether emancipated Negroes, or Negroes born of parents who had become free before the birth of their children, were citizens of a state in the sense in which the word "citizen" is used in the United States Constitution.

The Court considered the question who were citizens of the states when the Constitution was adopted; and who, at that time, were recognized as "the people" whose rights and liberties had been violated by the British government.

[5] 21 How. 506 (U.S. 1859).   [6] 19 How. 393 (U.S. 1857).

In his opinion for the Court, Chief Justice Taney said that neither slaves nor their descendants, whether free or not, were then considered a part of the people;

they had for more than a century before been regarded as beings of an inferior race, and altogether unfit to associate with the white race, either in social or political relations, and so far inferior that they had no rights which the white man was bound to respect, and that the Negro might justly and lawfully be reduced to slavery for his benefit.

The judgment of the Court was that "people of the United States" and "citizens" mean the same thing; that *free Negroes were not part of the people and not citizens;* that they could claim none of the rights and privileges which the Constitution provides for and secures to citizens of the United States; that, whether slaves or freedmen, Negroes were subject to the authority of white persons, "and had no rights or privileges but such as those who held the power the government might choose to grant them."

It was in the light of these cases, said Harlan, that the amendments were adopted.

The Statute under the Thirteenth Amendment, According to Harlan

The Thirteenth Amendment, he said, wiped out slavery; it was followed by the 1866 act which conferred national citizenship on Negroes. Negroes were citizens, therefore, before the Fourteenth Amendment was adopted. While the power of Congress to enforce the master's right to have his slave delivered up on claim was implied from the recognition of that right in the Constitution, the power conferred by the Thirteenth Amendment does not rest upon implication or inference; the power to enforce the amendment by appropriate legislation was expressly granted. The Court had uniformly held that the national government has the power, whether expressly given or not, to secure and protect the rights conferred or guaranteed by the Constitution. "That doctrine," said Harlan, "ought not now to be abandoned when the inquiry is not as to an implied power to protect the master's rights, but what may Congress, under power expressly granted, do for the protection of freedom and the rights necessarily inhering in a state of freedom."

Did the freedom established by the Thirteenth Amendment involve nothing more than exemption from actual slavery?

Was it the purpose of the nation simply to destroy the institution, and then remit the race, theretofore held in bondage, to the several states for such protection, in their civil rights, necessarily growing out of freedom, as those states, in their discretion, might choose to provide? Were the states against whose protest the institution was destroyed, to be left free, so far as national interference was concerned, to make or allow discriminations against that race, as such, in the enjoyment of those fundamental rights which, by universal concession, inhere in a state of freedom?

Congress, contended Harlan, had the power by direct and primary legislation to eradicate burdens and disabilities which are the badges and incidents of slavery and servitude. He said:

I do not contend that the Thirteenth Amendment invests Congress with authority, by legislation, to define and regulate the entire body of civil rights which citizens enjoy, or may enjoy, in the several states. But I hold that since slavery, as the court has repeatedly declared, was the moving or principal cause of the adoption of that amendment, and since that institution rested wholly upon the inferiority, as a race, of those held in bondage, their freedom necessarily involved immunity from, and protection against, all discrimination against them, because of their race, in respect of such civil rights as belong to freemen of other races.

Congress could pass laws to protect Negroes against deprivation, because of their race, of any civil rights granted to other freemen in the same state; and such legislation might operate against officers and agents of the state, *"and also, upon, at least, such individuals and corporations as exercise public functions and wield power and authority under the state."* [7]

According to Harlan, then, the power of Congress under the

[7] Italics added.

Thirteenth Amendment was not restricted to legislation against slavery as an institution. It might be extended to the protection of *Negroes against discrimination in respect of civil rights belonging to freemen where such discrimination is based upon race.*

What, then, would the legal rights of Negroes be in respect of public conveyances, inns, and places of public amusement?

Harlan pointed out that it had been held by the Court that a common carrier exercises a sort of public office and has public duties to perform. Railways are public highways, established by authority of the state for public use; they are intended for public use and benefit; a railway corporation is a government agency, subject to control for the public benefit; the government may regulate the rates of fares, all matters relating to the convenience and safety of the public; it may prohibit discriminations and favoritism.

Such being the relations these corporations held to the public, it would seem that the right of a colored person to use an improved public highway, upon the terms accorded to freemen of other races, is as fundamental . . . as are any of the rights which my brethren concede to be so far fundamental as to be deemed the essence of civil freedom.

Blackstone had said that the power of locomotion is an element of personal liberty.

But of what value is this right of locomotion, if it may be clogged by such burdens as Congress intended by the act of 1875 to remove? They are burdens which lay at the very foundation of the institution of slavery as it once existed. They are not to be sustained, except upon the assumption that there is, in this land of universal liberty, a class which may still be discriminated against, even in respect of rights of a character so necessary and supreme, that, deprived of their enjoyment in common with others, a freeman is not only branded as one inferior and infected, but, in the competitions of life, is robbed of some of the most essential means of existence; and all this solely because they belong to a particular race which the nation has liberated.

The same observations made as to railways, said Harlan, apply to inns. An innkeeper may not select his guests. Innkeepers are a sort of public servant, exercising a quasi-public employment. The law gives the innkeeper special privileges, and, in consideration of these, he is charged with certain duties to the general public. He may not discriminate against any person asking admission as a guest on account of the person's race or color.

Places of public amusement, Harlan pointed out, are established and maintained under direct license of the law. The authority to establish and maintain them comes from the public. "The colored race is part of that public. The local government granting the license represents them as well as all other races within its jurisdiction."

In brief, it was Harlan's contention that discrimination practiced by individuals in the exercise of public or quasi-public functions "is a badge of servitude" which Congress may prevent under the Thirteenth Amendment.

The Statute under the Fourteenth Amendment, According to Harlan

Harlan went on to remind the majority that in an earlier case the Court had said that the one pervading purpose found in all the Civil War amendments, lying at the foundation of each, and without which none of them would have been suggested, was "the freedom of the slave race, the security and firm establishment of that freedom, and the protection of the newly-made freeman and citizen from the oppression of those who had formerly exercised unlimited dominion over him." Positive rights and privileges, he said, were intended to be secured by the Fourteenth Amendment.

Section 5 of the amendment gives power to Congress to enforce by appropriate legislation provisions of the amendment. However, the majority of the Court in this case held that Section 5 limits Congress to the power to legislate only for the purpose of carrying into effect the prohibition on state action. But for this purpose, Harlan argued, the judicial power is adequate: the courts could nullify all hostile state proceedings. The section grants not judicial but legislative power—power to Congress, he said.

Nor is the amendment merely a prohibition upon state action. For the first clause of the first section provides that "all persons born or naturalized in the United States, and subject to the jurisdiction thereof, are citizens of the United States, and of the state wherein they reside." This provision is of an affirmative character: it grants Negroes citizenship in the United States and in the states wherein they reside. This provision introduced the Negroes into the political community known as the "people of the United States." It extended to them the provisions of Article IV, Section 2: *"the citizens of each state shall be entitled to all the privileges and immunities of citizens in the several states."*

"No state," said Harlan,

can sustain her denial to colored citizens of other states, while within her limits, of privileges or immunities, fundamental in republican citizenship, upon the ground that she accords such privileges only to her white citizens and withholds them from her colored citizens. The colored citizens of other states, within the jurisdiction of that state, could claim . . . every privilege and immunity which that state secures to her white citizens. . . . A colored citizen of Ohio or Indiana, while in the jurisdiction of Tennessee, is entitled to enjoy any privilege or immunity, fundamental in citizenship, which is given to citizens of the white race in the latter state. It is not to be supposed that any one will controvert this proposition.

What was secured to Negro citizens by the grant to them of state citizenship by the nation? At least exemption from race discrimination in respect of any civil right belonging to citizens of the white race in the same state—"unless the recent amendments be splendid baubles, thrown out to delude those who deserved fair and generous treatment at the hands of the nation." As was stated in four previous opinions of the Court, the purpose of the amendments was to raise Negroes from the condition of inferiority and servitude to perfect equality of civil rights with all other persons. "It is fundamental in American citizenship that, in respect of such rights, there shall be no discrimination by the state, or its officers, *or by individuals or corporations exercising public functions or authority,* against any citizen because of his race or previous condition of servitude." [8]

If exemption from discrimination in respect of civil rights is a new constitutional right, why may not Congress guard, protect, and enforce that right? Congress may protect and enforce any right derived from or created by the Constitution. The Court said in an earlier case that "rights and immunities created by and dependent upon the Constitution of the United States can be protected by Congress." The means to be adopted to protect such rights and immunities are within the discretion of Congress:

it is for Congress, not the judiciary, to say that legislation is appropriate —that is—best adapted to the end to be attained. The judiciary may not, with safety to our institutions, enter the domain of legislative discretion, and dictate the means which Congress shall employ in the exercise of its granted powers. That would be sheer usurpation of the functions of a co-ordinate department, which, if often repeated, and permanently acquiesced in, would work a radical change in our system of government.

The principle of construction or interpretation when a constitutional provision is before the Court should be different from the one applied to a private contract. "Are constitutional provisions, enacted to secure the dearest rights of freemen and citizens, to be subjected to that rule of construction, applicable to private instruments, which requires that words to be interpreted must be taken most strongly against those who employ them?"

Prior to the amendments, Congress, with the sanction of the Court, passed the most stringent laws, operating upon the states, their officers, and agents, and also upon individuals, in vindication of slavery and the rights of the master; but now the Court has decided that Congress may not, by legislation of like char-

[8] Italics added.

acter, guard, protect, and secure the freedom established by the amendments. Congress may, said Harlan,

> without transcending the limits of the Constitution, do for human liberty and the fundamental rights of American citizenship, what it did, with the sanction of this court, for the protection of slavery and the rights of masters of fugitive slaves. If fugitive slave laws, providing modes and prescribing penalties, whereby the master could seize and recover his fugitive slave, were legitimate exercises of an implied power to protect and enforce a right recognized by the Constitution, why shall the hands of Congress be tied, so that—under an express power, by appropriate legislation, to enforce a constitutional provision granting citizenship—it may not, by means of direct legislation, bring the whole power of this nation to bear upon states and their officers, *and upon such individuals and corporations exercising public functions* as assume to abridge, impair, or deny rights confessedly secured by the supreme law of the land? [9]

The fact that the Fourteenth Amendment prohibited states from making or enforcing laws abridging privileges and immunities of citizens of the United States furnishes no reason for maintaining that the Fourteenth Amendment was intended to deny to Congress the power, by legislation, to protect the citizens of the several states, being also United States citizens, against all discrimination, in respect of their rights as state citizens, founded on race, color, or previous condition of servitude. In other words, the fifth section of the amendment confers upon Congress the power, by legislation, to enforce not merely the prohibition upon the states but all previous provisions of the amendment.

> It was perfectly well known that the great danger to the equal enjoyment by citizens of their rights, as citizens, was to be apprehended not altogether from unfriendly state legislation, but from the hostile action of corporations and individuals in the states. And it is to be presumed that it was intended, by that section, to clothe Congress with power and authority to meet that danger.

[9] Italics added.

Harlan foresaw in the decision of the Court the future development of Jim Crowism and other forms of race discrimination, and the passivity of the federal government in the face thereof. If it be adjudged, he said,

that *individuals and corporations, exercising public functions, or wielding power under public authority,* may, without liability to direct primary legislation on the part of Congress, make the race of citizens the ground for denying them that equality of civil rights which the Constitution ordains as a principle of republican citizenship; then . . . we shall enter upon an era of constitutional law, when the rights of freedom and American citizenship cannot receive from the nation that efficient protection which heretofore was unhesitatingly accorded to slavery and the rights of the master.[10]

Assuming with the majority that the amendment was intended to be directed only against action by the states and their officers, agents, and instrumentalities, Harlan argued that "keepers of inns, and managers of places of public amusement are agents or instrumentalities of the state, because they are charged with duties to the public, and are amenable, in respect of their duties and functions, to government regulation." *A denial by them of equality of civil rights is a denial by the state.* "If it be not, then the race is left, in respect of the civil rights in question, practically at the mercy of corporations and individuals wielding power under the states." The 1875 act endeavored to protect legal, not social, rights. It endeavored to provide that no state, nor officers of a state, *nor any corporation or individual wielding power under state authority for the public benefit or public convenience,* shall discriminate against citizens in their civil rights because of race.

It will be recalled that the Court reserved the question whether Congress, in the exercise of its power to regulate interstate commerce, might or might not pass a law regulating rights in public conveyances moving in interstate commerce. But this question,

[10] Italics added.

said Harlan, should not have been reserved, for it was directly presented in one of the cases, in which a citizen of Mississippi bought a ticket from Tennessee to Virginia. Might not the 1875 act apply at least to this situation?

The underlying purpose of the legislation was to enable the Negro to take the rank of citizen accorded to him by the Fourteenth Amendment.

At every step, in this direction, the nation has been confronted with class tyranny. . . . If the constitutional amendments be enforced, according to the intent with which, as I conceive, they were adopted, there cannot be, in this republic, any class of human beings in practical subjection to another class, with power in the latter to dole out to the former just such privileges as they may choose to grant.

Summary of Bradley's Decision

The purpose of the 1875 act was to declare that in the enjoyment of accommodations and privileges of inns, public conveyances, theaters, and other places of public accommodation or amusement, no distinction shall be made between citizens differing in race or color. It is directed against action by individuals not acting as officers, agents, or instrumentalities of states or their political subdivisions. But the Fourteenth Amendment is directed only against action by states, their political subdivisions, and their officers, agents, and instrumentalities acting on their behalf. The subject matter of the act is confined to the states.

The Thirteenth Amendment, however, is not a limitation on state action only. Congress may pass legislation under this amendment directed against individuals who impose slavery or involuntary servitude upon another person. But a denial to a person of admission to the accommodations and privileges of an inn, a public conveyance, or a theater is not a subjection of that person to slavery or involuntary servitude. The inseparable incidents of slavery are compulsory work; restraint of movements; disability to hold property, make contracts, have standing in courts, act as a witness against a white person; and to be subject to severer punishments than those imposed upon white persons. These, and similar burdens and incapacities, differentiate the slave from the freeman, and only these were outlawed by the Thirteenth Amendment. The amendment has not outlawed all race or color distinctions.

Summary of Harlan's Dissent

Constitutional rights should not be construed narrowly. The Thirteenth Amendment involves more than exemption from actual slavery. Under its provisions Congress may undertake to eradicate burdens and disabilities which are the badges and incidents of slavery and involuntary servitude. Such civil rights as belong to freemen of other races now belong to the Negro, too. Congress may pass laws to protect Negroes against their deprivation of civil rights granted to other freemen in the state, and such laws may operate against the officers and agents of the state, and upon such individuals as exercise public functions and wield power and authority under state law, license, or grant.

Operators of public conveyances, inns, and places of public amusement exercise a sort of public office and have public duties to perform. Such accommodations are intended for public use and benefit, and are subject to public control or regulation in all matters affecting the public safety and convenience.

The Fourteenth Amendment prohibits states from abridging the privileges or immunities of citizens of the United States; but the amendment also provides, in positive rather than in prohibitive terms, that all persons born or naturalized in the United States are citizens of the United States and of the state wherein they reside. It says, too, that Congress shall have the power to enforce, by legislation, the provisions of the amendment. Congress, therefore, has the power, by direct and positive legislation, to protect state citizenship, not merely against *state* interference or abridgment, but against *all* interference or abridgment.

Negroes, by becoming citizens, are entitled to all the privileges and immunities of citizens in the several states. This means that a Negro citizen of Ohio is entitled, while in Tennessee, to enjoy all the privileges and immunities granted by Tennessee to its white citizens.

The grant of state citizenship implies, at least, freedom from race discrimination in respect of the civil rights enjoyed by white citizens, or, at any rate, from such discrimination practiced by the state, its officers, or by individuals exercising public functions or authority (such as innkeepers, carriers, theater owners).

Assuming with the majority that the Fourteenth Amendment was intended to be directed only against action by states, their officers, agents, and instrumentalities, then keepers of inns, carriers, and theater owners come within its terms. For a denial by them of equality of civil rights is a denial by the state. The denial, in contemplation of the amendment, is state action.

Significance of the Decision

The decision in the *Civil Rights Cases* of 1883 is one of the most far-reaching in the social history of the people of the United States. Had Justice Harlan's views prevailed, the American people would have been spared much heartache. Yet the opinion of Justice Bradley, as we shall see in the next chapter, contains some elements that, when taken with others, may one day become "a firebrand plucked out of the burning."

Civil Rights in The District of Columbia

Mr. Justice Bradley said that as to territories and the District of Columbia, Congress has plenary power, implying that if the Civil Rights Act of 1875 were not of national scope, but limited to the District of Columbia, it might be constitutional. The cases presented, however, came from the states and not from the district, and so the question of the constitutionality of congressional civil rights legislation for the District of Columbia was not passed upon.

The fact is, however, that Congress in 1869 passed an anti-discrimination act for the District of Columbia, applying to places of public accommodation. The act provided that it shall not be lawful for any person having a license to give a lecture, concert, exhibition, circus performance, theatrical entertainment, or to conduct a place of public amusement of any kind to make any distinction on account of race or color as regards admissions to any part of the room, hall, or place, as long as the person will conduct himself in an orderly and peaceable manner. The penalty for violation was $20. An amendment in 1870 increased the penalty to $50. Other amendments enacted in 1870 provided against racial discrimination by keepers of licensed restaurants, taverns, and hotels. Legislation of 1872 provided against racial discrimination by any person who maintains a hotel, ice cream parlor, barbershop or bathhouse. The penalty was a fine of $100 and forfeiture of the license. Finally, legislation of 1873 provided that any person who operates a licensed restaurant, barroom, ice cream parlor, or soda fountain shall serve all "well-behaved and respectable persons" in the same room or rooms and at the same posted prices.[11]

After 1873 these laws appeared to be dead letters, but finally in 1953 the United States Supreme Court upheld a prosecution under this legislation.[12] Until then, racial discrimination in the nation's capital had made the district a symbol of rampant racism rather than an emblem of democracy. American and foreign persons of color were not admitted to hotels, restaurants, churches, hospitals, soda fountains, lunch counters (except at certain ones

[11] Act of June 10, 1869, ch. 36, §§ 1, 2, at 22, Corp. Laws of Wash. 66th Council; Act of March 7, 1870, ch. 42, §§ 1, 2, at 22, Corp. Laws of Wash. 67th Council; Leg. Assem., June 20, 1872, § 3; 3 Leg. Assem., June 26, 1873, ch. 46, § 3. D.C. CODE (1955 Supp.) §§ 33–604 to –607.
[12] Thompson Co. v. District of Columbia, 346 U.S. 100 (1953), *rev'g* 203 F.2d 579 (D.C. Cir. 1953); see also 214 F.2d 210 (D.C. Cir. 1954). See also Central Amusement Co. v. District of Columbia, 121 A.2d 865, 1 RACE REL. L. REP. 554 (1956).

where they were served only if they stood), theaters, auditoriums, and even department stores. The color line was rigid—in public accommodations, housing, employment, in every activity and relationship. Washington was described as the "Capital of White Supremacy." [13]

Following the Court's decisions in the public accommodations case of 1953 and in the school desegregation case of 1954— the one that came up from the District of Columbia [14]—the picture in Washington changed radically. Helpful in bringing about the changes was the position taken by President Eisenhower in his State of the Union message to Congress in 1953. "I propose," he said, "to use whatever authority exists in the office of the President to end segregation in the District of Columbia." [15] The dramatic, radical changes in Washington should alone suffice to disprove the assertion, often heard, that one cannot change morals —by which is meant race relations—by law or legal institutions or government. Speaking just before the Senate passed the Civil Rights Act of 1960, Senator Fulbright told the Senate that "legislation to regulate men's mores [meaning race relations] is doomed to failure from the day it is introduced." [16] All that he needed to do to prove to himself that there was no basis for this judgment was to go out of the Senate chamber and observe what went on in the hotels, restaurants, movie theaters, and other places of public accommodation in the city of Washington, and contrast the scene with what he had observed only a few years before. Whether people were less prejudiced, we cannot tell; but that they did not act out their racial prejudices by practicing discrimination—this was clear; and it was equally clear that a major factor in bringing about this change was the government's position: the existence of civil rights legislation, enforcement by the executive, and the judgments of the courts upholding the statutes.

[13] NATIONAL COMM. ON SEGREGATION IN THE NATION'S CAPITAL, SEGREGATION IN WASHINGTON (1948).
[14] Bolling v. Sharpe, 347 U.S. 497 (1954). See NAIRO, CIVIL RIGHTS IN THE NATION'S CAPITAL—A REPORT ON A DECADE OF PROGRESS (1959).
[15] HANSEN, MIRACLE OF SOCIAL ADJUSTMENT 19 (1957).
[16] 106 CONG. REC. 7185 (daily ed. April 8, 1960).

Chapter 5

NOT SEPARATE, BUT EQUAL

The student sit-in demonstrations at lunch counters, begun in 1958, have brought to the fore the debate in Congress over the Civil Rights Act of 1875 and the debate in the Supreme Court over the *Civil Rights Cases* of 1883. To understand more fully these debates, focused on the student demonstrations, let us briefly note certain constitutional developments that have a strong bearing on the issues and on future lines of action.

School Desegregation

As the Civil Rights Act of 1875 passed the Senate, it contained a provision regarding schools. The bill provided that all persons should be entitled to the full and equal enjoyment of the accommodations and privileges of "all common schools and public institutions of learning or benevolence supported in whole or in part by general taxation and also institutions known as agricultural colleges endowed by the United States." It did, however, contain a significant proviso, stating that if separate schools are supported, "giving equal educational advantages in all respects for different classes of persons entitled to attend such schools and institutions," then such separate schools shall be deemed sufficient compliance with the law.[1]

What this school provision in the Senate bill seems to have meant was that while Congress favored racially integrated schools, separate but equal schools would be accepted as compliance with the statute.

As we have noted, the House struck from the bill all reference

[1] 3 CONG. REC. 1010 (1875).

to schools. The feeling there seems to have been that the public schools had not yet won firm roots in the South, and so there was fear that the statutory demands included in the bill passed by the Senate might have the effect of breaking up the schools altogether. The threat was made that the public schools would be closed if the Senate bill were enacted; then, while the white citizens would have the resources to open and support private schools, Negro children would go without any schooling. Even some Negro members of Congress accepted this threat as real and stated that they were willing to see the school provision omitted.

The argument of Congressman Burrows was impressive. The school provision, he said, could become the greatest obstacle ever put in the way of Negro education. He cited the 1870 census that showed that while one out of five white children attended school, only one out of twenty-seven Negro children did so. Although one twelfth of the white population was illiterate, over one half of the Negroes were.[2] This was not the appropriate time, therefore, to offer inducements to further weaken public education, to the special detriment of the Negroes. Even separate but equal schools, when made mandatory by law, might destroy public education in the South—so weak was that institution in 1875. But while Congress refused to enact legislation to outlaw school segregation or to permit separate but equal schools, the Supreme Court in time accomplished both of these ends.

The "separate but equal" doctrine probably originated in 1849 in the *Roberts* case in Massachusetts.[3] Before that year, under the abolition impetus, many cities and towns in Massachusetts had abolished racially segregated schools, but such schools continued in Boston. In 1846 Negroes petitioned the Boston authorities for the abolition of the Jim Crow public school. The request was denied.[4] Controversy over the issue divided the authorities, the Negroes, and the community.

[2] *Id.* at 999.   [3] Roberts v. Boston, 5 Cushing (59 Mass.) 198 (1849).
[4] See Levy & Phillips, *The* Roberts *Case—Source of the "Separate but Equal" Doctrine,* 56 Am. Hist. Rev. 510 ff. (1951).

Benjamin Roberts, a Negro, sought to have his five-year-old daughter admitted to a white primary school (five such schools were nearer his home than was the Negro school). When the school officials refused, he brought an action for damages, under a state statute. Charles Sumner undertook Roberts's case and argued that school segregation was in violation of the state constitution, which commands "the equality of men before the law." He cited the Declaration of Rights of the state constitution, which provided:

All men are born free and equal, and have certain natural, essential and unalienable rights, among which may be reckoned the right of enjoying . . . their lives and liberties. . . . No man, . . . or association of men, have any other title to obtain advantages, or particular and exclusive privileges, distinct from those of the community, than what arises from the consideration of services rendered to the public.

"These," said Sumner, "are not vain words." They allow no distinction established by birth.

He also argued that the state legislature, in providing for an educational system, had made no provision for segregated schools, and the state courts had never countenanced any racial discrimination in the schools.

The school board, he contended further, had no power to segregate the races and thereby "brand a whole race with the stigma of inferiority and degradation." The board was not above the constitution: it could consider only matters relating to age, sex, and moral and intellectual fitness in assigning pupils; it could not start with the presumption that an entire race possess characteristics which made necessary their separate classification.

The Negro pupils were entitled, not to separate but equal schools, but to "precise Equality"—the same schools. Schools should further social understanding, and segregated schools would breed ignorance and prejudice. "The whites themselves," he said, are injured by the separation. . . . With the law as their monitor . . . they are taught practically to deny that grand revelation of

Christianity—the Brotherhood of Mankind. Their hearts, while yet tender with childhood, are necessarily hardened by this conduct, and their subsequent lives, perhaps, bear enduring testimony to this legalized uncharitableness. Nursed in the sentiment of Caste, receiving it with the earliest food of knowledge, they are unable to eradicate it from their natures. . . . The school is the little world in which the child is trained for the larger world of life. It must, therefore, cherish and develop the virtues and sympathies which are employed in the larger world . . . beginning there those relations of equality which our Constitution and laws promise to all. . . . Prejudice is the child of ignorance. It is sure to prevail where people do not know each other. Society and intercourse are means established by Providence for human improvement. They remove antipathies, promote mutual adaptation and conciliation, and establish relations of reciprocal regard.[5]

Chief Justice Shaw, perhaps the leading state jurist of his day, delivered the opinion for the unanimous Supreme Judicial Court of the state, which held that the school board had the legal right to enforce segregation. His opinion made the point that by providing the Negro child with a primary school equal in all respects to other such schools, the state had not unlawfully excluded the child from public school instruction. The issue, Shaw said, was one of power: if the school board had the legal authority to provide primary education, "the expediency of exercising it in any particular way is exclusively with them." The school officials had the right to make racial classifications of pupils. The "great principle" that "all persons without distinction of age or sex, birth or color, origin or condition are equal before the law," when applied "to the actual and various conditions of persons in society," does not lead to the conclusion that all persons "are legally clothed with the same civil and political powers." Laws may be enacted that are "adapted" to the "respective relations and conditions" of people or classes of people.

As happened so often in the debate over abolition and civil rights of Negroes, the fact that at that time women did not enjoy

[5] *Id.*, quoted at 514.

civil and political equality with men led to the conclusion that the law could also make distinctions between the races—that the law could make special provision for women, children, and Negroes without violating the commandment of equality. Shaw's opinion followed this line of reasoning, a line of reasoning then so commonplace that abolitionists felt compelled to join the women's suffrage movement, if only to bring to an end the glib legal analogy of the Negro race to the female sex.

After the Civil War and the end of Reconstruction, federal and state courts turned to Shaw's opinion as a precedent for upholding racially segregated schools (a federal and a New York court in 1883, an Arkansas court in 1885, a Missouri court in 1890, a Louisiana court in 1893, a West Virginia court in 1896).[6] The United States Supreme Court expressed its approval of Shaw's reasoning in an *obiter dictum* in 1877,[7] and squarely in *Plessy v. Ferguson* in 1896.[8] While the last-cited case involved Jim Crow in public conveyances, the majority opinion, in upholding racial segregation in transportation, placed Jim Crow cars on a constitutional parity with segregated public schools, and seems to have argued from the latter to the former. In his opinion for the Court, Mr. Justice Brown said that the question ultimately was whether racial segregation was a reasonable regulation, and with respect to this

there must necessarily be a large discretion on the part of the legislature. In determining the question of reasonableness, it is at liberty to act with reference to the established usages, customs, and traditions of the people, and with a view to the promotion of their comfort, and the preservation of the public peace and good order. Gauged by this standard, we cannot say that a law which authorizes or even requires the separation of the two races in public conveyances is unreasonable, or more obnoxious to the fourteenth amendment than the acts of Congress requiring separate schools for colored children in the District of Columbia, the constitutionality of which does not

[6] *Id.* at 517. [7] Hall v. DeCuir, 95 U.S. 485 (1877).
[8] Plessy v. Ferguson, 163 U.S. 537 (1896).

seem to have been questioned, or the corresponding acts of state legislatures.

In his classic dissent in this case, Mr. Justice Harlan refused to accept "the guise" of "equal accommodations," under which Negroes were forced "to keep to themselves." Segregation, he argued, placed the Negro in an inferior caste, and the whites became "a dominant race, a superior class of citizens, which assumes to regulate the enjoyment of civil rights, common to all citizens, on the basis of race." Americans, he said,

boast of the freedom enjoyed by our people above all other people. But it is difficult to reconcile that boast with a state of the law which, practically, puts the brand of servitude and degradation upon a large class of our fellow citizens, our equals before the law.

Justice Harlan did not believe that racial segregation would contribute to public peace and order. On the contrary, the best guaranty

of peace and security of each race is the clear, distinct, unconditional recognition by our governments, national and state, of every right that inheres in civil freedom, and of equality before the law of all citizens of the United States without regard to race. State enactments, regulating the enjoyment of civil rights, upon the basis of race, and cunningly devised to defeat legitimate results of the [Civil] war, under the pretense of recognizing equality of rights [separate but equal facilities], can have no other result than to render permanent peace impossible and to keep alive a conflict of races, the continuance of which must do harm to all concerned.

Sharply, Justice Harlan told the Court: "Our Constitution is color-blind, and neither knows nor tolerates classes among citizens."

Massachusetts, in 1855, six years after the decision in the *Roberts* case, and despite the great prestige of Chief Justice Shaw, and despite the fact that free Negroes represented no political force in that state, passed a law to provide that no school, in determining the admission qualifications of pupils, should make any distinction "on account of the race, color, or religious opinions of the applicant or scholar." And as we shall see later, other states were more impressed with Harlan's dissenting opinions in the *Civil Rights Cases* of 1883 and in *Plessy v. Ferguson* (1896) than with the majority opinions, and proceeded to enact civil rights acts. Congress, however, refused to act, on the basis of the United States Constitution, to undo these decisions; and the Supreme Court from 1883 to 1954 almost uniformly decided cases on the premise that separate but equal facilities met the constitutional demands of due process and equal protection.

Then, in 1954, in *Brown v. Topeka,*[9] and in a companion case, *Bolling v. Sharpe,*[10] the Supreme Court concluded that "in the field of public education the doctrine of 'seperate but equal' has no place." In the second *Brown*[11] decision, in 1955, the Court spoke of this doctrine as constituting "racial discrimination in public education," and declared that "all provisions of federal, state, or local law requiring or permitting such discrimination" are unconstitutional. Lower federal courts were directed to follow such proceedings as might be necessary and proper to admit to public schools on a racially nondiscriminatory basis "with all deliberate speed the parties to these cases."

The "deliberate speed" mandate was perhaps an echo of the doctrine of the American Anti-Slavery Society, when, at its founding in 1833, it defined immediate emancipation as gradual emancipation immediately begun;[12] or the doctrine of *gradual immediatism* or "immediate emancipation gradually accomplished,"[13] formulated by the New York Committee for a National Anti-Slavery Society in 1831.

Six years after the 1954 decision no school integration had even been started in five states: Alabama, Georgia, Louisiana,

[9] Brown v. Topeka, 347 U.S. 483 (1954).
[10] Bolling v. Sharpe, 347 U.S. 497 (1954).
[11] Brown v. Topeka, 349 U.S. 294 (1955).
[12] DUMOND, ANTISLAVERY ORIGINS OF THE CIVIL WAR IN THE U.S. 27 (1939).
[13] ELKINS, SLAVERY 179 (1959).

Mississippi, and South Carolina. Only token integration—500 of 800,000 Negro pupils—had taken place in four states: Arkansas, Florida, North Carolina, and Virginia. Integration was reported accomplished only in the District of Columbia and West Virginia, and largely accomplished in five states: Delaware, Kentucky, Maryland, Missouri, and Oklahoma.[14] Six years after the 1954 decision, fifty-six cases were pending in the courts protesting school segregation in thirteen Southern and border states.[15] On the sixth anniversary of the decision, only six percent of the South's Negro pupils were attending schools with white pupils.[16] One can speak of "deliberate speed" against this six-year record only in an Aesopian sense. To make the Constitution the supreme law of the land remains a remote ideal, largely because the Court has had practically no support from the other branches of the government.

In any case, the constitutional record is now clear and straight. What Congress would not state through legislation in 1875 has been declared by the Supreme Court through decisions: racial segregation in public education is racial discrimination banned by the Constitution, as it was interpreted by Justice Harlan in his dissenting opinions.

Now that the "separate but equal" doctrine has been discarded, it is important to recall and to emphasize that this doctrine was not an absolute evil. Rather, it was an imperfect good; for it did give recognition to the ideal of equality. The aim, constitutionally, was almost always equality, not separation. Constitutionally, the stress was not on separation but on equality. Harlan a long time ago prophetically saw that separation and equality were contradictory; almost three quarters of a century later the Court unanimously came around to accepting his position. In this process the Court itself practiced "gradualism" and provided an illustration of the truth of Tagore's judgment:

[14] Lewis, N.Y. Times, March 6, 1960; Sitton, N.Y. Times, May 22, 1960; Southern School News, June, 1960.
[15] N.Y. Times, June 4, 1960.   [16] Southern School News, May, 1960.

An imperfection which is not all imperfection, but which has perfection for its ideal, must go through a perpetual realisation. Thus, it is the function of our intellect to realise the truth through untruths, and knowledge is nothing but the continually burning up of error to set free the light of truth. Our will, our character, has to attain perfection by continually overcoming evil, either inside or outside us, or both; . . . our moral life too has its fuel to burn.[17]

Public Conveyances

While schools were omitted from the Civil Rights Bill of 1875 as it was finally enacted, public conveyances were mentioned. Yet the opinion of the Supreme Court in 1883, however, did not except public conveyances from the holding that the 1875 act was unconstitutional. After the decision of the Court in the *School Cases* in 1954, however, it became clear that Jim Crow in transportation, if supported by police enforcement, was unconstitutional. As to interstate carriers, the Interstate Commerce Commission abandoned the "separate but equal" doctrine in interpreting the Interstate Commerce Act. "Former decisions applying the separate-but-equal principle . . . strongly reflected views of public policy then prevailing" and, said the Commission, no longer prevailing.[18]

As to intrastate or local carriers, since the *Brown* decision courts have enjoined transportation companies when they have attempted to enforce state statutes or local ordinances requiring racial segregation. The most notable case involving a local carrier was, perhaps, the one involving Montgomery, Alabama. In this case, coming before the United States district court in 1956, the constitutionality of the Alabama statutes and the city ordinances was attacked. "We cannot in good conscience," said the court,

---

[17] TAGORE, SADHANA—THE REALISATION OF LIFE 53 (1921). See Konvitz, *The Use of Intelligence in Advancement of Civil Rights,* in KONVITZ & ROSSITER, ASPECTS OF LIBERTY 79, 89 (1958).

[18] NAACP v. St. Louis & S.F. Ry., 1 RACE REL. L. REP. 263 (1955); Keys v. Carolina Coach Co., 1 RACE REL. L. REP. 272 (1955).

perform our duty as judges by blindly following the precedent of *Plessy v. Ferguson,* when our study [of the law] leaves us in complete agreement . . . that the separate but equal doctrine can no longer be safely followed as a correct statement of the law. In fact, we think that *Plessy v. Ferguson* has been impliedly, though not explicitly [because the *Brown* decision involved schools, not transportation], overruled, and that, under the later decisions, there is now no rational basis upon which the separate but equal doctrine can be validly applied to public carrier transportation within the City of Montgomery and its police jurisdiction. The application of that doctrine cannot be justified as a proper execution of the state police power.[19]

The court held that the state statutes and city ordinances requiring Jim Crow in common carriers violated the due process and equal protection clauses of the Fourteenth Amendment. This decision was affirmed by the United States Supreme Court.

Enforced Segregation in Public Facilities

The reasoning in the *Montgomery Bus Case* has been applied in other cases involving segregation enforced by law in the use of public facilities. It is now well settled that racial segregation in the use of public facilities is unconstitutional if the segregation is required by state or local law or is enforced by law. A number of cases will illustrate the scope of the decisions against such segregation affirmed by the Supreme Court since 1954.

The Maryland courts had upheld segregation of the races in the public parks of Baltimore on the theory that the city park officials had the power to make rules for the preservation of order within the city parks, that separation of the races was normal racial treatment in Maryland, and that the regulation was justified as an effort on the part of the authorities to avoid conflict from racial antipathies.

[19] Browder v. Gayle, 142 F. Supp. 707, 1 RACE REL. L. REP. 668 (1956), *aff'd per curiam,* 352 U.S. 903 (1956).

The United States court of appeals rejected these views. "It is now obvious," said the court,

that segregation cannot be justified as a means to preserve the public peace merely because the tangible facilities furnished to one race are equal to those furnished to the other. The Supreme Court expressed the opinion in *Brown* . . . that it must consider public education in the light of its full development and its present place in American life, and therefore could not turn the clock back to 1896 when *Plessy v. Ferguson* was written, or base its decision on the tangible factors only of a given situation, but must also take into account the psychological factors recognized at this time, including the feeling of inferiority generated in the hearts and minds of Negro children, when separated solely because of their race from those of similar age and qualification. With this in mind, it is obvious that racial segregation in recreational activities can no longer be sustained as a proper exercise of the police power of the State; for if that power cannot be invoked to sustain racial segregation in the schools, where attendance is compulsory and racial friction may be apprehended from the commingling of the races, it cannot be sustained with respect to public beach and bathhouse facilities, the use of which is entirely optional.

The United States Supreme Court affirmed the decision.[20]

Negroes in Harris County, Texas, brought an action in the federal district court to restrain county officials and the lessee of a restaurant operated in the county courthouse from denying service in the restaurant to Negroes. The defense was that the restaurant was leased to a private individual and that the lessee could legally restrict his service to whomever he chose.

The federal court held that the county, having undertaken to provide a restaurant, could not escape from its constitutional obligations under the equal protection clause of the Fourteenth Amendment by turning over the operation of the restaurant to a private entrepreneur. Said the court:

The equality of the races before the law, and their entitlement to equal enjoyment of State and municipally-operated facilities for edu-

[20] Dawson v. Baltimore, 220 F.2d 386 (4th Cir. 1955), 1 RACE REL. L. REP. 162, *aff'd per curiam*, 350 U.S. 887 (1955).

cation, recreation, etc., are now fully recognized and enforced. It is common knowledge that efforts at segregation under varying circumstances have been stricken down in the public schools, in municipally-owned golf courses and swimming pools, and public parks and beaches.

In view of the foregoing authorities, there can be little doubt that plaintiffs are entitled to relief.

The court of appeals affirmed this decision, holding that the acts of the lessee in operating the restaurant were as much "state action" as if the county itself were the operator. The United States Supreme Court refused to review the decision.[21]

These cases may be taken as typical examples of the dynamism of the Supreme Court's opinion and decision in the 1954 *School Cases*. The force of that decision has been such as to invalidate legally enforced racial segregation in governmentally owned facilities or property—whatever the governmental unit may be—and in interstate and local transportation facilities.

The Student Sit-in Demonstrations

We have seen thus far that: (1) without benefit of a school integration provision in the Civil Rights Act of 1875, racial segregation in public education has been outlawed by decision of the Supreme Court, in *Brown v. Topeka* (1954); (2) though the reference to public conveyances in the Civil Rights Act of 1875 was included in the sweep of unconstitutionality as declared by the Supreme Court in the *Civil Rights Cases* of 1883, racial segregation in public conveyances has been condemned as unconstitutional, following *Brown v. Topeka;* (3) without benefit of federal or state legislation, all racial segregation or discrimination in governmentally owned facilities or property, or all compulsory racial segregation in facilities or property owned or operated by any government agency, or ordered by government in

---

[21] Plummer v. Case, later Derrington v. Plummer, 240 F.2d 922 (5th Cir. 1956), 1 RACE REL. L. REP. 532, 2 RACE REL. L. REP. 117, 2 RACE REL. L. REP. 300 (1957).

privately operated facilities, have been declared unconstitutional as "state action," following *Brown v. Topeka.*

Now, referring again to the Civil Rights Act of 1875, we find that no constitutional development has expressly affected the provision of that act against racial discrimination in inns, theaters, and other places of public amusement, when operated and owned by private individuals. The opinion of the Supreme Court in the *Civil Rights Cases* of 1883, which made a sharp distinction between state action and private action, condemned the 1875 act for its attempt to regulate "purely" or "merely" private action. The student sit-in demonstrations at novelty store lunch counters have brought to the fore once more, after a lapse of some eighty years, public and constitutional policy affecting such places of public accommodation or resort.

The legal challenge to the exclusion of Negroes, solely because of their color, from lunch counters began in 1958, when high school units of the National Association for the Advancement of Colored People in Oklahoma City launched a campaign of sit-in demonstrations to secure service at lunch counters in chain stores. From Oklahoma City the movement spread to other cities in Oklahoma and to Wichita, Kansas. In two years fifty-six eating places were opened to Negroes in Oklahoma City.

The challenge gained in dramatic effect when, on February 1, 1960, four Negro college students in Greensboro, North Carolina, took seats at a lunch counter in a chain store there and asked for service. They were refused. They remained sitting.

This demonstration started a movement that within four months spread to more than seventy Southern cities. Participants were mainly Negro college and high school students, with some white students lending support, and with sympathetic demonstrations by Negro and white students in the North. About fifteen hundred participants were arrested and about two hundred fifty were convicted on a variety of charges, including trespass, disorderly conduct, fire law violations for blocking aisles,

and refusal to leave a business establishment when requested by
the operator to do so, a misdemeanor under laws specially
enacted to meet the situation.

In almost every instance the demonstrators acted peacefully,
in accordance with the Negro Students' Code, drawn up by
Negro college students in Nashville, Tennessee.

> Don't strike back or curse if abused.
> Don't laugh out.
> Don't hold conversations with floor workers.
> Don't block entrances to the stores and the aisles.
> Show yourself courteous and friendly at all times.
> Sit straight and always face the counter.
> Remember love and non-violence.
> May God bless each of you.[22]

In formulating this code of conduct, the students professed to be
following the teachings of Gandhi, and also those of the Reverend Martin Luther King, Jr., who led the 1955–1956 Montgomery bus boycott in the spirit of nonviolent resistance to segregation.

The reaction to the demonstrations varied from place to place.
At times the Negroes were met with violence and insults; at times
they were arrested; at times the stores discontinued the lunch
counters altogether. Some stores adopted Harry Golden's suggestion of "vertical integration" (in 1959 Golden made this suggestion in a spirit of cynicism, saying that since whites objected
to sitting with Negroes but did not seem to object to standing
alongside them in shops and in other public places, the stores
should remove all seats and serve everyone standing at the
counters; and in 1960 some stores seriously adopted the device).

In eight Southern cities lunch counters were desegregated in
the first four months of the 1960 demonstrations. The cities were
Austin, Corpus Christi, Dallas, San Antonio, and Galveston,
Texas; Nashville, Tennessee; and Winston-Salem and Salisbury,

[22] N.Y. Times, March 2, 1960.

North Carolina. In at least thirty cities in the South, community organizations were set up to seek peaceful solutions to the problem of the sit-in demonstrations.[23]

A statement made by LeRoy Collins, Governor of Florida, on the moral issue of the demonstrations, attracted wide attention and undoubtedly lent support to the students. Collins said:

> I don't mind saying that I think that, if a man has a department store and he invites the public generally to come into his department store and trade, then it is unfair and morally wrong to single out one department and say he does not want or will not allow Negroes to patronize that one department.
>
> Now, he has a legal right to do that, but I still don't think that he could square that right with moral, simple justice.[24]

We accept, of course, Governor Collins's statement of the moral issue, but on the legal question we believe he was wrong; and to that question we now turn.

The demonstrators cannot be charged with violation of any law requiring racial segregation, for such laws would not survive a constitutional test. A statute or ordinance requiring segregation of the races clearly constitutes "state action" and therefore falls under the ban of the *Brown* decision and that in the later cases. Segregation imposed by a private individual in obedience to a mandatory state or municipal act is not private but state action. For example, a bus driver required a Negro passenger to change his seat in accordance with a state law. The federal court of appeals held that the driver was engaging thereby in state action: the state had constituted bus drivers police officers for enforcement of the state's segregation policy.[25] The same reasoning would apply to a law making segregation mandatory at lunch counters, or in restaurants, hotels, theaters, or any other facility, even if privately owned or operated.

[23] Report of Southern Regional Council, N.Y. Times, June 6, 1960.
[24] U.S. News & World Report, April 4, 1960, p. 87.
[25] Flemming v. South Carolina Elec. & Gas Co., 224 F.2d 752 (5th Cir. 1955), 1 RACE REL. L. REP. 183 (1956).

The issue of social equality, flowing in part from the majority opinions in the *Civil Rights Cases* and in *Plessy v. Ferguson,* is a false one. When the Civil Rights Act of 1875 was before Congress, proponents of the measure rightly contended that the bill was not intended to give the Negro social equality. Its only purpose was to protect all persons in their enjoyment of *public rights* or *common rights,* without regard to race or color. Places of public accommodation or resort are obviously not places where one has the right to expect privacy or to express his whims—or to assert his racial or religious prejudices. The twenty-four state civil rights acts, discussed in the next chapter, are all based on these patent distinctions, on the policy on which Congress grounded the Civil Rights Act of 1875. If these statutes are constitutional—and they are, as we shall see—then much of the Court's reasoning in the *Civil Rights Cases* of 1883 was obviously without substance; for a state can no more invade the realm of the purely or merely private, or compel social equality, than can Congress.

When a man opens the door of his novelty shop or of any business or store, he is not expecting the same consequences as when he closes the door of his home. Suppose the business operator were to put up a sign that he would not sell to or serve Jews or Roman Catholics or persons of Irish or Italian origin, would not the courts strain their legal resources, methods, and processes to find that his action was not a strictly private one, that his action was one that takes place in the open market place, and that therefore, it was not one that could be claimed to be as private as an action in his home might be?

Relevant at this point is the argument made by Adolf A. Berle, Jr., in *Power Without Property,* that economic power, governmental *or private,* "must not be joined to or controlled by —nor may it control—any other form of power." For example,

if the Standard Oil Company of New Jersey were ever (it has not) to indulge the inconceivable folly of decreeing that no Negro should buy its gasoline at any of its stations—adding to its economic function of supplying oil the quite different function of regulating race relations—it would violate just this same principle. Probably it would promptly be prevented from doing so by political intervention in the form of law.

. . . The primary consideration is not that the State shall not have economic power. It is that economic power exercised either by the State or by non-Statist [*private*] organizations shall not be combined with any other form of power, or used for other than economic ends.[26]

Violation of this principle, says the author, is "a nail in the coffin of individual freedom . . . an inherent danger to individuality, which our government and our economic system are designed to serve." [27] Berle says that such actions may appear to be permissible under rules of technical law but are not acceptable "according to the standards and principles of the public consensus." [28]

How does one determine "the public consensus" on a matter such as segregation in places of public accommodation? The Supreme Court did not look for that consensus in the Southern states when the question of school segregation was before it. But surely the existence of civil rights acts in twenty-four states, representing the majority of our population, are an index to the consensus of the whole.

The courts, since *Brown v. Topeka,* have said that when racial segregation is looked into today, the examination can no longer be limited to the tangible factors of a given situation. The courts must also take into account the psychological factors, "including the feeling of inferiority generated in the hearts and minds of Negro children, when separated solely because of their race from those of similar age and qualification." [29] The same feelings are generated whether the public act is performed by a governmental

[26] BERLE, POWER WITHOUT PROPERTY 96, 97 (1959).

[27] *Ibid. Cf.* Greenberg, *A Case Against Jim Crow Eating,* New Leader, March 14, 1960.

[28] BERLE, *op. cit. supra* note 26, at 116. See also p. 123.

[29] Case cited note 20 *supra.*

agency or by a private entrepreneur. To the Negro who finds himself barred and humiliated, it makes no difference whether the facility is operated governmentally or privately; so long as it is a public facility or place of public accommodation or resort, the slap on his face stings just the same.

Indeed, when the opinion of Justice Bradley in the *Civil Rights Cases* of 1883 is read carefully with this issue in mind, it will disclose the fact that the majority of the Court were aware of these considerations. The Court simply assumed that the Negroes would have adequate remedies against discrimination in the state courts. The Court said that in a refusal to accommodate the Negro,

if it is violative of any right of the party, his redress is to be sought under the laws of the State; or if those laws are adverse to his rights and do not protect him, his remedy will be found in the corrective legislation which Congress has adopted, or may adopt, for counteracting the effect of State laws, or State action, prohibited by the Fourteenth Amendment. . . . Innkeepers . . . by the laws of all the States, so far as we are aware, are bound, to the extent of their facilities, to furnish proper accommodation to all unobjectionable persons who in good faith apply for them. If the laws themselves make any unjust discrimination, amenable to the prohibitions of the Fourteenth Amendment, Congress has full power to afford a remedy under that amendment and in accordance with it.

Furthermore, we should note that since *Brown v. Topeka* and *Bolling v. Sharpe,* the single most comprehensive civil right, protected by the Constitution against governmental action, is that there be no classification of persons according to race or color. Now again, if we look into Bradley's opinion in the *Civil Rights Cases* of 1883 with this civil right in mind, the following passage would seem to leave the door open, to some extent, for relief against racial discrimination in places of public accommodation. It is proper to state, said Bradley, that

civil rights, such as are guaranteed by the Constitution against State aggression [including, now, the broad civil right stated above], cannot be impaired by the wrongful acts of individuals, unsupported by

State authority in the shape of laws, customs, or judicial or executive proceedings. The wrongful act of an individual, unsupported by any such authority, is simply a private wrong, or a crime of that individual; an invasion of the rights of the injured party, it is true, whether they affect his person, his property, or his reputation; but if not sanctioned in some way by the State, or not done under State authority, his rights remain in full force, and may presumably be vindicated by resort to the laws of the State for redress.

In the case of lunch counter segregation, it is obvious that even if no use be made of a state segregation law, the segregation is clearly supported by "State . . . customs." The proprietor does not practice segregation as an isolated private person. He acts in response to and in accordance with the policy of the state or municipality, just as if he were enforcing a state or local law. But even more than this is involved, for the state or local government, by arresting the sit-in demonstrators against the lunch counter segregation, acts to enforce the governmental policy or "State . . . customs" compelling racial segregation.

At this point it will help us to understand the constitutional requirement of "state action" if we consider the very important case of *Shelley v. Kraemer.*[30]

There is no question but that action of a state legislature is "state action." But suppose the action is that of a court? In a case decided in 1880 the United States Supreme Court held that when a state court judge in Virginia excluded Negroes from state juries, in violation of federal law, his action was "state action." [31]

The most important decision on this question came in 1948 in *Shelley v. Kraemer.* The Supreme Court considered consolidated cases from Missouri and Michigan. In the Missouri case, thirty owners of property had agreed to restrict for fifty years the use of the property "by any person not of the Caucasian race, it being intended hereby to restrict the use of said property for said period of time against the occupancy as owners or tenants

[30] Shelley v. Kraemer, 334 U.S. 1 (1948).
[31] *Ex parte* Virginia, 100 U.S. 339 (1880).

of any portion of said property for resident or other purposes by people of the Negro or Mongolian race." Despite this agreement or restrictive covenant, Negroes obtained a warranty deed to a parcel of the property, whereupon owners of other parcels subject to the agreement brought suit in the state courts of Missouri to restrain the Negroes from taking title. The state supreme court directed the trial court to enforce the agreement. The court found that the restrictive covenant, if enforced, would not violate the rights of Negroes under the United States Constitution.

The Supreme Court of the United States reversed this decision and held that it is state action, in violation of the equal protection clause of the Fourteenth Amendment, for a state court to enforce a racially restrictive covenant. The Court unanimously [32] held that while such covenants are private, their enforcement by state courts is state action and, as such, is unconstitutional.

In his opinion for the Court, Chief Justice Vinson observed that

these covenants do not seek to proscribe any particular use of the affected properties. Use of the properties for residential occupancy, as such, is not forbidden. The restrictions of these agreements, rather, are directed toward a designated class of persons and seek to determine who may and who may not own or make use of the properties for residential purposes. The excluded class is defined wholly in terms of race or color; "simply that and nothing more."

The Court reasoned that the restrictive covenants, standing alone, are not violative of any constitutional rights. "So long as the purposes of those agreements are effectuated by voluntary adherence to their terms," there is no state action and the Fourteenth Amendment has not been violated. But, said the Court,

here there was more [than voluntary compliance]. These are cases in which the purposes of the agreements were secured only by judicial enforcement by state courts of the restrictive terms of the agreements. . . .

[32] Justices Reed, Rutledge, and Jackson did not participate in the case.

These are not cases . . . in which the States have merely abstained from action, leaving private individuals free to impose such discriminations as they see fit. Rather, these are cases in which the States have made available to such individuals the full coercive power of government to deny to petitioners, on the grounds of race or color, the enjoyment of property rights.

The broad constitutional principle from which the Court proceeded is worthy of note.

The historical context in which the Fourteenth Amendment became a part of the Constitution should not be forgotten. Whatever else the framers sought to achieve, it is clear that the matter of primary concern was the establishment of equality in the enjoyment of basic civil and political rights and the preservation of those rights from discriminatory action on the part of the States based on considerations of race or color.[33]

Following this decision, the Court, in another case, held that the restrictive covenant was barred also in the District of Columbia (against enforcement by federal courts),[34] and the last loophole was closed when the Court, in 1953, held that one party to a restrictive covenant may not recover damages from another party who has broken the covenant.[35]

In brief, racial restrictive covenants are not enforceable either by injunction or by action for damages, in either state or federal courts. Parties may voluntarily observe the terms of their agreements, but no court may aid them; for such aid constitutes state action—the enforcement of racial discrimination by the state.

Before we try to apply the rationale of *Shelley v. Kraemer* to the lunchroom sit-ins, we wish to note another decision of the Supreme Court that will help us in our attempt to think through the problem.

Marsh v. Alabama[36] involved a conviction of a Jehovah's Wit-

[33] It may be noted that in Corrigan v. Buckley, 271 U.S. 323 (1926), the Court had upheld racially restrictive covenants.

[34] Hurd v. Hodge, 334 U.S. 24 (1948).

[35] Barrows v. Jackson, 346 U.S. 249 (1953).

[36] Marsh v. Alabama, 326 U.S. 501 (1946).

ness for entering and remaining on the premises of a private person after having been warned by the owner not to do so, in violation of an Alabama statute. The property was that of a company town, privately owned. The Jehovah's Witness sought to distribute religious literature at a place where a notice showed that the property was private and where solicitation, without written permission, was prohibited. She was told that she would not be given permission; she tried to distribute her literature just the same. She was arrested and convicted of violation of the state statute against trespassing or entering and remaining on the property of another after a warning by the owner not to do so.

The Supreme Court set aside the conviction on the ground that the state act was used here to accomplish an unconstitutional restriction on freedom of religion and the press.

Now, in the lunchroom sit-ins the owner of the shop can do one of the following: (1) he can close down the lunch counter; (2) he can remove the seats and serve all customers as they stand at the counter; or (3) he can call the police and have the student demonstrators arrested on one of the charges previously noted.

It is only when the proprietor acts in the third way that the question of state action arises. A strong case can be made for the proposition that the use of the police and courts under these circumstances constitutes a violation of the Constitution under the precedents we have discussed.

That there is state action when a student demonstrator is arrested and convicted cannot be denied. If this is not state action, then the phrase has no meaning. The difficult question, however, remains, and that is: Is it state action in violation of the Constitution?

That there are these two separate questions was made clear by the Supreme Court in *Rice v. Sioux City Memorial Park Cemetery* (1955).[37] This was an action for damages brought by

[37] Rice v. Sioux City Memorial Park Cemetery, 349 U.S. 70 (1955).

Mrs. Rice in an Iowa court to compensate her for mental suffering claimed to flow from the defendant cemetery's refusal to bury
her husband, a Winnebago Indian, after services had been conducted at the grave site and the burial party had disbanded. She
founded her action on breach of a contract whereby the cemetery
had agreed to afford plaintiff the right of burial in a specified
plot. The contract also provided that "burial privileges accrue
only to members of the Caucasian race." The Iowa court ruled
that the restrictive covenant in the contract was not void but
was unenforceable. Though unenforceable, it might, however,
be relied on as a defense, said the court, and went on to say that
the action of the state court in permitting the use of the covenant
as a defense does not constitute state action contrary to the
Foureenth Amendment.

The Supreme Court granted *certiorari*. The Court was evenly
divided, and so the Iowa court's decision was affirmed without
an opinion. Then a petition for a rehearing was filed, and the
Court now dismissed the writ of *certiorari* as improvidently
granted, with three Justices dissenting. The reason for the dismissal was that after the commencement of the litigation Iowa
enacted a statute that prohibited cemeteries from denying the
right of burial solely by reason of race or color. This statute
made the action before the Supreme Court, said Justice Frankfurter in his opinion for the majority of the Court, one with
"such an isolated significance that it would hardly have been
brought here [before the Supreme Court] in the first place."

Frankfurter pointed out that cases such as this one involve
two questions. The first is "the threshold problem" of whether
what the state did through its courts amounted to state action.[38]
After this question is answered in the affirmative, the second
question, "the ultimate substantial question," is whether, in the

[38] This, said Frankfurter, "is a complicated problem which for long has divided opinion in this Court." He cited several cases, but not *Shelly v. Kraemer*.
He did cite *Barrows v. Jackson,* but in this case only one Justice dissented.

circumstances of the case, "the action complained of was condemned by the Fourteenth Amendment."

When a state or a municipality resorts to the use of trespass, disorderly conduct, fire hazard, vagrancy, or other statutes or ordinances for the purpose of indirectly enforcing the state's "custom" of racial discrimination, then the action is condemned by the Fourteenth Amendment. In such police action, the state pursues a conscious, deliberate policy of racial discrimination. It enforces what it assumes to be the policy and will of a majority of its people, or at least of its white population.

In the *Rice* case, it may be noted, the questions raised within the constitutional framework involved a defense in an action for a civil remedy. Had Mrs. Rice succeeded in burying the corpse of her husband and had she been prosecuted for the act, then her case would be close to the case of the prosecuted student demonstrators, for the criminal law clearly is an expression of state policy—much more so than permitting a defense to a civil suit—and use of the criminal law in specific prosecutions clearly raises questions involving the guarantees of the Fourteenth Amendment.

The owner of a business who resorts to the police power of the state to carry out racial policies is not, in such action, merely carrying on his business according to his own business notions, nor is he seeking protection against ordinary actions of trespass. He seeks to implement the state's or municipality's custom of racial discrimination, and the police and court actions are state actions and discriminatory acts that are violative of the Fourteenth Amendment.

Indeed, the case for the students is constitutionally stronger than was the case for the Negroes in the restrictive covenant cases, for in the latter what was involved was the sought remedies in private actions and the acquisition or retention of title to private property—what one might call classic instances of private rights. But in the case of the students, it is public rights that are involved—rights in places of public accommodation, where the doors are open for all interested persons of the general public. There is no question here of the alleged right to choose one's neighbors, however arbitrary or willful the choice. One does not choose the fellow members of the public with whom one goes into a novelty shop or any other place of public accommodation or resort, whether to buy pins and needles, or a cup of coffee, or a soda. And the calling of the police to enforce a racial policy is not resort to a private remedy but to the use of the state's police power on behalf of the state's custom or policy of racial discrimination.

The theory of civil remedies is that the interest of the state in the protection of property and contract rights is ordinarily secondary to that of the individual citizen, that the extent to which the protection of the law is obtained for them is largely discretionary with him, and that the sanction of private damages adequately safeguards them. As compared with the implementing of civil remedies, a criminal statute is an expression of state policy of a much higher order. In theory the state pursues purposes of its own in criminal legislation and is itself chiefly offended when such statutes are violated. Thus it could easily be said that where a criminal statute is turned to the service of what are usually classified as private rights it adopts as the policy of the state the motives of private interests which call for its enforcement.[39]

Bearing in mind the distinction drawn by Justice Frankfurter in the *Rice* case, we would say that the state is only formally involved in every case in which a court acts: a court's judgment is always state action, but only in a formal sense. Such action becomes state action under the Fourteenth Amendment not when small, narrow private rights or claims are involved, but when it is a question of broad social policy, such as ghettoization of races subject to restrictive covenants, though enforced by civil remedies in the courts, or racial discrimination in places of public

[39] Comment, 45 MICH. L. REV. 733 (1947).

accommodation or resort, especially when enforced by criminal sanctions.

The criminal statutes are not in themselves unconstitutional, but their misuse to enforce racial policies makes them, in the circumstances, unconstitutional. In *Yick Wo v. Hopkins* [40] the Supreme Court declared unconstitutional a municipal ordinance that on its face validly regulated laundries but that in its enforcement discriminated against Chinese. So, too, a state's trespass or other criminal laws may be valid, but they become unconstitutional when used to enforce racial discrimination.

Where private racial discrimination is effective without help from the government, then the principle of *Shelley v. Kraemer* has no application. But where the private racial discrimination cannot be implemented without governmental aid, then such aid is within the rationale of *Shelley v. Kraemer,* [41] and is a violation of the Fourteenth Amendment. Racial discrimination in places of public accommodation or resort often is ineffective without the support of criminal sanctions. The use of such sanctions brings the state within the condemnation of *Shelley v. Kraemer.* In such cases, the police do not act disinterestedly, merely to protect neutral property rights. [42] They act to carry out the social judgment of the state that condemns racial integration in public places; but the Fourteenth Amendment condemns this social judgment as unconstitutional. Racial discrimination, when it pervades public places and characterizes the public environment, and is then enforced by criminal sanctions—police and courts— is then the state's custom or policy, and then the courts' acts are state acts, formally and substantively—and unconstitutionally.

[40] Yick Wo v. Hopkins, 118 U.S. 356 (1886).
[41] Note, 44 CALIF. L. REV. 718 (1956).
[42] Note, 52 NW. U.L. REV. 774 (1958). Case comment, 45 CORNELL L.Q. 104 (1959). See also Horowitz, *Misleading Search for "State Action" Under Fourteenth Amendment,* 30 SO. CAL. L. REV. 208 (1957); Glenn Abernathy, *Expansion of the State Action Concept Under the Fourteenth Amendment,* 43 CORNELL L.Q. 375 (1958).

When the action of the state, in enforcing the will—even the arbitrary will—of a private person does not imply important social consequences or important public policies, no constitutional issue is involved. If the state,

> by enforcing my property rights, gives effect to my arbitrary refusal to have a Catholic or a Protestant or a Jew or a Negro or a Republican in my house, the sound reason why the Fourteenth Amendment is not violated is not that state action is lacking, but that state action to enforce property rights cannot be regarded as arbitrary, however arbitrary the whim of the owner, *provided that carrying out the owner's will does not involve some matter of high public importance.*[43]

The distinction between an owner's rights in his private property, e.g., his home, and his rights in his public property, e.g., his department store, is consequential. While he may arbitrarily order me from his home, and even call a policeman to aid him, he cannot do this when I am in his store except for good cause; and when the cause is the policy of racial discrimination which is the custom of the state, then a "matter of high public importance" is involved, and the state's aid is state action in violation of the Constitution.

This view of the law is consonant with the Court's opinion in the *Civil Rights Cases* of 1883. Again we call attention to the fact, often overlooked, that the Court assumed that the acts of the carriers and of the innkeepers which discriminated against the Negroes were violations of state law. They were not state acts because they were not "authorized" or "sanctioned" by state law, and hence they were not violations of the Fourteenth Amendment. The Court assumed that the Negroes had rights under state law which they could vindicate in the state courts.[44] We quote once more the following key passage from Justice Bradley's opinion:

[43] HALE, FREEDOM THROUGH LAW 370 (New York 1952). Italics added.
[44] *Id.* at 320, 327.

civil rights, such as are guaranteed by the Constitution against State aggression, cannot be impaired by the wrongful acts of individuals, unsupported by State authority in the shape of laws, customs, or judicial or executive proceedings. The wrongful act of an individual, unsupported by any such authority, is simply a private wrong, . . . but if not sanctioned in some way by the State, or done under State authority, his rights remain in full force, and may presumably be vindicated by resort to the laws of the State for redress.

The distinction between public wrong and private wrong, between state aid of a private act and state aid of a private act that involves important public consequences is contained in the following passage from Thomas Aquinas: "Human law cannot forbid all and everything that is against virtue; it is enough that it forbids deeds against community life; the remainder it tolerates almost as if they were licit, not indeed because they are approved, but because they are not punished." [45]

The student demonstrations at lunch counters compel a re-reading of Justice Bradley's opinion; they also compel a re-reading of Justice Harlan's dissenting opinion, especially the passages in which he argued that the Thirteenth Amendment outlawed all the badges and incidents of slavery. "I hold," it will be recalled Justice Harlan's saying,

that since slavery . . . was the moving or principal cause of the adoption of that amendment, and since that institution rested wholly upon the inferiority, as a race, of those held in bondage, their freedom necessarily involved immunity from, and protection against, all discrimination against them, because of their race, in respect of such civil rights as belong to freemen of other races.

Congress, Harlan maintained, had the power to carry out the intent of the Thirteenth Amendment by adopting legislation to protect civil rights, at least against "such individuals and corporations as exercise public functions and wield power and authority under the state." Considering the temper of Congress to-

[45] Thomas Aquinas, Summa Theologicae I, 27, 2 a–2 a e. *Cf.* Hale, *op. cit. supra* note 43, at 376.

day when it comes to enacting civil rights acts, it would be utopian to expect it to pass civil rights legislation of the scope of the act of 1875. It is, however, not unreasonable to ask the federal courts to apply the rationale of the *Shelley v. Kraemer* decision to the states when they seek, by police and court action, to perpetuate the incidents and badges of slavery, along with the view that the Negro race is by nature inferior, and that, therefore, while the Negro may no longer be a slave, he must continue to wear and show the incidents and badges of slavery.[46]

[46] For the purposes of the Thirteenth Amendment, see JACOBUS TENBROEK, ANTISLAVERY ORIGINS OF THE FOURTEENTH AMENDMENT 148 ff. (1951). See also opinion of Justice Field in Slaughter-House Cases, 16 Wall. 36, 90 (U.S. 1873).

STATE LAW AGAINST DISCRIMINATION

Chapter 6

PUBLIC ACCOMMODATIONS

We have seen that the United States Supreme Court in the *Civil Rights Cases* of 1883 held that federal power under the Fourteenth Amendment did not extend to passing or enforcing laws requiring nondiscriminatory conduct of individuals, unless they were exercising some form of state authority. Discriminatory acts by individuals, the Court said were "within the domain of state legislation." The victim of discriminatory conduct on the part of another individual was directed by the Court to "resort to the laws of the State for redress."

There was no disagreement between the majority of the Court and Mr. Justice Harlan concerning the basic power of the states, "which they have always had to define and regulate the civil rights which their own people, in virtue of state citizenship, may enjoy within their respective limits."

Let us look at the early beginnings of state efforts to deal with the problem which the Supreme Court in 1883 placed beyond the reach of congressional regulation.

The Situation before 1883

Prior to 1883, there was very little civil rights legislation on the books.

On May 16, 1865, Massachusetts enacted the first state law in the country banning distinctions or restrictions based on race or color in any licensed place of public accommodation. (Ten years earlier, as we saw in chapter 5, the commonwealth had outlawed racial criteria in the admission of students to public schools.[1]) Since it was the forerunner of many similar statutes, we set out the Massachusetts statute in full.

Section 1. No distinction, discrimination or restriction on account of color or race shall be lawful in any licensed inn, in any public place of amusement, public conveyance or public meeting in this commonwealth.

Section 2. Any person offending against the provisions of this act shall be punished by a fine not exceeding fifty dollars.[2]

The following year, 1866, "theatres" were included in the list in Section 1, but the statute was weakened somewhat by the added condition that there should be no exclusion "except for good cause." [3]

Almost a decade later, in 1874, New York became the second state to enact a civil rights law with a statute prohibiting race distinctions at inns, public conveyances on land and water, theaters, other places of amusement, common schools, public institutions of learning, and cemeteries.[4] In 1881, the law was amended to add hotels, taverns, restaurants, and place of public resort.[5]

One other state passed a civil rights law before the federal law of 1875 was declared unconstitutional in 1883. On April 25, 1874, the governor of Kansas signed a bill prohibiting any distinctions based on race, color, or previous condition of servitude in any state university, college, or other school of public instruction, or in any licensed inn, hotel, boarding house, or any place of public entertainment or amusement, or in any steamboat, railroad, stagecoach, omnibus, streetcar, or any other means of public carriage for persons or freight, under penalty of a fine of $1,000.[6]

[1] See pp. 129–30 *supra*.
[2] Mass. Stat. 1865, ch. 277; Laws of Mass., 1864–65, at 650.
[3] Laws of Mass., 1866, at 242.
[4] N.Y. Stat. at Large, vol. IX, at 583–84.
[5] N.Y. Laws of 1881, vol. I, at 541.
[6] Laws of Kan., 1874, ch. 49, § 1.

The Situation after 1883

Immediately after the federal Civil Rights Act of 1875 was declared unconstitutional and the problem of discrimination by one individual against another was relegated to the exclusive jurisdiction of the states, many state legislatures outside the South adopted laws modeled on the federal Civil Rights Act. Connecticut, Iowa, New Jersey, and Ohio passed such laws in 1884; Colorado, Illinois, Indiana, Michigan, Minnesota, Nebraska, and Rhode Island in 1885; Pennsylvania (1887), Washington (1890), Wisconsin (1895), and California (1897) joined the parade before the turn of the century. By 1900, eighteen Northern, Eastern and Western states had legislated a public policy against discrimination for reasons of race or color in places of public accommodation.

In recent years, Oregon (1953), Montana (1955), New Mexico (1955), Vermont (1957), and Maine (1959) passed similar statutes. Alaska joined the Union with a civil rights act already on its books, bringing the total to twenty-four.[7]

The wording of all the early state statutes is essentially the same: all persons (citizens in Alaska, California, and Ohio) within the jurisdiction of the state, regardless of race, color, or previous condition of servitude, are entitled to the full and equal advantages, facilities and privileges of the various places of public accommodation, resort, or amusement listed. Individuals who defy the law are subject to fine or imprisonment (criminal sanction) or are responsible in damages to the party aggrieved (civil sanction). In some states both remedies are available, but an action for one bars an action for the other. Places listed in

[7] During February and March, 1961, while this volume was in production, Idaho, North Dakota, and Wyoming enacted legislation prohibiting discrimination in places of public accommodation. Thus, the number of states with such statutes rose to twenty-seven.

Although forty-six state legislatures were scheduled to be in session during 1961, whatever action they may have taken, could not be included, for the addition of new material to this section of the book was terminated in March, 1961.

the various state laws include inns, taverns, restaurants, eating
houses, boarding houses, cafés, chophouses, lunch counters, hotels, motels, saloons, soda fountains, ice cream parlors, bathhouses, barber shops, theaters, concert and music halls, skating
rinks, bicycle rinks, churches (Colorado), public meetings
(Massachusetts), elevators (Illinois), public conveyances, colleges and universities, schools and places of public instruction,
places of public amusement, resort or entertainment, places
where refreshments are served, and public places kept for hire,
gain, or reward.

Early State Court Decisions

Perhaps the first case in the United States under a state civil
rights statute arose in Massachusetts in 1866, when a Negro
was refused permission to play in a billiard room. The report
does not mention the name of the city. The law required equal
treatment in "places of public amusement." The highest court
of Massachusetts held that in the absence of proof that the billiard room was licensed, there was no violation of the statute.
"It cannot be supposed," the opinion said, "that it was the intention of the legislature to prescribe the manner in which persons should use their own premises or permit others to use
them." [8] Another early case arose in New York City in 1881,
involving the meaning of the terms "inn" and "restaurant." At the
time, the state statute listed "inns" and the defense was that a
restaurant was not included within the term "inn." The court rejected this defense, defining "inn" as a place that provides food,
lodging, or both to guests, and hence encompassing a restaurant
that provides only food.[9]

An interesting case was decided by the highest court of Indiana
in 1896, the same year that the United States Supreme Court

[8] Commonwealth v. Sylvester, 13 Allen (95 Mass.) 247 (1866).
[9] Kopper v. Willis, 9 Daly 460 (N.Y. 1881).

pronounced the "separate but equal" principle in *Plessy v. Ferguson*.[10] The University of Indiana had a Negro player on its football team that year. A hotel clerk at the Nutt House in Crawfordsville, Indiana, barred the Negro from using the hotel's eating facilities with his teammates but offered to feed him separately and apart from the white members of the team. The Negro student brought suit under the civil rights law and the court held that the offer of separate accommodations did not satisfy the statutory requirements of full and equal advantages, privileges, and facilities.[11]

Strict Construction by the Courts

Although state civil rights laws have been described as a proper exercise of the police power to compel recognition of the equal right of citizens to the enjoyment and use of services and facilities afforded to the general public,[12] many courts have severely limited the effectiveness of these statutes by strict interpretation.

Three principal grounds have been used to justify strict construction of civil rights laws: (1) such statutes are in derogation of the common law; (2) they are penal in nature; and (3) they impose restrictions on the control or management of private property.

Actually, there is considerable authority for the argument that with respect to innkeepers and common carriers the civil rights statutes merely restate the common law. English common law, for centuries, has required the managers of such public accommodations to furnish their facilities to all unobjectionable persons who, in good faith, apply for them. Railroads have been regarded as public highways established and owned by private corporations for the public use and, therefore, invested with some

[10] 163 U.S. 537 (1896).

[11] Fruchey v. Eagleson, 43 N.E. 146 (Ind. 1896).

[12] Johnson v. Auburn & Syracuse Elec. R.R., 222 N.Y. 443 (1918); Jones v. Kehrlein, 49 Cal. App. 646, 194 Pac. 55 (1920).

of the unique powers of government itself—the power of eminent domain, for example.[13] The innkeeper, too, was vested with special privileges and charged with specific responsibilities to the public that he served. An old English case summarizes these responsibilities thus:

An indictment lies against an innkeeper who refuses to receive a guest, he having at the time room in his house; and either the price of the guest's entertainment being offered him, or such circumstances occurring as will dispense with that tender. This law is founded in good sense. The innkeeper is not to select his guests. He has no right to say to one, you shall come to my inn; and to another, you shall not; as everyone coming and conducting himself in a proper manner has a right to be received; and for this purpose innkeepers are a sort of public servants.[14]

Under the Fourteenth Amendment, as interpreted by the Supreme Court in the *Civil Rights Cases,* neither state legislation nor state court decisions could make "any unjust discrimination" between the rights of whites and Negroes with respect to the accommodations of innkeepers and common carriers. Any such "unjust discrimination" would be action by the state and hence prohibited by the amendment.

Since owners and managers of places of public accommodation, resort, or amusement (other than innkeepers and common carriers) were not prohibited at common law from picking and choosing among would-be patrons, early decisions interpreting the state civil rights statutes resorted to strict interpretation on the ground that these statutes created rights and obligations unknown to the common law.[15]

A second argument used by many courts to limit the ap-

[13] New Jersey Steam Nav. Co. v. Merchants' Bank, 6 How. 344 (U.S. 1848); Inhabitants of Worcester v. Western R.R. Co., 4 Met. (45 Mass.) 564 (1842).

[14] Rex v. Ivens, 32 E.C.L. 495, 7 C. & P. 213 (1835).

[15] Brown v. J. H. Bell Co., 146 Iowa 89, 123 N.W. 231 (1909); People *ex rel.* Barnett v. Bartlett, 169 Ill. App. 304 (1912); Rhone v. Loomis, 74 Minn. 200, 77 N.W. 31 (1898); Kellar v. Koerber, 61 Ohio St. 388, 55 N.E. 1002 (1899).

plicability of the state civil rights laws was the rule that "penal statutes" must be strictly construed. Thus, for example, where the title of a statute referred to "all citizens" and the body to "all persons," the Nebraska court held that it must be alleged and proved that the person deprived of the right was a citizen in order to entitle him to the protection of the act.[16]

Traditionally, courts in common law countries have imposed strict construction of statutes which limit the use of private property. When two Negroes, who were refused service in a New York saloon because of their color, sued under the New York Civil Rights Law in 1917, the court of appeals applied the strict construction principle to rule that a saloon was "closer to a tobacco and cigar shop" than to a restaurant, and hence not a "place of public accommodation within the letter or spirit of the statute." [17]

In another New York case, the plaintiffs charged that they had been refused the use of the defendant's golf course because they were Negroes. But the Civil Rights Act, under which they sued for damages, did not expressly include golf courses in its enumeration of places of public accommodation or amusement. The plaintiffs proved that on a previous occasion one of them had been permitted to play on the course upon the payment of a fee; and, further, that signs on the highway and on the grounds indicated that the course was a public one. The defendant contended that the course was a private club, and so not within the terms of the statute. It argued that on a previous occasion, when one of the plaintiffs had played, the rules of the club had been relaxed, but that the relaxation of the rules was only temporary. As to the signs, it argued that they had been put up by a group of businessmen in the neighboring town, not by the

[16] Messinger v. State, 25 Neb. 674, 41 N.W. 638 (1889).

[17] Gibbs v. Arras Bros., 222 N.Y. 332, 118 N.E. 857 (1918). See also Chochos v. Burden, 74 Ind. App. 242, 128 N.E. 696 (1921); Darius v. Apostolos, 68 Colo. 323, 190 Pac. 510 (1920).

club, and that while they indicated that the course was "public," they stipulated it was "under club rules."

The court held that the plaintiffs had failed to sustain the burden of proving that the golf course was a place of public accommodation, resort, or amusement, and that in any case, the statute did not (then) specifically name golf courses among such public places. In view of the fact that the act enumerates public places, the court stated, one may say that the legislature intended to limit its application to the places enumerated, and if there is to be an extension of the list, the legislature, rather than the courts, should extend it.

Finally, said the court, the act being penal and restrictive of property rights, it is not to be extended through implication or by analogy.[18]

Another legal rule of interpretation, *ejusdem generis*, states that general references following an enumeration of specific items should be interpreted as encompassing only the same kind of items which are expressly specified. Thus, for example, laws which enumerate specific places, followed by the words "and all other places of public accommodation," have been held not to include a bootblack stand,[19] a retail store,[20] a drugstore where soda water was sold,[21] an apartment or family hotel,[22] or a beauty parlor.[23] Restaurants and lunchrooms were not deemed included within the Kansas civil rights statute prohibiting discrimination in any "inn, hotel, or boarding house, or any place of entertainment or amusement for which a license is required by the municipal authorities," even though a state license is required for the operation of restaurants.[24]

As limiting court decisions resulted in an ever-growing list of

[18] Delaney v. Central Valley Golf Club, 28 N.Y.S.2d 932 (1941), *aff'd*, 31 N.Y.S.2d 834, *appeal* denied, 32 N.Y.S.2d 1016 (1942).
[19] Burks v. Bosso, 180 N.Y. 341, 73 N.E. 58 (1905).
[20] Harvey, Inc. v. Sissle, 53 Ohio App. 405, 5 N.E.2d 410 (1936).
[21] Cecil v. Green, 161 Ill. 265, 43 N.E. 1105 (1896).
[22] Alsberg v. Lucerne Hotel Co., 46 Misc. 617, 92 N.Y. Supp. 851 (1905).
[23] Campbell v. Eichert, 155 Misc. 164, 278 N.Y. Supp. 946 (1935).
[24] State v. Brown, 112 Kan. 814, 212 Pac. 663 (1923).

amendments, civil rights statutes grew longer and longer. Also, as the years went on, an increasing number of establishments came to be considered within the category of public accommodations. The New York Civil Rights Law, which is probably the most detailed of the twenty-seven state statutes, includes the following list of places covered by the act, in addition to a general prohibition against discrimination in places of public accommodation, resort, or amusement: inns, taverns, roadhouses, hotels, "whether conducted for the entertainment of transient guests or for the accommodation of those seeking health, recreation or rest," restaurants, eating houses, "or any place where food is sold for consumption on the premises," buffets, saloons, barrooms, "or any store, park or enclosure where spirituous or malt liquors are sold," ice cream parlors, confectioneries, soda fountains, "and all stores where ice cream, ice and fruit preparations or their derivatives, or where beverages of any kind are retailed for consumption on the premises," retail stores and establishments, dispensaries, clinics, hospitals, bathhouses, barber shops, beauty parlors, theaters, motion picture houses, air dromes, roof gardens, music halls, race courses, skating rinks, amusement and recreation parks, fairs, bowling alleys, golf courses, gymnasiums, shooting galleries, billiard and pool parlors, public libraries, kindergartens, primary and secondary schools, high schools, academies, colleges, universities, extension courses, "and all educational institutions under the supervision of the regents of the state of New York, and any such public library, kindergarten, primary and secondary school, academy, college, university, professional school, extension course, or other educational facility, supported in whole or in part by public funds or by contributions solicited from the general public," garages, all public conveyances operated on land or water, and the stations and terminals thereof, public halls and public elevators of buildings and structures "occupied by two or more tenants, or by the owner and one or more tenants."

Institutions for the care of neglected or delinquent children, if supported "directly or indirectly, in whole or in part," by public funds, are by the act prohibited from refusing their accommodations to any person "on account of race or color." The statute specifically avoids including religion in this connection, thus permitting neglected children, "when practicable," to be placed in institutions under the control of persons of the same religious faith as the child.[25]

The New York Civil Rights Law, in an excess of caution, expressly excepts "any institution, club or place of accommodation which is in its nature distinctly private." This exception does not apply, however, to a club or place of accommodation which sponsors or conducts amateur athletic contests or sparring exhibitions "and advertises or bills such contests or exhibitions as a New York state championship contest or uses the words 'New York State' in its announcements."

The tendency of the courts to construe the acts strictly has necessitated frequent amendments of the civil rights laws by the state legislatures in order to overcome restrictive decisions; these amendments, in turn, are used by the courts as an argument against liberal construction. Thus, the New York law was amended to include saloons after a decision held that saloons are not included in places of public accommodation, resort, or amusement; a later decision prompted the addition of beauty parlors;[26] yet another resulted in having golf courses expressly covered by the law.[27] The process, apparently, is an endless one.

Clearly, the practice of listing every place of public accommodation which the statute means to cover is cumbersome and requires constant amendment. Recently a different approach to the matter was attempted. In 1953, Connecticut amended its Civil Rights Law striking out the enumeration of places covered

[25] See: N.Y. CHILDREN'S COURT ACT § 26; SOCIAL WELFARE LAW § 373; DOMESTIC RELATIONS COURT ACT § 83.
[26] Campbell v. Eichert, *supra* note 23.
[27] Delaney v. Central Valley Golf Club, *supra* note 18.

by the statute and substituting "any establishment . . . which caters or offers its services or facilities or goods to the general public." [28]

In 1959, Section 51 of the Civil Code of California was amended for the first time in thirty-six years. Prior to amendment, the section protected the right of all "citizens" to the full and equal accommodations, advantages, and facilities of "inns, restaurants, hotels, eating-houses, places where ice cream or soft drinks of any kind are sold for consumption on the premises, barber shops, bath houses, theaters, skating rinks, public conveyances and all other places of public accommodation or amusement." The new statute substituted the following language:

> All citizens within the jurisdiction of this State are free and equal, and no matter what their race, color, religion, ancestry or national origin are entitled to the full and equal accommodations, advantages, facilities, privileges, or services in all business establishments of every kind whatsoever.
>
> This section shall not be construed to confer any right or privilege on a citizen which is conditioned or limited by law or which is applicable alike to citizens of every color, race, religion, ancestry, or national origin.

It remains to be seen whether civil rights statutes written in broad, general terms will overcome the roadblocks that law courts have traditionally erected against statutes listing specific places. While several opinions by state attorneys general have given broad interpretations to the new statutes, no court decisions have been reported.

Other Restrictive Interpretations

In 1918 a white man entered a restaurant in Harlem, accompanied by a Negro, and was refused service because the restaurant had a policy against serving "mixed parties." The white man brought an action under Section 40 of the New York Civil

[28] CONN. GEN. STATS. § 3267(d).

Rights Law. The Appellate Term of the New York Supreme
Court held that the law "is penal and must be strictly construed,"
and may not be extended "by inference or by implication." Since
the white plaintiff and his colored companion were both refused
service, "it could not have been on account of color," the court
said. The restaurant's rule that mixed parties would not be
served applied to white customers as well as to Negroes; hence
the court found "no discrimination as to one color in favor of the
other." The court argued that if the plaintiff had been alone or
if he had been willing to separate himself from his companion,
he would have been served. A dissenting opinion was filed by
Justice Nathan Bijur, who was convinced that the Civil Rights
Law had been violated. He interpreted the proprietor as saying
to the plaintiff: "If you were colored and came here with your
[Negro] companion, you would be served; but being white,
we will not serve you." Therefore, Bijur held the plaintiff was
refused service because of his color. Since the statute was designed to prevent discrimination on the grounds of race or color,
the dissenting justice maintained, there was a violation of Section
40.[29] A recent case, involving a mixed couple refused accommodations at a hotel, adopted the reasoning of the dissenting
opinion.[30]

Disrespectful treatment, unaccompanied by a refusal of service, was held to be insufficient to bring an action under a statute
that barred a denial of accommodations, advantages, or privileges for reasons of race.[31]

Civil rights statutes traditionally specify that race, color, creed,
or religion may not be used as the basis for denial of public accommodations. More recently, national origin and ancestry have
been added to the list. However, these statutes do not prohibit
owners or managers of public places from excluding patrons for
other reasons.

[29] Cohn v. Goldgraben, 103 Misc. 500, 170 N.Y. Supp. 407 (1918).
[30] Hobson v. York Studios, 208 Misc. 888, 145 N.Y.S.2d 162 (1955).
[31] Seward v. New York Cent. R.R., 133 Misc. 584, 233 N.Y. Supp. 411 (1928).

In a case decided in 1897, the New York Court of Appeals held that the Civil Rights Act did not guarantee a race track enthusiast against being ruled off the turf for violating the rules and regulations of the jockey club. After quoting the language of the statute as amended in 1895, the court said:

We think the purpose of the statute now under consideration was to declare that no person should be deprived of any of the advantages enumerated, upon the ground of race, creed or color, and that its prohibition was intended to apply to cases of that character, and to none other. It is plain that the legislature did not intend to confer upon every person all the rights, advantages and privileges in places of amusement or accommodation, which might be enjoyed by another. Any discrimination not based upon race, creed or color does not fall within the condemnation of the statute. Neither the statute authorizing the holding of races or race meetings, nor the rules of the jockey club, made any such distinction, as the penalties for a breach of the rules of the club or of the usages of the turf are applicable to all alike.

The Westchester Racing Association was justified, the court ruled, in excluding the plaintiff from races open to the general public, even though he expressed a willingness to abide in the future by the rules and regulations of the club.[32]

In a later case (1916), a drama critic on the staff of the New York *Times,* wrote a review of a play which gravely displeased the owners of the theater in which the play was being shown. In retaliation, the owners barred the critic from one of their theaters and threatened to exclude him from all. The plaintiff sued to enjoin the defendants from such action.

The New York Court of Appeals held that the defendants were within their rights at common law, and that a theater, "while affected by a public interest which justified licensing under the police power or for the purpose of revenue, is in no sense public property or a public enterprise." The proprietor is not bound by law, as is a common carrier or public utility, to serve

[32] Grannan v. Westchester Racing Ass'n, 153 N.Y. 449 (1897).

all who request service. He has the right to decide who shall and who shall not be admitted. While these common law rights of theater proprietors were restricted by the Civil Rights Act of 1895, which established penalties for denial of "the full enjoyment of any of the accommodations, advantages, facilities or privileges . . . except for reasons applicable alike to all citizens of every race, creed or color, and regardless of race, creed or color," the court concluded that discrimination not based upon "race, creed or color" did not fall within the condemnation of the statute.[33]

Although the courts in most of the states with civil rights statutes have interpreted them strictly, the courts in California, Iowa, Michigan, New Jersey, Pennsylvania, and Washington have regarded their laws as remedial in nature, though penal in form, and hence have not resorted to strict construction with respect to either interpretation or remedy.[34] Also, a recent New York case held that the Civil Rights Law "is a remedial statute and must be liberally construed." [35]

Advertising

In 1913 the New York Civil Rights Law was amended to prohibit the owners of places of public accommodation from advertising that the patronage of any particular race, creed, or color was "unwelcome, objectionable or not acceptable, desired or solicited." The purpose of the amendment was to combat a practice which had developed since the enactment of the original law, whereby the proprietors of some places, principally resort hotels, clearly within the class of establishments covered by the law, used advertising media to inform prospective patrons that the

[33] Woollcott v. Shubert, 217 N.Y. 212 (1916).
[34] Orloff v. Los Angeles Turf Club, 30 Cal. 2d 110, 180 P.2d 321 (1947); Humbard v. Crawford, 128 Iowa 743, 105 N.W. 330 (1905); Bolden v. Grand Rapids Operating Corp., 239 Mich. 318, 214 N.W. 241 (1927); Raison v. Board of Educ., 103 N.J.L. 547, 137 Atl. 847 (1927); Everett v. Harron, 380 Pa. 123, 110 A.2d 383 (1955); Browning v. Slenderella, 154 Wash. 556 (Adv. Shts. 1959).
[35] Camp-of-the-Pines v. New York Times Co., 184 Misc. 389, 53 N.Y.S.2d 475 (1945).

resort was restricted on the basis of race, color, or religion. This tactic obviated the need actually to turn away guests, since most people tend to avoid using facilities or inviting abuse when they know they are unwelcome. The court of appeals said that "the purpose of the act as amended is to give greater efficacy to the policy of the original statute, to forbid the accomplishment of the discrimination barred by the statute, not only by direct exclusion, but also by the indirect means specified." [36]

Eventually Colorado, Illinois, Maine, Massachusetts, Michigan, New Jersey, Oregon, Pennsylvania, Washington, and Wisconsin joined New York in banning discriminatory advertising as well as discriminatory selection of patrons.

New Hampshire prohibits advertising "intended or calculated to discriminate against any religious sect, class, or nationality, or against any member thereof, as such, in the matter of board, lodging or accommodation, privilege or convenience offered to the general public at places of public accommodation." Two Southern states, Florida and Virginia, ban advertisements that express any religious limitation or discrimination (but not limitations on race or color). Since these three states have no equivalent prohibitions against the *practice* of discrimination itself at places of public accommodation, they are not included among the states with civil rights statutes.

A study of resort advertising in the New York *Herald Tribune* and in the New York *Times* revealed that from 1928 to 1936 frequent use was made of such phrases as "Gentile patronage," "Christian patronage," and the like. These direct statements of discriminatory guest selection tended to disappear by 1936, but they were replaced in the newspaper ads with terms such as "restricted" and "selected clientele." [37]

In 1943 the district attorney of New York County informed the newspapers published in his area that, in his opinion, such terms as "restricted" and "selected clientele" in advertisements

---

[36] Woollcott v. Shubert, *supra* note 33.
[37] N.Y. SCAD, In the Matter of Alleged Unlawful Resort Hotel Advertising re Location of Churches (mimeo.), March, 1953.

were "generally understood and intended to mean that guests of Jewish faith or colored persons were not wanted by such hotels and resorts," and that he would prosecute newspapers which published such advertisements.

An interesting case arose in 1943 when the Camp-of-the-Pines, a summer resort located on Lake Champlain in New York State, asked the New York *Times* to publish a series of advertisements describing the facilities and resort activities offered at the resort. Included in the text submitted to the newspaper were the words "selected clientele." On the basis of the district attorney's letter, the New York *Times* refused to print the advertisement as submitted and substituted in the place of "selected clientele" the words "congenial following." The Camp-of-the-Pines sued the New York *Times* for breach of contract and asked the court for an injunction to restrain the *Times* from editing the advertising text submitted by the resort. The New York Supreme Court, Special Term, Albany County, dismissed the action.

The court was convinced that the camp conducted by the plaintiff was a place of public accommodation within the statute and not a private club. Furthermore, the court felt that both the district attorney and the newspaper were correct in interpreting the words "selected clientele" as a "mask and a subterfuge . . . a cloak and disguise and an indirect means to hide discrimination."

The court held that the contract, asserted by the plaintiff as the basis for its cause of action against the *Times,* was illegal and void, injurious and offensive to morals and in contravention of the Civil Rights Law. A contract which is against public policy is void and unenforceable.

In conclusion, the court said:

The statute is definite, clear and unambiguous that there must be no discrimination, directly or indirectly, by reason of race, color or creed in excluding persons from places of public accommodation, resort or amusement. Our Constitution guarantees every citizen the right to life, liberty and the pursuit of happiness. It sternly prohibits religious intolerance. Section 40 of the Civil Rights Law is a laudable effort to blot out racial hatred. It strikes at the bigot and all promoters of discord and unhappiness. Every effort is made and should be made, and it is the duty of the courts to prevent, so far as is humanly possible, social and economic ostracism.[38]

Civil Rights Laws and Public Policy

One of the most significant developments in recent years has been the acceptance by the courts of state civil rights laws as an expression of public policy against racial or religious discrimination. This doctrine was enunciated clearly in California in *James v. Marinship Corp.*[39]

A group of California Negroes, denied equal membership rights in a local labor union, obtained a preliminary injunction against the union and the employer, restraining the defendants from discharging or causing the discharge of the plaintiffs because they were not members of the union with which the company had a closed shop agreement. The defendants argued that where individuals denied other individuals equality of treatment, no legal relief was available unless the specific acts of discrimination were prohibited by state law. Since the California Civil Rights Law did not expressly or by implication prohibit discrimination by labor unions or by employers, the defendants urged the California Supreme Court to dissolve the injunction and dismiss the action.

The court reasoned, however, that the Civil Rights Law established the "public policy" of the state and that the situation created by a union monopoly of the labor market through closed shop agreements was comparable to the public service businesses expressly regulated by the civil rights statute. In its opinion the court said:

[38] Camp-of-the-Pines v. New York Times Co., *supra* note 35.
[39] 25 Cal. 2d 721, 155 P.2d 329 (1944).

The analogy of the public service cases not only demonstrates a public policy against racial discrimination but also refutes defendants' contention that a statute is necessary to enforce such a policy where private rather than public action is involved.

The court restated this position two years later in another case involving discrimination against Negro workers by the International Brotherhood of Boilermakers:

Where persons are subjected to certain conduct by others which is deemed unfair and contrary to public policy, the courts have full power to afford necessary protection in the absence of statute.[40]

In a case involving the denial of service to a Negro by a dentist, however, the Appellate Department of the Superior Court of Los Angeles refused to follow the reasoning.[41]

Constitutionality

Are state statutes prohibiting discrimination in the enjoyment of civil rights constitutional? By implication, the Supreme Court answered the question affirmatively in the *Civil Rights Cases;* but strictly speaking, the Court held only that federal legislation on the subject, when directed against *individual* conduct, as distinguished from state action, is unconstitutional. It was not until 1945 that one could look to a closer Supreme Court decision on this point.[42]

Among the civil rights acts passed by New York State was one providing that no labor organization shall deny anyone membership for reasons of race, color, or creed, or deny any of its members equal opportunity for employment or promotion for the same reasons.[43] The New York Court of Appeals unanimously sustained the constitutionality of the act,[44] as did the United States Supreme Court on final appeal.

[40] Williams v. International Bhd. of Boilermakers, 27 Cal. 2d 586, 165 P.2d 901 (1946).
[41] Coleman v. Middlestaff, 147 Cal. App. 2d 833, 305 P.2d 1020 (1957).
[42] Railway Mail Ass'n v. Corsi, 326 U.S. 88 (1945).
[43] N.Y. CIVIL RIGHTS LAW § 43.
[44] Railway Mail Ass'n v. Corsi, 293 N.Y. 315 (1944).

The union in this case took the position that the act offended the due process clause of the Fourteenth Amendment and abridged its property rights and liberty of contract by interfering with its right to select its own members. In his opinion for the Court, Mr. Justice Reed said:

A judicial determination that such legislation violated the Fourteenth Amendment would be a distortion of the policy manifested in that amendment which was adopted to prevent state legislation designed to perpetuate discrimination on the basis of race or color. We see no constitutional basis for the contention that a state cannot protect workers from exclusion solely on the basis of race, color or creed by an organization, functioning under the protection of the state, which holds itself out to represent the general business needs of employees.

Mr. Justice Frankfurter, in a concurring opinion, said:

Of course a state may leave abstention from such discriminations to the conscience of individuals. On the other hand, a state may choose to put its authority behind one of the cherished aims of American feeling by forbidding indulgence in racial or religious prejudice to another's hurt. To use the Fourteenth Amendment as a sword against such state power would stultify that amendment. Certainly the insistence by individuals on their private prejudices as to race, color or creed, in relations like those now before us, ought not to have a higher constitutional sanction than the determination of a state to extend the area of non-discrimination beyond that which the Constitution itself exacts.

Reed spoke of an organization "functioning under the protection of the state," and Frankfurter spoke of private prejudices "in relations like those now before us"; but one need not consider these statements as words of limitation. The Supreme Court opinion which passed on the constitutionality of the federal Civil Rights Act of 1875 declared repeatedly that the protection of civil rights against violation by individuals was left entirely to the states. If the matter belongs to the states, the only constitutional limitation on their defining the content and scope of civil rights is that such definition should not deprive others of constitutional protections. The characterization of the Railway Mail Association as an organization "functioning under the protection of the state" was, therefore, not relevant to the decision.

In 1907 the Supreme Court had an opportunity to pass upon this question but failed to do so.[45] In 1948 the Court was faced with the issue of the constitutionality of a state civil rights statute as applied to a common carrier engaged in "foreign commerce." The Bob-Lo Excursion Company owned almost all of Bois Blanc Island, which for many years had served as an amusement park for Detroit's population. The island is located just above the mouth of the Detroit River and is part of the province of Ontario, Canada. The company also owned and operated two steamships used to transport people from Detroit to Bois Blanc Island and back.

In June, 1945, one of a group of people who had planned an excursion to the island was asked to leave the steamship because she was a Negro. The Bob-Lo Excursion Company was prosecuted criminally for violating Michigan's Civil Rights Law, which prohibits owners or employees of any place of public accommodation from withholding its advantages or privileges from any person because of race, creed or color. Places of public accommodation are defined to include "public conveyances on land and water." The Michigan Supreme Court held that the defendant operated a "public conveyance" by water and that the Civil Rights Act was applicable.[46]

Mr. Justice Rutledge, who wrote the opinion for the United States Supreme Court, limited the issue to "the single and narrow question" of whether the commerce clause of the federal Constitution bars a state from attempting to regulate, through a civil rights law, the business of a steamship company engaged

[45] In Western Turf Ass'n v. Greenberg, 204 U.S. 359 (1907), it was argued that the California Civil Rights Act deprived the defendant, a corporation, of liberty without due process of law. The court held that the constitutional prohibition against deprivation of liberty without due process applies only for the protection of natural persons.

[46] Bob-Lo Excursion Co. v. Michigan, 317 Mich. 686 (1947).

in "foreign" commerce. The defendant's ships sailed from a port in the United States, across the international boundary, to an island under the sovereignty of a foreign country. The Court held that the facts indicated a very limited type of "foreign" business. The island to which the defendant's ships transported passengers was really "an amusement adjunct of the City of Detroit," completely insulated from all commerce or social intercourse with Canada and from the normal flow of foreign commerce. The defendant's enterprise was described as "highly closed and localized" although conducted in Canadian waters. "If therefore in any case a state may regulate foreign commerce, the facts here would seem clearly to justify Michigan's application of her civil rights act." [47]

The language of the 1948 *Bob-Lo* opinion indicates a Supreme Court conclusion that civil rights statutes requiring nondiscriminatory treatment of passengers would in no way conflict with the federal power to regulate interstate and foreign commerce under the commerce clause. Thus, for example, Rutledge said:

It is difficult to imagine what national interest or policy, whether of securing uniformity in regulating commerce, affecting regulations with foreign nations or otherwise, could reasonably be found to be adversely affected by applying Michigan's statute to those facts or to outweigh her interest in doing so. Certainly there is no national interest which overrides the interest of Michigan to forbid the type of discrimination practiced here. And, in view of these facts, the ruling would be strange indeed, to come from this Court that Michigan could not apply her long-settled policy against racial and creedal discrimination to this segment of foreign commerce, so peculiarly and almost exclusively affecting her people and institutions.

Mr. Justice Douglas's concurring opinion argued that the decision should have been predicated expressly upon the broader ground, namely, that no state statute requiring nondiscriminatory treatment of passengers could possibly conflict with the

[47] Bob-Lo Excursion Co. v. Michigan, 333 U.S. 28 (1948).

federal government's responsibility to regulate interstate commerce.

It is unthinkable to me that we should strike down a state law which requires all carriers—local and interstate—to transport all persons regardless of their race or color. The common-law duty of carriers was to provide equal service to all, a duty which the Court has held a State may require of interstate carriers in the absence of a conflicting federal law [citing cases]. And the police power of a State under our Constitutional system is adequate for the protection of the civil rights of its citizens against discrimination by reason of race or color. *Railway Mail Ass'n v. Corsi,* 326 U.S. 88.

Douglas did not believe that there was any danger of a burden on interstate commerce from state statutes prohibiting discriminatory treatment of passengers. As he interpreted the Constitution, a different conclusion was indicated if a state undertook to bar Negroes from passage on public carriers, since that action would violate the Fourteenth Amendment: "The only constitutional uniformity is uniformity in the Michigan pattern."

A dissent was filed by Mr. Justice Jackson, with whom Chief Justice Vinson agreed. They argued that the Michigan statute could not be applied to commerce set apart under the Constitution for exclusive regulation by Congress. Once it was conceded that the commerce involved was interstate or foreign, the dissenters argued, state regulation was unconstitutional. Under the *School Segregation Cases* and subsequent Supreme Court decisions, clearly a state cannot now use its authority to enforce racial segregation in any form of transportation, interstate or intrastate.

The constitutionality of civil rights acts has been passed on by a number of state courts.[48] In all cases, they have been sustained as constitutional; but frequently the scope of the decisions has been rather narrow, upholding the act "as to all kinds of busi-

[48] Bolden v. Grand Rapids Operating Corp., *supra* note 34; People v. King, 110 N.Y. 418 (1888); Piluso v. Spencer, 36 Cal. App. 416, 172 P. 412 (1918); Browning v. Slenderella, *supra* note 34.

ness, of a public or quasi-public character," [49] or as the regulation of certain businesses "in which the public have an interest." [50]

Almost all of the decisions were based on the state's right to regulate places of public entertainment, amusement or resort, rather than on the state's right to define and protect civil rights as an exercise of the police power. Thus, because a barber shop is a place of public resort, a civil rights act applying to such shops was sustained; [51] similarly, because a bootblack stand is a public accommodation, a civil rights act applying to such an activity was sustained. [52]

While state legislatures have recognized the existence of civil rights as such, and have undertaken the regulation of businesses in the interests of such rights, courts have not, apparently, been eager to give clear and definite recognition of the right of a state to define and protect such rights.

Inherent Weaknesses in State Civil Rights Laws

As we have seen, the typical civil rights statute prohibits owners of places of public accommodation, resort, or amusement from refusing to make their facilities available to prospective patrons on the grounds of race, color, or religion. Some state laws also prohibit advertisements that expressly or impliedly say that the patronage of members of certain religious, racial, or ethnic groups is unwelcome. Enforcement of such statutes is in the form of civil actions for damages and penalties or criminal prosecutions which could result upon conviction in fines or imprisonment. Several states have held that an action for an injunction to restrain future violations of the law is also available as a sanction even though the statute does not expressly authorize that remedy. [53] The prevailing view, however, is that the remedies

---

[49] Rhone v. Loomis, Brown v. J. H. Bell Co., *supra* note 15.
[50] Picket v. Kuchan, 323 Ill. 138, 153 N.E. 667 (1926).
[51] Messinger v. State, *supra* note 16.   [52] Burks v. Bosso, *supra* note 19.
[53] Orloff v. Los Angeles Turf Club, Everett v. Harron, *supra* note 34; Kenyon v. City of Chicopee, 320 Mass. 528, 70 N.E.2d 241 (1946).

enumerated in the civil rights statutes are exclusive and that no remedy not expressly given by the statute is available to a complainant.[54] The courts rely upon the principle that the inadequacy of a remedy provided by a statute is a matter for legislative correction.

The enforcement of civil laws by requiring violators to pay money either as a fine to the state or as damages to the party aggrieved, is ordinarily not effective. Unless the amount is substantial, say a thousand dollars, it neither deters future violations nor heals the wound inflicted upon the individual who has been rejected. Some of the state civil rights laws have retained the same limit upon money damages that they had when they were originally enacted in the 1880s. These damages were inadequate then and inflation has merely served to make them more so now. Owners of places of public accommodation tend to regard the occasional fine or civil penalty which they are forced to pay for violations of civil rights laws as a kind of "license fee" for the privilege of continuing to practice discrimination. Because actions based on the civil rights statutes are rarely instituted, and when instituted are frequently lost or compromised, the "fee" is not deemed exorbitant.

Our earlier discussions of some state cases has indicated that those who attempt to circumvent the law not infrequently receive aid and comfort from the courts. The burden of proof, as in all litigation, is on the one charging violation of law and, by the very nature of the kind of offense involved in civil rights cases, the complainant is likely to be a member of one of the lower socioeconomic groups in the community. This factor compounds the difficulty of winning the lawsuit.

When the owner of a place of public accommodation is hailed into court for an alleged violation, his lawyer knows that the defendant will have a good chance of winning the verdict if business-

[54] Fletcher v. Coney Isl., Inc., 165 Ohio St. 150, 134 N.E.2d 371 (1956); White v. Pasfield, 212 Ill. App. 73 (1918); Woollcott v. Shubert, 169 App. Div. 194, 154 N.Y. Supp. 643 (1915), *aff'd*, 217 N.Y. 212 (1916).

men are on the jury; and usually, if not always, some businessmen are on such juries. The appeal, overt or subtle, to the jury is: "If you owned a restaurant (or hotel, or other place of public accommodation) and catered to a white patronage, would you hazard losing your customers by opening your doors to Negroes"? Such an appeal to a combination of racial prejudice and selfish economic interests frequently works; and Negro complainants often lose their cases even when the evidence is clearly in their favor. The defendant wins either with the judge, or if the judge lets the case go to the jury, with the jury.

Another difficulty standing in the way of effective enforcement of the civil rights laws is that it costs money to institute a lawsuit and to see it through to termination. Not many Negroes can afford the luxury of involvement with the law and frequently they must look for a lawyer who is willing to take the case as an act of public service rather than for a fee, or they must ask a local legal aid society, a branch of the National Association for the Advancement of Colored People, or a local chapter of some other civil rights organization to secure a lawyer to handle the case. Under such circumstances, it can be expected that only a few, highly selected cases will be undertaken.[55]

In those states where the violation of the civil rights law is made a criminal offense, an additional obstacle to effective enforcement emerges. District attorneys, normally concerned with sensational crimes of violence, tend to look with disdain and annoyance at violations of civil rights statutes.

Now and then, and more so during the past fifteen years than in any comparable period, the owner of a place of public accom-

[55] Fewer than twenty-five cases involving alleged violations of the Civil Rights Acts were reviewed by the California Supreme Court and the district courts of appeal between 1897 and 1958. Klein, *The California Equal Rights Statutes in Practice,* 10 STAN. L. REV. 253, 260 n.41 (1958). The New York State Commission Against Discimination, on the other hand, ruled on over 350 complaints of discrimination in places of public accommodation between July 1, 1952, when it was given responsibility over such discrimination, and December, 1959. SCAD, "Churches Nearby"—A Survey of Its Purposes and Uses in Resort Advertising (mimeo.), Dec., 1959.

modation pays a penalty, but the vast majority of violators are left undisturbed under the conventional civil rights statute. The existence of such a law on the statute books does not, therefore, necessarily mean that discrimination has been eliminated. A statute guaranteeing equal rights in places of public accommodation, resort, or amusement should be deemed only the beginning of the struggle for equality of opportunity.

New Remedies

The origin and development of fair employment practice legislation is treated in the next chapter. The FEP movement, however, resulted in expanding and improving the legal remedies available for the enforcement of state civil rights laws, and we now turn to a discussion of those new remedies.

New Jersey was the first state to extend to the field of public accommodations the jurisdiction of its administrative agency originally established to handle charges of discrimination in employment. In 1949 the provisions of the Law Against Discrimination [56] were broadened to provide that "all persons shall have the opportunity to obtain . . . all the accommodations, advantages, facilities and privileges of any place of public accommodation, without discrimination because of race, creed, color, national origin or ancestry." [57] The original FEP law was amended to reorganize the Division Against Discrimination into two sections, one to deal with complaints of discrimination in employment, and the other to deal with complaints charging "other unlawful acts of discrimination." The 1949 amendatory act also contained a series of changes which made the various administrative procedures available in all cases of "unlawful discrimination." "Place of public accommodation" was defined in the definition section of the law to mean:

Any tavern, roadhouse, or hotel, whether for entertainment of transient guests or accommodation of those seeking health, recreation or

[56] Laws of 1945, ch. 169.   [57] Laws of 1949, ch. 11.

rest; any retail shop or store; any restaurant, eating house, or place where food is sold for consumption on the premises; any place maintained for the sale of ice cream, ice and fruit preparations or their derivatives, soda water or confections, or where any beverages of any kind are retailed for consumption on the premises; any garage, any public conveyance operated on land or water, or in the air, and stations and terminals thereof; any public bathhouse, public boardwalk, public seashore accommodation; any auditorium, meeting place, or public hall; any theater, or other place of public amusement, motion-picture house, music hall, roof garden, skating rink, swimming pool, amusement and recreation park, fair, bowling alley, gymnasium, shooting gallery, billiard and pool parlor; any comfort station; any dispensary, clinic or hospital; and any public library, any kindergarten, primary and secondary school, trade or business school, high school, academy, college and university, or any educational institution under the supervision of the State Board of Education, or the Commissioner of Education of the State of New Jersey.

There followed the customary exception for "any institution, *bona fide* club, or place of accommodation, which is in its nature distinctly private" and for "any educational facility operated or maintained, by a *bona fide* religious or sectarian institution."

It was made an "unlawful discrimination" for

any owner, lessee, proprietor, manager, superintendent, agent, or employee of any place of public accommodation directly or indirectly to refuse, withhold from or deny to any person any of the accommodations, advantages, facilities or privileges thereof, or to discriminate against any person in the furnishing thereof, or directly or indirectly to publish, circulate, issue, display, post or mail any written or printed communication, notice or advertisement to the effect that any of the accommodations, advantages, facilities, or privileges of any such place will be refused, withheld from, or denied to any person on account of the race, creed, color, national origin, or ancestry of such person, or that the patronage or custom thereat of any person of any particular race, creed, color, national origin or ancestry is unwelcome, objectionable or not acceptable, desired or solicited, and the production of any such written or printed communication, notice or advertisement, purporting to relate to any such place and to be made by any owner, lessee, proprietor, superintendent, or manager thereof, shall be presumptive evidence in any action that the same was authorized by such person.

Any person claiming to be aggrieved by an unlawful discrimination at a place of public accommodation may file a complaint with the Division Against Discrimination and thus invoke the administrative machinery of the state agency. He may also proceed under the old civil rights act since a saving clause in the 1949 amendment expressly provided that nothing therein "shall be deemed to repeal any of the provisions of the civil rights law or of any other law of this state relating to discrimination because of race, creed, color, national origin or ancestry." However, as to acts defined as unlawful in the new public accommodations law, the administrative procedure was to be "exclusive" while pending, and a final determination under the Law Against Discrimination would bar "any other action, civil or criminal based on the same grievance of the individual concerned."

The administrative procedure is identical with that for cases of discrimination in employment: complaint; investigation; finding of probable cause to credit the charges or dismissal; attempt to eliminate the discrimination by conference, conciliation, and persuasion; public hearing; findings of fact and issuance of appropriate order either dismissing the complaint or directing the respondent to cease and desist from the unlawful discriminatory conduct. If necessary, the Division Against Discrimination could ask the courts to enforce compliance with its cease and desist order. Also, a respondent may seek judicial review of the administrative orders. The division was renamed in 1960 the Division on Civil Rights.

The leadership of New Jersey in extending the jurisdiction and procedures of its administrative agency to discrimination in places of public accommodation was followed the same year (1949) by Connecticut, which renamed its Interracial Commission the Commission on Civil Rights, and the next year by Massachusetts, which renamed its Fair Employment Practice Commission the

Massachusetts Commission Against Discrimination. In 1952 New York and Rhode Island fell into line; in 1957, Colorado, Oregon, and Washington; in 1961, Pennsylvania. This is a trend which will continue as additional states discover how much more effective the administrative agency can be in reducing and eliminating discrimination in places of public accommodation.

The first complaint of discrimination under the new public accommodations law, which the New Jersey Division Against Discrimination was unable to adjust satisfactorily by conciliation, involved a dispute as to whether the Hightstown Swimming Pool was a public facility or a private club. In the summer of 1949, the parents of three Negro children charged that their children had been excluded from the use of the pool because of their race. The facility in question, privately owned, claimed that it was being operated on a "club plan" and was, therefore, within the exception provided in the statute for a "place of accommodation, which is in its nature distinctly private."

When preliminary investigation established probable cause to credit the allegations of the complaint, attempts were made to eliminate the discrimination by conference, conciliation, and persuasion. The owner of the pool was adamant and a public hearing was ordered. On the basis of the evidence adduced at the hearing, the commissioner of education found that the complainants' children had been excluded from the pool because of their race. He also found that the exclusion was pursuant to a consistent policy on the part of the owner to keep out Negroes, and that this policy had been in effect at the pool since the present owner purchased it in 1947. Finally, he found that the pool had at all times since the summer of 1948 been "a place of public accommodation" and not, as claimed, a private club. The evidence introduced at the hearing established that patronage was solicited from the public generally, that the requirement of "membership" in the "club" served no bona fide purpose, since it was available to any white person who tendered the admission fee, that "members' " endorsements were issued without any investigation, and that they were issued principally by the owner's employees.

The commissioner ordered the owner of the Hightstown Swimming Pool to cease and desist from unlawfully discriminating against colored persons desiring admission to his pool and to extend immediately the full and equal privileges of the pool to all persons regardless of race. The order also required the owner to abandon any requirement of recommendations, references, or membership in any organization as a condition for admission to the pool and to report to the division within twenty days how he had complied with the order.

This private club subterfuge was also attempted by a vacation resort in Greene County, New York, which called itself The Westkill Tavern Club. As a condition for the acceptance of reservations, this resort required "club membership," which was obtained through an application form to be completed by prospective guests. The application requested information pertaining to religion, color, and citizenship. The brochure accompanying the application also featured the "club" as "one of the few remaining Wayside Inns in America with the old traditional charm and hospitality impossible for modern ingenuity to create or even copy." Advertising material noted that the "club" catered to "a strictly selected clientele in a Christian community."

A proceeding was instituted in 1953 against The Westkill Tavern Club before the New York State Commission Against Discrimination, charging that the "club" was a place of public accommodation and therefore subject to the provisions of the 1952 amendment to the Law Against Discrimination.

In July, 1953, the State Commission Against Discrimination, after an investigation of the matter, concluded that The Westkill Tavern Club was a place of public accommodation and not a private club. The order, issued through a conciliation agreement, required the discontinuance of the "membership" procedures and the elimination of the statement in the brochure referring to "selected clientele." The disposition further required that all personnel employed by the resort be informed of the policy requiring "full, equal and unsegregated accommodations . . . to all persons regardless of their race, creed, color or national origin." [58]

Later in the same year, the New York State Commission Against Discrimination announced that it would hold its first public hearing under the public accommodations provisions of the Law Against Discrimination. The complaint, brought by two New York City residents, charged that the Castle Hill Beach Club was a public accommodation, and that it had denied them admission because of their color. Following the filing of the complaint, the commission sought to adjust the matter through the process of conference and conciliation. The beach club maintained, however, that it was a "private" organization and not a "place of public accommodation" subject to the jurisdiction of the commission.

As a result of the testimony produced at the hearing, the tribunal made 154 findings of fact, including the following significant ones. From 1928 through 1950 concededly the premises had been operated as a public bathing and recreation park. In 1950 the Castle Hill Beach Club was organized as a membership corporation; it became the operator of the facility. The persons actually in control did not change, although the corporate form did. The Castle Hill Beach Club leased the premises from the Bronx–City Island Realty Corporation, which, under the lease, had the option to collect as rent either $50,000 or the total income received from seasonal and guest admissions, less operating costs and taxes. The landlord had exercised the second option in 1951, 1952, and 1953. There had been a commingling

[58] American Jewish Comm. v. Flick d/b/a Westkill Tavern Club, 1953 N.Y. SCAD REPORT 22.

of the funds of the predecessor corporation which operated the public accommodation and the newly formed membership corporation.

The bylaws of the membership corporation provided for two types of members, seasonal and permanent, and since its organization it had had six permanent members, all of whom were associated prominently with the landlord corporation and three of whom continued to occupy the same positions, perform the same functions, and receive the same salary as they did when employed by the predecessor corporation, which operated the facility in question as a public bathing park. The seasonal members, of whom there were about 13,000, had no actual voice in the management of the membership corporation, did not vote for officers, directors, permanent members or seasonal members, and continued to use the premises in all respects as they had before the formation of the membership corporation. A so-called members governing committee had no actual function other than to approve actions taken by the president and secretary of the "club" in accepting or rejecting applications.

Ever since its opening in 1928, the facility had applied for and received a license from the City of New York "for the operation of a public bathing establishment." For many years (including the period when the facility claimed to be operating as a private club) a "commercial beer license" had been obtained for the premises. (Bona fide clubs are eligible for a special club license.) Prior to 1950, the facility had been listed in the local classified telephone directory as the Castle Hill Bathing Park under the heading "Bathing Beaches—Public." After its conversion to a membership corporation, the name was changed to Castle Hill Beach Club, Inc., but it continued to be listed, with the apparent knowledge of its officers, under the heading of "Bathing Beaches —Public," notwithstanding the fact that the directory also contained a heading entitled "Clubs."

On the basis of all the evidence, and considering the record as a whole, two of the three commissioners who sat as the hearing tribunal concluded that although the respondent was a membership corporation in form, in fact it was operating a place of public accommodation, resort, or amusement within the meaning of the Law Against Discrimination.

The State Commission Against Discrimination thereupon entered an order requiring the Castle Hill Beach Club to cease and desist from withholding or denying its accommodations, facilities, or privileges from the complainants, and from all others similarly situated, on the grounds of race or color. In addition, the respondent was ordered to post a conspicuous notice that the facility was a public accommodation available on an equal and unsegregated basis to all who tender the necessary fee. All its officers, agents, and employees were required to be advised that the establishment was to comply fully with the Law Against Discrimination. Finally, a written report to the commission was required within thirty days of the steps taken by the respondent to comply with the order.

The club petitioned the state supreme court to annul the cease and desist order, while the state commission filed a cross petition seeking court enforcement. Justice Martin M. Frank reviewed the record, including the testimony taken at the hearing, and concluded that it was overwhelmingly established that the complainants had been excluded from the facilities of the club because of their color. He ruled that judicial review of the findings of the administrative agency was limited by law to whether such findings, upon the entire record, are supported by substantial evidence. He held that the commission's findings were so supported, notwithstanding the dissent by one of the three-member hearing tribunal.

Turning to the question of whether the club was a public accommodation or a private club, the court found that despite the creation of the membership corporation, actual control continued to reside in the hands of the original individual owners of the pool, and not in the hands of those patronizing it as "members." He rejected the contention that the club was a bona fide membership corporation and said that "the Commission had the power and the duty, as have the courts, to lift the corporate veil to ascertain the facts." The court, thereupon, dismissed Castle Hill's petition and granted SCAD's request for an enforcement mandate.[59]

An appeal was taken to the appellate division, which unanimously affirmed the supreme court decision.[60] Finally, in 1957, the court of appeals handed down a unanimous decision affirming the lower courts and upholding the cease and desist order of the State Commission Against Discrimination. The court reviewed the evidence relied upon by SCAD to determine that the Castle Hill Beach Club was a public facility rather than a private club, and said:

It may be that the telephone listing, etc., as isolated facts, do not justify the conclusion that the membership corporation was a mere sham designed to conceal the true public nature of the enterprise. But, in our judgment, the record, considered as a whole, leads to that conclusion. The various aspects of a plan or scheme, when considered singly, may very well appear innocent. The true nature of the plan or scheme is revealed only when the various aspects are viewed as a totality. Such is this case.[61]

It must be conceded that there will be some close cases in which a real difficulty exists in determining whether a particular facility is *public* or *private* as these terms are used in state civil rights or public accommodations statutes. But assuming that to be true, it should be possible to establish some criteria to help decide into which category a particular facility falls. Consideration should be given to the following.

Advertising widely on billboards, car cards, or in the news-

[59] Castle Hill Beach Club v. Arbury, 208 Misc. 35, 142 N.Y.S.2d 432 (1955).
[60] Castle Hill Beach Club v. Arbury, 1 A.D.2d 943, 150 N.Y.S.2d 367 (1956).
[61] Castle Hill Beach Club v. Arbury, 2 N.Y.2d 596, 608, 142 N.E.2d 186 (1957).

papers that the facility solicits patrons or guests from the public generally is a factor tending to establish that the facility is a place of public accommodation, resort, or amusement rather than a private club.[62]

The corporate charter, bylaws, and other basic organization documents may indicate clearly whether the facility was created as a public or private facility. If a change is claimed from the originally stated objectives of the organization, the burden of proving such change would be on those asserting it.

If a license is required from state or local authorities for the operation of the facility, reference to the terms and conditions of the license and to the provisions of the statute or ordinance under which it is issued may help to establish whether the facility is public or private.[63]

Bona fide clubs are normally controlled by their members, whereas privately owned facilities, which are really public accommodations seeking to evade their responsibilities under civil rights statutes, are controlled by an owner or his employees. Therefore, it is very significant to discover whether the membership, as distinct from the owner or his employees, exercises any control over the policies of the facility. Whether the enterprise is a commercial establishment or a private club can generally be shown by the answers to questions like the following: Does the membership have control over the enterprise? Who establishes policy for the use of the facilities, the membership or the owners? Are membership meetings held? How often? What is discussed at such meetings? Are minutes kept? Who actually owns the property? Who fixes the salary for employees? Who selects the officers and for how long do they serve?

An enterprise cannot be a "distinctly private club" if it exercises no real control over membership. An important factor, therefore, is the method of selecting members. Is there a membership

---

[62] McKaine v. Drake Business School, 107 Misc. 241, 176 N.Y. Supp. 33 (1919).

[63] Bowlin v. Lyon, 25 N.W. (Iowa) 766 (1885).

committee or board? What are the qualifications for membership other than race or religion? Is the membership committee or board distinct from the ownership? Does membership selection actually rest with the members or with the owners?

Information about other operations, unrelated to admissions, sometimes casts considerable light on the true nature of the enterprise. For example, what kind of telephone listing does the establishment have in the classified directory? Who is authorized to sign checks? How many signatures are necessary to withdraw funds? How were these authorizations established? Who attended and voted at the meeting at which these decisions were reached? What kind of tax returns are filed with the state and federal tax collectors?

The answers to such questions will help determine, in each case, whether the facility in question is a public accommodation, catering to the public generally and forbidden from discriminating under state civil rights statutes, or whether it is a "distinctly private" facility permitted to choose its members in any way it wishes. Moreover, a state agency, such as a state commission against discrimination, vested with all of the authority and prestige of the state, is far more likely to get the answers to such questions than is a private litigant who seeks to invoke the sanction of a traditional civil rights law.

The Connecticut Civil Rights Commission undertook an educational campaign from 1953 to 1955 to inform many important groups subject to the public accommodations statute of their obligations and responsibilities under the law. This type of activity, peculiarly within the competence of an administrative agency, probably does as much to effectuate the state's public policy against discrimination as the complaint procedure created by the statute, essential as the latter is.

In September, 1953, letters were sent by the Connecticut commission to all police chiefs in the state and to all taverns and restaurants which had state permits to dispense alcoholic beverages.

The attention of the police chiefs was called to the recently amended public accommodations law barring discrimination on the basis of race, creed, or color in places of public accommodation and making such discrimination a misdemeanor. The letter went on to state that persons refused service might summon a police officer to help them. The police chiefs were, therefore, requested to advise all their officers of the change in the law. The letter to taverns and restaurants holding liquor licenses advised the recipients that their places of business were places of public accommodation under the Connecticut law and offered additional information concerning the operation of the law.

Letters were mailed over the joint signatures of the chairman of the Commission on Civil Rights and the state commissioner of health to all hairdressers, cosmetologists, and hospitals in the state, calling attention to the Law Against Discrimination and stating that an operator of the type of establishment named might set standards for the acceptance of clients but that these standards could not lawfully include race, creed, or color.

A letter was also sent over the signatures of the chairman of the Commission on Civil Rights and the state barber examiner to all barber shops in the state. This letter, like the others, informed the barbers that while they might set standards for the acceptance of clients, such standards could not legally include race, creed, or color or operate as a device to exclude members of a particular racial or religious group.

A letter was sent jointly by the chairman of the Commission on Civil Rights and the state commissioner of health to all owners of convalescent homes and homes for the aged. Finally, a letter was sent to all dentists in the state calling their attention to the fact that the public accommodations statute contained provisions barring discrimination by any establishment which caters or offers its services or facilities to the general public. The letter pointed out that a dentist may accept patients on the basis of the nature of the professional services he offers to the general public, but that he may not deny his services to any person solely by reason of race, creed, or color.

These letters, typical of the educational activities carried on by state commissions against discrimination, serve to bring home to the operators of many types of places of public accommodation that fact that there is a law against discrimination and that they must comply with that law or face the consequences, including the possible loss of their licenses.

Civil Rights Divisions in Offices of Attorneys General

Another recent development at the state level has been the creation of civil rights divisions in the offices of the attorneys general. Thus, for example, Illinois provides:

There is created in the office of the Attorney General a Division to be known as the Division for the Enforcement of Civil and Equal Rights. The Division, under the supervision and direction of the Attorney General, shall investigate all violations of the law relating to civil rights and the prevention of discrimination against persons by reason of race, color, or creed, and shall whenever such violations are established, undertake necessary enforcement measures.[64]

Other states which have created similar divisions in the attorney general's office are California, Massachusetts, Michigan, and New York.

If there is any doubt that the general laws give investigative powers to the office of the state attorney general, the statute creating the civil rights division should expressly provide that that division has the power to investigate whenever the attorney general has reason to believe that some individual or group of individuals may have been deprived of a civil right or have been subjected to discrimination in education, employment, housing, or public accommodations. The right to subpoena witnesses and records should also be provided. In addition, the attorney general

[64] ILL. REV. STATS., ch. 14.

should be vested with power to commence actions to enjoin violations of existing laws and to institute proceedings before the appropriate state or local licensing authority to suspend or revoke the license of any person or establishment which violates the public policy of the state as expressed in its constitution and laws.

While the creation of these new divisions in the offices of the attorneys general has not yet produced much of substantial value in the enforcement of civil rights, it is too early to decide that such divisions cannot play a significant role in protecting and expanding equality of opportunity. Certainly, in those states which have commissions against discrimination, there is an opportunity for close cooperation between the office of the attorney general and the administrative agency.

Chapter 7

FAIR EMPLOYMENT PRACTICES

The serious shortage of labor during the Second World War, and the judicious application of political pressure by a group of Negro leaders, including Walter White, Channing Tobias, Mary McLeod Bethune, Lester Granger, and A. Philip Randolph, the last of whom organized a Negro "March on Washington" scheduled for July 1, 1941, caused President Franklin D. Roosevelt to promulgate Executive Order 8802 on June 25, 1941, and thus prevent the demonstration.[1] That order established the first Fair Employment Practices Committee, consisting of five nonsalaried members, "to promote the full and equitable participation of all workers in defense industries, without discrimination because of race, creed, color or national origin." [2] The committee, originally in the Office of Production Management and later transferred to the War Manpower Commission, was reconstituted on May 27, 1943, by Executive Order 9346, as an independent agency in the Executive Office of the President.[3]

The later order asserted that the successful prosecution of the war required "the maximum employment of all available workers regardless of race, creed, color, or national origin," and that it was the policy of the government "to encourage full participation in the war effort by all persons in the United States . . . in the firm belief that the democratic way of life within the nation can be defended successfully only with the help and support of all groups within its borders."

[1] RUCHAMES, RACE, JOBS AND POLITICS ch. 1 (1953); ROSS, ALL MANNER OF MEN 19–20 (1948); WHITE, A MAN CALLED WHITE 189–93 (1948).
[2] 6 Fed. Reg. 3109 (1941).   [3] 18 Fed. Reg. 7183 (1943).

As President, and as Commander in Chief of the Army and Navy, Mr. Roosevelt reaffirmed "the policy of the United States that there shall be no discrimination in the employment of any person in war industries or in Government." All employers, the several federal departments and agencies, "and all labor organizations" were directed to eliminate discrimination in hiring, tenure, terms or conditions of employment, and in union membership.

Executive Order 9346 required contracting agencies of the government to include a provision in all of their contracts obligating the contractor and his subcontractors not to discriminate against any employee or applicant for employment; and all departments and agencies of the government engaged in vocational and training programs for war production were required to take measures to assure that their training programs were administered without discrimination.

The Committee on Fair Employment Practices, or FEPC as it was known popularly, was increased from five to seven members and was authorized "to formulate policies to achieve" the purposes of the executive order and "to make recommendations to the various Federal departments and agencies" regarding steps to be taken to comply with the order. FEPC was given power to receive and investigate complaints of discrimination prohibited by the executive order, to conduct hearings, make findings of fact, "and to take appropriate steps" to eliminate discrimination. The committee was also authorized to use the services of other federal departments and agencies, to accept the services of state and local officials, and to promulgate rules and regulations necessary to carry out the provisions of the order.

The Committee on Fair Employment Practices was the first administrative agency established in the United States to protect and enforce the rights of all Americans to equality of opportunity in employment.[4] It was the forerunner of state fair employment

[4] FEPC, First Report (1945); FEPC, Final Report (1947); National

practices laws, which were a giant step forward in the struggle for civil rights.

When Congress refused to make the Fair Employment Practices Committee a permanent agency of the government, President Truman created the Committee on Government Contract Compliance to police the nondiscrimination clause in government contracts for goods or services.[5] In 1953, President Eisenhower promulgated a new executive order declaring that nondiscrimination in employment on government contracts was "government policy" and creating the Committee on Government Contracts, with the Vice President as its chairman.[6] This committee was authorized to receive complaints against government contractors charging discrimination in employment, upgrading, demotion, or transfer; in recruitment or recruitment advertising; in layoff or termination; in rates of pay or other forms of compensation; or in selection for training, including apprenticeship. The committee was required to send such complaints to the federal agency holding the contract with directions to investigate the charges and take appropriate action to eliminate any discrimination found to exist.

In 1955, President Eisenhower set up the Committee on Government Employment Policy to supervise the nondiscrimination program within the federal establishment.[7] This order replaced President Truman's Fair Employment Board, created within the Civil Service Commission in 1948. The Committee on Government Employment Policy was authorized to determine whether the departments and agencies of the government were carrying out the nondiscrimination policy with respect to their own employment practices and to make such inquiries and investigations as

---

COMMUNITY RELATIONS ADVISORY COUNCIL, F.E.P.C. REFERENCE MANUAL 36–42 (1948); Maslow, *FEPC—A Case History in Parliamentary Maneuver,* 13 U. CHI. L. REV. 407 (1946); RUCHAMES and ROSS, *op. cit. supra* note 1.

[5] Exec. Orders 9346, 8 Fed. Reg. 7183 (1943), and 10308, 16 Fed. Reg. 12303 (1951).

[6] Exec. Order 10479, 18 Fed. Reg. 4899 (1953).

[7] Exec. Order 10590, 20 Fed. Reg. 409 (1955).

were necessary in order to carry out responsibilities assigned it.

On March 6, 1961, President Kennedy issued Executive Order 10925 vesting the functions of both presidential committees in a newly created Committee on Equal Employment Opportunity with the Vice President as chairman and the Secretary of Labor as vice chairman. The expanded duties and strengthened powers of the new committee were spelled out in considerable detail in the executive order.

The First State FEPC

Prior to 1945, thirteen states had statutes prohibiting discrimination in various fields of employment, although no state had a fair employment practices law.[8] These laws were directed against discriminatory employment by state civil service, in home or work relief, by public works contractors, in war industries, and by trade unions. In New York State, a 1909 law prohibited discrimination in the right to practice law;[9] a 1918 law prohibited discrimination in "any state employment";[10] a 1932 law prohibited inquiries about the religious affiliation of persons seeking employment in public education;[11] a 1933 law prohibited discrimination in employment by utility companies;[12] a 1935 law required all public works contracts to contain a clause against discrimination.[13]

In 1938, the New York State Constitutional Convention recommended and the voters adopted a novel provision in the bill of rights of the state constitution. This section provides as follows:

Equal protection of laws; discrimination in civil rights prohibited. Sec. 11. No person shall be denied the equal protection of the laws of this state or any subdivision thereof. No person shall, because of race, color, creed or religion, be subjected to any discrimination in his civil rights by any other person or by any firm, corporation, or institution, or by the state or any agency or subdivision of the state.[14]

[8] FEPC, FIRST REPORT 148–49 (1945).
[9] JUDICIARY LAW § 460.
[10] PENAL LAW § 514.
[11] CIVIL RIGHTS LAW § 40-a.
[12] CIVIL RIGHTS LAW § 42.
[13] LABOR LAW § 220-e.
[14] Art. I, § 11.

In introducing this amendment to the constitutional convention, the chairman of its Bill of Rights Committee, said:

Thus, the state alone can make laws dealing with discriminatory practices of those within its jurisdiction. . . . An examination of the constitutions of our sister states discloses that not a single one of them contains any provision seeking to prohibit discrimination on the part of individuals, firms or corporations upon racial, religious or any other ground.[15]

This provision of the state constitution was not self-executing; it required action by the legislature to define civil rights and to provide the administrative or judicial machinery to enforce the constitutional principle.

After 1938 the New York legislature passed a number of additional laws intended to protect equal rights and to implement the constitutional guarantee. Thus, for example, a 1939 law prohibited discrimination in public housing; [16] a 1940 law prohibited discrimination by labor organizations [17] and in public relief or on public work projects; [18] a 1941 law made any offense against Article I, Section 11 of the constitution a misdemeanor [19] and another statute forbade discrimination in employment by firms engaged in defense work; [20] and a 1943 law prohibited discrimination in the sale or delivery of alcoholic beverages.[21]

In 1944 the New York legislature established a twenty-three–member temporary commission to study the "practices of discrimination against any of the inhabitants of the state because of race, color, creed or national origin, and in connection therewith to make studies of existing laws and to make recommendations designed to eliminate such discrimination." [22] On the basis of its preliminary studies, the temporary commission concluded that a permanent state agency should be created to deal with the various

[15] N.Y. State Constitutional Convention, 2 Revised Record 1068 (1938).
[16] Public Housing Law § 223.   [17] Civil Rights Law § 43.
[18] Penal Law § 772-a.   [19] Penal Law §§ 700, 701.
[20] Civil Rights Law § 44; Penal Law § 514.
[21] Alcoholic Beverage Control Law § 65.
[22] Laws of 1944, ch. 692, § 3.

aspects of racial and religious discrimination; to enforce the
state's policy and to organize formal and informal educational
programs against such practices; and to encourage the development of local citizens' councils. A draft of proposed legislation
to accomplish those objectives was sent in early November, 1944,
to leaders of government, education, labor, business, and industry
and to bar associations and social, civic, and religious groups,
with invitations to participate in a series of public hearings to
discuss the commission's findings and proposals. As a result of
that series of public discussions, a number of changes were made
in the proposed legislation, which was eventually introduced into
the New York legislature as the Ives-Quinn Bill.

On March 12, 1945, Governor Thomas E. Dewey signed into
law the first state fair employment practices statute enacted in
the United States. It became effective on July 1, 1945.[23]

The Law Against Discrimination, as the New York statute
is known, states that the act shall be deemed an exercise of the
police power of the state, for the protection of the public welfare,
health, and peace of the people of the state, and in fulfillment of
the provision in the 1938 constitution concerning civil rights. It
creates a State Commission Against Discrimination, with power
to eliminate and prevent discrimination in employment because
of race, creed, color, or national origin, by employers, labor
unions, and employment agencies. Opportunity for employment
without discrimination is declared to be a civil right.

The commission consists of five members, appointed by the
governor, by and with the consent of the state senate. Each commissioner originally received an annual salary of $10,000; this
has been substantially increased.

The law defines "unlawful employment practices" as being the
following:

(1) For an employer, because of the race, creed, color or national origin of an individual, to discharge, to refuse to hire or

---

[23] Laws of 1945, ch. 118.

otherwise to discriminate against him with respect to compensation or terms, conditions or privileges of employment;

(2) For a labor organization to exclude a person from membership or to discriminate in any way against any of its members or against an employer;

(3) For an employer or an employment agency to advertise concerning employment opportunities, to use application forms, or to elicit information in such a manner or of such a character as to indicate discrimination because of race, creed, color or national origin;

(4) For an employer, employment agency or labor organization to discriminate against a person because he has opposed any practice forbidden by the law or because he has filed a complaint or testified in a proceeding concerning any discrimination outlawed by the act; or

(5) For any person to aid, abet, incite or compel the doing of any act forbidden by the law, or to attempt to do so.

A person claiming to be aggrieved by an unlawful employment practice is required to file a verified complaint. One of the commissioners is then appointed to make an investigation. If he determines that probable cause for the complaint exists, he must attempt to eliminate the practice through persuasion. If he fails, a formal hearing is held, at which he may have no part other than as a witness. If the commission finds that the respondent violated the law, it issues a cease and desist order which may be enforced by court decree. Any refusal to obey such a court mandate would be punishable as contempt of court. The law also provides for judicial review of the commission's orders at the instance of "any complainant, respondent or other person aggrieved by such an order." In any court proceeding based upon a commission order, "the findings of the commission as to the facts shall be conclusive if supported by sufficient evidence on the record considered as a whole."

Willful resistance or interference with the commission or any of its members in the performance of their duties, is made a misdemeanor, punishable by imprisonment for not more than one year or by fine of not more than $500 or both. The act does not apply to employers with fewer than six workers, or to social, fraternal, religious, educational, and charitable organizations, if not organized for private profit. The commission is also charged with the duty of creating advisory agencies, or conciliation councils, throughout the state, to study the problems of discrimination in specific fields or in specific instances, and to foster cooperation and good will among the various groups in the state. Citizens serving on the councils receive no pay.

The New York Law Against Discrimination was amended in 1958 to add age to the other types of discrimination prohibited by the law.[24]

Other State FEPCs

In 1945, hard on the heels of New York, New Jersey passed a fair employment practices law establishing a Division Against Discrimination in the Department of Education. Massachusetts outlawed discrimination in employment in 1946 and created an independent Fair Employment Practices Commission. In 1947, Connecticut vested its previously established Interracial Commission with jurisdiction over complaints of discrimination in employment. The number of FEP states was doubled when, in 1949, New Mexico established a Fair Employment Practices Commission, Oregon vested jurisdiction over discrimination in employment in its Bureau of Labor, Rhode Island established an independent Commission Against Discrimination, and Washington created a state Board Against Discrimination. Three more states, Michigan, Minnesota, and Pennsylvania, joined the growing number of FEP states in 1955, and California and Ohio passed their laws in 1959.

Although Wisconsin enacted a statute as early as 1945 con-

[24] Laws of 1958, ch. 738, § 1, EXECUTIVE LAW § 296.

demning discrimination in employment and authorizing efforts to counteract it, no provision in the original act outlawed such discrimination or empowered the Fair Employment Practices Division of the Wisconsin Industrial Commission to issue cease and desist orders. The statute, however, was amended in 1957 to conform to the models provided by the other FEP states. Colorado also adopted a limited statute in 1951—limited with respect to enforcement machinery to so-called public employment. In 1957, Colorado amended its law and vested full enforcement authority over employment discrimination generally in its Anti-Discrimination Commission. Alaska, which outlawed discrimination in employment in 1953 and gave its commissioner of labor jurisdiction to enforce the law, brought the number of states with fully enforceable FEP laws to sixteen when it was admitted to statehood in 1959. Delaware raised the total to seventeen in July, 1960, when a bill to outlaw discrimination in employment on the grounds of age was amended to include discrimination based on race, color, religion, or national origin.

There are numerous differences among the state FEP laws. Some establish independent commissions while others vest jurisdiction in a branch or division of an established department. Some provide for paid, full-time commissioners while others establish lay advisory boards. Two state FEP laws cover discrimination practiced by an employer of one or more employees, while one requires the employer to hire at least twelve employees before he is brought under the statute, and the other laws vary widely within these extremes. Some statutes expressly declare the right to employment without discrimination to be "a civil right" and others are silent on this point. Some specify a 90-day statute of limitations on complaints, some provide for a one-year statute, and several provide no specific time limit. Eight states include age among the grounds on which discrimination is prohibited, while one (New Jersey) includes liability for military service.

The fully enforceable FEP laws, with the sole exception of

Delaware, have the following provisions in common: they declare discrimination in public and private employment on racial, religious, or ethnic grounds to be illegal; they authorize a state administrative agency to receive and investigate complaints; they empower the agency to eliminate, by persuasion and mediation, any discrimination found to exist; if unsuccessful in such efforts, the agency is authorized to proceed by public hearings, findings of fact and law, and cease and desist orders, which are enforceable by court decree; judicial review is available to a person claiming to be aggrieved by an agency ruling; and finally, the state agency is responsible for an educational program intended to reduce and eliminate discrimination and prejudice.

The Delaware statute does not expressly provide for an educational program, for the use of persuasion and mediation before resort is had to more drastic sanctions; nor does it expressly provide for public hearings and cease and desist orders. Since violations are made a crime and since the labor department is vested with jurisdiction to enforce the act, it must, however, be classified as an enforceable Fair Employment Practices Law.

Two states, Indiana and Kansas, have FEP laws without enforcement machinery. In 1945 Indiana passed a law condemning discrimination in employment and conferring on the Division of Labor the duty to seek the removal of such discrimination through studies and voluntary means. Likewise, the Kansas law passed in 1953, seeks to discourage discrimination in employment by the establishment of an Anti-Discrimination Commission to conduct a program of education, mediation, and cooperation with public and private organizations and with employers, labor organizations, and employees. These have been characterized as "educational" or "voluntary" laws.

FEPC in the Courts

The first court case under a state fair employment practices law arose in Connecticut in 1949. A Negro student in New

Haven, Oscar Draper, answered a newspaper advertisement for "Boys Wanted" and was told that the job was filled. He filed a complaint with the Connecticut Interracial Commission, charging the Clark Dairy with refusing to hire him because of his race. The commission assigned the matter for investigation by one of its field representatives and reached the conclusion that there was probable cause to believe that an unfair employment practice had occurred. Following unsuccessful attempts to conciliate the complaint, as required by the statute, the matter was noticed for a public hearing before a hearing tribunal of three examiners, none of whom had been involved in the proceedings to that point. A three-day hearing brought out that the respondent operated a wholesale and retail milk, ice cream, and ice cream products business and had four dairy stores. An advertisement was inserted in a daily newspaper reading: "Boys, 18 years or over. Experience unnecessary. Evening work. Apply 3 to 5 or after 6 P.M. Clark Dairy, 74 Whitney Avenue, City." Draper was the first applicant interviewed by the store manager on the same day that the advertisement appeared. There was no discussion of the kind of employment or of the wages or hours involved. Several other applicants, all white, who answered the advertisement later, secured jobs as dishwashers or fountain men in Clark's milk and ice cream stores. The hearing established that the employer had several job openings on the day Draper applied, that no special qualifications were required other than that the applicant be at least eighteen years of age and willing to work nights. Draper met these qualifications. The Clark Dairy had no Negro employees in its stores except a girl who appeared to be white. About seven months after the event occurred, the hearing tribunal issued an order addressed to Clark Dairy, stating: "You are hereby ordered to cease and desist forthwith from refusing to employ Oscar S. Draper." The respondent appealed to the Superior Court, New Haven County, on the following grounds: (1) the applicant for employment should have been made a party to the proceedings; (2) the hearing tribunal's findings were arbitrary and contrary to law and fact; and (3) if the findings were sustained, then the form of order was improper. An objection to the statute on constitutional grounds was withdrawn at the time of oral argument and was not briefed. Since this was the first court test of an FEP law, *amici curiae* briefs were filed by the American Jewish Committee, the Anti-Defamation League of B'nai B'rith, the Connecticut Committee on Civil Rights, the United Labor Committee of the C.I.O., the A.F.L., and the International Association of Machinists.

On October 10, 1950, the superior court held that the primary purpose of the fair employment practices law is to secure equal opportunity for employment for qualified persons regardless of race, color, religious creed, national origin, or ancestry. When a a complainant files a complaint charging discrimination under the law, he sets the machinery of the statute in motion and "his function in the proceeding ceases." The entire procedure established by the statute is intended to make the commission the adversary of the employer charged with violating the law. Hence, the law gives no right or interest to the complainant "which makes him a necessary party."

Passing to the second issue, the court cited the provision of the statute that "the findings of the hearing tribunal as to the facts, if supported by substantial and competent evidence, shall be conclusive." From all of the evidence before it, the tribunal drew the inference that the real (although unexpressed) reason for the respondent's refusing to hire Draper was his race. "An examination of the record," the court said, "warrants the conclusion that the finding [of discrimination] is proper and should stand."

Turning to the final argument, namely that the form of the order was improper, the court pointed out that the complainant was not a party to the proceeding and hence the commission's order could not be binding upon him. In view of the seven-month interval between the dates of the unfair employment practice and of the commission's order, intervening factors might have made employment of the complainant by the respondent impossible. Draper might no longer be interested in employment by Clark Dairy, but he was neither in a position nor under any duty to make this known. The form of the commission's order was too broad. The statute authorizes the commission to require a respondent to "cease and desist from *such* unfair employment practice" as the commission may find after investigation and hearing. That means only to stop henceforth from doing the objectionable thing done in the past. The court thereupon modified the commission's order to read: "In the event that Oscar S. Draper, now or formerly of 285 Starr Street, New Haven, Connecticut, presents himself for employment, you are hereby ordered to cease and desist from refusing, because of his race, to employ him." [25]

The respondent did not appeal from the superior court decision. In November, 1950, the Interracial Commission was advised by Draper that he was no longer interested in the job at Clark Dairy because he was attending day school and employed evenings. Thus, the first court test of a fair employment practices law vindicated the statute and its application by the administrative agency to a discriminatory refusal by an employer to hire because of race. Although the Connecticut Interracial Commission, to its credit, acted with all possible speed on the complaint, the time lapse between the date of the unfair employment practice and the final court ruling deprived the complainant of the satisfaction of seeing his civil right vindicated in fact as well as in theory.

The case is significant because it accepts the legislative scheme which gives a state agency primary responsibility for combating discrimination in employment and protecting the civil rights of individuals. The statutory scheme differs markedly from that of the civil rights laws which we discussed early in ch. 6 in that the burden is removed from the shoulders of the person victimized

[25] Draper v. Clark Dairy, Inc., 17 Conn. Supp. 93 (1950).

by discrimination and placed on those of the state agency. Under the fair employment practice scheme, as the Connecticut court noted, the adversaries are the state commission and the respondent-employer.

The Connecticut case is also significant because it sustains the role of the commission as fact-finder. The statute provides that "the findings of the hearing tribunal as to the facts, if supported by substantial and competent evidence, shall be conclusive." The court recognized that whether it would come to the same or to some other conclusion, upon the evidence considered by the commission, was immaterial. The court was not empowered under the statute to substitute its discretion for that of the hearing tribunal. Hence, the findings of fact upon which the hearing tribunal predicated its order were deemed binding upon the court unless a reading of the total record justified the conclusion that the commission acted arbitrarily or capriciously.

The first litigated controversy under the New York Law Against Discrimination to reach the court of appeals, the highest appellate court of that state, involved a complaint against an employment agency.[26] Helena Holland was charged with an unlawful employment practice in that she used an application form that asked questions about the former name of job applicants. The complainant, Rue Lehds, also charged that when she answered a newspaper advertisement for a secretary, she was asked orally by the respondent about the religion of one of her former employers, about the maiden name of the latter's wife and about the complainant's national origin. When efforts to settle the complaint by conciliation and persuasion failed, the New York State Commission Against Discrimination held a formal hearing, during the early stages of which the respondent and her attorney withdrew, without availing themselves of their right to cross-examine witnesses and raise legal objections. At the conclusion of the hearing, SCAD found that the employment agency had

[26] Holland v. Edwards, 307 N.Y. 38, 119 N.E.2d 581 (1954).

engaged in an unlawful employment practice and issued an order
directing the respondent to cease and desist from making any
inquiries concerning race, creed, color, or national origin when
interviewing or when receiving applications from persons seeking employment; from considering such factors in referring applicants to prospective employers; and from using application
forms which include questions about an applicant's change in
name. The respondent was also ordered not to furnish information to prospective employers concerning an applicant's race,
creed, or color, and not to accept or service job orders which
contained discriminatory specifications. Finally, the order directed the employment agency to maintain and make available
to the commission records of all actions taken on employment
applications and job orders and "all other records relating to her
business, until such time as the commission should determine
that she was complying with the statute."

The employment agency commenced an action in the New
York Supreme Court, New York County, to annul the cease and
desist order, and in a counteraction SCAD, for the first time
since its creation in 1945, asked for judicial enforcement. The
lower court denied the employment agency's petition and granted
the commission's application.[27] The appellate division affirmed,[28]
and Holland appealed to the court of appeals.

The court's opinion, written by Judge Stanley H. Fuld, noted
that the state commission had been created by the legislature
"to effectuate its declared policy of combating the practice of
discrimination on the basis of race, creed, color or national
origin, as a threat to our democratic institutions." After summarizing briefly the procedure required by the statute, the court
ruled that SCAD was authorized to issue a cease and desist order
if it found, "upon all the evidence at the hearing," that the re-

---

[27] Holland v. Edwards, 116 N.Y.S.2d 264 (1952).
[28] 282 App. Div. 353, 122 N.Y.S.2d 721 (1953).

spondent had engaged in an unlawful employment practice. Judicial review of findings of the commission was "of course, limited to the question whether the findings are, upon the entire record, supported by evidence 'so substantial that from it an inference of the existence of the fact found may be drawn reasonably.'" There was no doubt of the presence of the required substantial evidence to sustain the commission's findings of an unlawful employment practice and so those findings were deemed "conclusive" upon the courts.

The respondent objected to the commission's ruling because the inquiry as to the change of name did not "necessarily" reflect a discriminatory purpose or design. In reply to that argument, Fuld stated that although in another setting and under other circumstances, an inquiry as to change of name might be appropriate, it was entirely reasonable for the commission to conclude that in the present case such inquiry, when considered along with the surrounding circumstances, disclosed a discriminatory intent.

The court added:

One intent on violating the Law Against Discrimination cannot be expected to declare or announce his purpose. Far more likely is it that he will pursue his discriminatory practices in ways that are devious, by methods subtle and elusive—for we deal with an area in which "subtleties of conduct play no small part. . . ." All of which amply justifies the legislature's grant of broad power to the commission to appraise, correlate and evaluate the facts uncovered.

The court also rejected the respondent's argument that the complainant could not be considered "aggrieved" since there was no evidence that she had been refused a referral because of discrimination by the respondent. Fuld pointed out that, apart from being made too late—the point should have been raised before the commission—this objection was without foundation because the New York law made the mere use by employment agencies of forms containing discriminatory questions an unfair practice whether or not such use caused the denial of employment or employment referral to a particular applicant.[29]

The New York state commission's authority was tested again in court in 1954, when an employment agency commenced an action for a declaratory judgment and an injunction to prevent the commission from requiring all employment agencies to post a notice, supplied by the state, advising the public of the provisions of the Law Against Discrimination.[30]

SCAD promulgated a regulation which read in part as follows:

Posting of Notices. Every employer, employment agency and labor organization, subject to the Law Against Discrimination, shall post and maintain at their establishment, notices furnished by the State Commission Against Discrimination, indicating the substantive provisions of the Law Against Discrimination, where complaints may be filed and such other information as the State Commission Against Discrimination deems pertinent.

The notice prepared by the commission contained the state seal and the legend THIS ESTABLISHMENT IS SUBJECT TO THE LAW AGAINST DISCRIMINATION. The notice then briefly stated the objectives of the law, advised that persons aggrieved may file complaints, and gave the addresses of the local offices of the state commission where people could get further information as to their rights under the law.

There was no dispute as to the facts. The only question raised by the lawsuit was a legal one—did the state commission have authority to adopt the regulation in question? The Massachusetts, Michigan, Ohio, and Rhode Island FEP statutes require every employer, employment agency, and labor union to post in a

[29] Judge Charles W. Froessel wrote a short concurring opinion, which was shared by three other members of the court. They agreed "in large measure" with Fuld's opinion, but expressed doubts as to the scope of some of the provisions of the cease and desist order, particularly the requirement that the respondent submit to the commission all job orders "which raise a question" whether there was a violation of the law.

[30] Ross v. Arbury, 206 Misc. 74, 133 N.Y.S.2d 62 (1954), *aff'd without opinion,* 285 App. Div. 886, 139 N.Y.S.2d 245 (1955).

conspicuous place on their premises a notice setting forth the major requirements of their laws, but the New York statute is silent on this point. The court found that the question was one of first impression because other state agencies which require the posting of notices either are expressly authorized by specific legislation to do so, or their authority has never been adjudicated. The court also refused to give any weight to the failure of the legislature to enact a bill, sponsored by the state commission, expressly delegating such power to the agency. "The rules of statutory construction on implications from legislative inaction must be applied cautiously," the court said, "particularly in instances where bills have not been reported to the floor, or where there is no record indicating the reasons for the disposition of them. Frequently, legislative bodies prefer to leave acts which they deem administrative to administrative agencies in the exercise of their rule-making power." After citing the objectives of the Law Against Discrimination, the court reasoned that the commission would be unable to carry out the purposes "of this entirely new legislation" unless it could bring the provisions of the statute to the attention of those intended to be protected.

The commission was held to have the power to issue regulations which fill in the administrative details omitted from the Law Against Discrimination. Finally, the court rejected the argument that the regulation was unreasonable because "everyone is presumed to know the law." That presumption is essential in any ordered society so as not to relieve members from the legal consequences of their wrongful acts or their contractual obligations. It is not a substitute "for educating the public as to the social measures intended for the benefit of all the people of the state."

Thus far, we have seen how state fair employment practice laws were invoked against an employer and against an employment agency which refused to obey the statute. We will now consider a case in which a labor union violated the law by discriminating against two Negro applicants for membership. It will show

how the ultimate sanction of contempt of court was invoked to protect the applicants' civil rights.

In March, 1949, in Hartford, Connecticut, Mansfield T. Tilley and Warren B. Stewart applied for membership in Local No. 35 of the International Brotherhood of Electrical Workers, A.F.L. Both applicants were high school graduates with two additional years of electrical training in a trade school. They had served in the armed forces where they did electrical work and earned honorable discharges. The I.B.E.W. never informed Tilley or Stewart what action, if any, was taken on their applications. After more than a year of waiting, complaints were filed with the state's Commission on Civil Rights charging racial discrimination. After a preliminary investigation and a finding of probable cause, unsuccessful efforts were made by the commission to persuade the I.B.E.W. to admit Tilley and Stewart. A public hearing was held before three hearing examiners and some 1,400 pages of testimony were taken. The union conceded that its admission practices were arbitrary, but contended that they could not be construed as discriminatory because they applied to all applicants, white and Negro, alike. The commission argued that the union's practice of giving preference to sons and relatives of present members acted as an absolute ban on Negro applicants, since Negroes had never been admitted to membership in the past. It also appeared at the hearing that the union had admitted several white applicants—it was claimed that they were either relatives or friends of union members—during the period in which it failed to act on the complainants' applications. The hearing tribunal concluded that Tilley and Stewart had been barred from union membership because of their race, and the commission issued an order directing the union to cease and desist from excluding them from the benefits of full membership.

The union appealed to the superior court, claiming that the decision and order of the commission were contrary to the facts, the evidence, and the law, and that the hearing tribunal acted arbitrarily and abused its discretion. The superior court dismissed the union's petition and ordered it to comply with the commission's cease and desist order. An appeal was taken to the Connecticut Supreme Court of Errors, which unanimously affirmed the superior court.[31]

Following the affirmance by the highest court of Connecticut, Tilley and Stewart again submitted membership applications to the union. The executive board of the I.B.E.W. submitted the applications, without recommendation, to the union membership which voted not to accept Tilley and Stewart, assigning no reason in the minutes for the decision. When the Commission on Civil Rights learned of the latest rejection of Tilley and Stewart by the union membership, a motion was made in the superior court to punish the I.B.E.W. and its officers for contempt of court for failure to obey the cease and desist order of the commission, as affirmed by the superior and supreme courts of Connecticut. The court found no new reasons to justify the exclusion of the complainants from union membership and, therefore, held the union in contempt of court. A fine of $2,000 was imposed upon the union for its past misconduct and it was given 30 days in which to admit the complainants to full union membership and benefits. The court ordered an additional fine of $500 for each week thereafter that the union continued to disregard the cease and desist order.

The *I.B.E.W.* case is significant because it was the first test of the ultimate sanction—punishment for contempt of court—available to state commissions against discrimination for the enforcement of FEP laws. The case also demonstrated the flexibility and effectiveness of punishment for contempt. The provision for the additional fine of $500 for each week, if the union should decide to continue to disregard the court's mandate, was effective. Tilley and Stewart were admitted to full membership and

[31] International Bhd. of Elec. Workers v. Commission on Civil Rights, 140 Conn. 537, 102 A.2d 366 (1953).

were assigned to union jobs before the 30-day period expired.

One other judicial decision deserves mention. A Negro, named Wendell A. Jeanpierre, charged Pan-American World Airways System with violating the New York Law Against Discrimination by refusing to hire him as an airline flight steward. The commissioner assigned by SCAD to investigate the charges concluded that there was no probable cause to credit the alleged racial discrimination and dismissed the complaint. Jeanpierre, believing that the commissioner's action deprived him of a civil right, commenced an action in the Supreme Court of New York County against the state commission alleging the improper dismissal of his complaint. The trial court reviewed the evidence upon which the commissioner acted and held that, on the record considered as a whole, he was justified in dismissing Jeanpierre's complaint.

The appellate division affirmed, but held in its majority opinion that the complainant had no right to judicial review of a determination of no probable cause by the investigating commissioner. A vigorous dissent was filed by two of the five justices.[32]

The New York Court of Appeals held unanimously in a *per curiam* opinion that the final dismissal of the complaint, by one commissioner on the ground that in his opinion probable cause did not exist to credit the charge of discrimination, was reviewable by the courts in an appropriate proceeding to challenge such action. The court said:

No intent to preclude judicial review of such determination may be found in the language contained in Article 15 of the Executive Law nor from its legislative history. The rule is well settled that, in the absence of a "clear expression by the Legislature to the contrary," the courts may review the discretionary act of an administrative officer or body to determine whether the discretion has been exercised in an arbitrary or capricious manner.

[32] Jeanpierre v. Arbury, 3 A.D.2d 514, 162 N.Y.S.2d 506 (1957).

The court of appeals then said that the record before it did not tend to establish that the commissioner acted arbitrarily in dismissing the complaint for lack of probable cause.[33]

The case is significant because it established the rule in New York that the acts of the State Commission Against Discrimination will be reviewed by the courts for arbitrariness and capriciousness, notwithstanding the fact that the enabling statute does not expressly provide for judicial review of the dismissal of a complaint for lack of probable cause. Since the dismissal of a complaint by the investigating commissioner finally disposes of the proceeding (as though there had been a hearing and dismissal on the evidence), a complainant is entitled, as a matter of due process of law, to have the courts review the action of the commissioner for legality and arbitrariness.

Other Activities of State FEP Agencies

In 1957 the New York State Commission Against Discrimination prepared and circulated a questionnaire addressed to twelve state FEP agencies [34] asking about their structure, scope, funds, and enforcement procedures. The agencies were also requested to describe their educational, research, and community relations programs. The results were published in pamphlet form by the American Jewish Committee for the Conference of Governors on Civil Rights.[35]

Almost all twelve states reported that they viewed education as their primary means of overcoming discrimination. In fact, the very process of settling fair employment cases was considered a valuable educational tool. The time devoted to community programs promoting fair employment practices varied.

Seminars, labor-management institutes and meetings, work-

[33] Jeanpierre v. Arbury, 4 N.Y.2d 238, 173 N.Y.S.2d 597 (1958).

[34] Colorado, Connecticut, Massachusetts, Michigan, Minnesota, New Jersey, New York, Oregon, Pennsylvania, Rhode Island, Washington, and Wisconsin.

[35] AMERICAN JEWISH COMM., FAIR EMPLOYMENT PRACTICES AT WORK IN TWELVE STATES (1958).

shops, conferences, training sessions for personnel managers and employment agency personnel, and community conferences with majority and minority group members were given as illustrations of educational activities. Materials included pamphlets, car cards, newsletters, special literature, bulletins, copies of the laws, FEPC rules and regulations, and posters. All of the states reported using mass media in their educational programs.

Ten of the commissions reported that they engaged in research. Their activities, however, suggested widely differing interpretations of the term "research." Only three states employed personnel specifically for research projects. The others relied on resources and findings of other governmental agencies or of private organizations, or they assigned nonresearch staff to such projects. Included as research were studies of apprenticeship, community profiles, the socioeconomic status of minority groups and educational opportunities for such groups. Housing studies also were conducted by several states.

An analysis of the state FEP laws reveals that research can usually be undertaken as an integral part of the agency's program. The relative lack of comprehensive research activities may be attributed to financial limitations.

The commissions sought in many ways to obtain the advice, counsel, and cooperation of the general public. New York reported the most extensive apparatus, with local and regional advisory councils; commerce and industry, and labor advisory committees; and special industry-wide committees. Rhode Island, on the other hand, had only one community council.

While all twelve states agreed that their laws against discrimination were effective, most of the states reported problems in achieving the maximum effectiveness of the law. The problem most frequently cited was that aggrieved individuals failed to file complaints, particularly in connection with upgrading and promotion.

Some of the states also pointed out that their small staffs were unable to cover the vast areas assigned to them. Others cited the limited number of skilled workers among minority group job-seekers. Most members of minority groups are not prepared to challenge discriminatory barriers, except in unskilled classifications where discrimination is least prevalent. Several states also reported that public "apathy" and "indifference" made full implementation difficult.

Seven commissions specified a variety of measures they felt necessary for greater effectiveness in their operations. New York, Oregon, and Washington wished coverage extended to employers now exempt. Massachusetts and New York sought reconsideration of the exemption of some, if not all, employers who, because of their charitable, sectarian, or private character, did not come under the jurisdiction of the commissions. In addition, New York sought the power to initiate complaints on its own motion, a power currently exercised by a majority of the state commissions. Pennsylvania asked for a provision that would allow civic agencies to initiate complaints, an extension of coverage to agricultural workers, and independence of the agency from its intra-departmental status.

The various state agencies charged with enforcing fair employment legislation were asked a series of questions concerning the attitudes toward the law on the part of employers, minority groups, and the general public. All states reported some opposition prior to the passage of the act. The reactions ranged from "no *organized* opposition" to "extensive opposition." In one state, opposition prevented passage of the act for ten years. In contrast, all states reported at least general satisfaction and no organized public opposition to their activities under the laws. Moreover, seven of the states reported that any attempt to broaden the legislation would elicit either no opposition at all, some opposition, or only covert opposition. The remaining five states either indicated uncertainty about the opposition or stated their conviction that there was no need to strengthen the laws, an opinion which rendered the question moot.

Ten of the states indicated that minority group organizations were either "satisfied" or "generally satisfied" with the operation of the laws. Only New Jersey and New York reported that such organizations felt the law should be strengthened. The reactions of the general public led to two conclusions: On one hand, the public was "generally favorable" or gave "good support" or "tacit acceptance" to the law. On the other, there still appeared to be extensive "ignorance" about the law, "passivity," and, to some extent, "indifference." This lack of knowledge and concern, especially among minority groups, presented a major problem for every one of the commissions.

Constitutionality of FEP Laws

As we saw earlier in this chapter, the Bill of Rights of the New York State Constitution of 1938 provides that no person shall, because of race, color, creed, or religion, be subjected to any discrimination in his civil rights by any other person, firm, corporation or institution, or by the state or any state agency. The New Jersey State Constitution of 1947 contains a similar provision which states:

No person shall be denied the enjoyment of any civil or military right, nor be discriminated against in the exercise of any civil or military right, nor be segregated in the militia or in the public schools, because of religious principles, race, color, ancestry or national origin.[36]

Neither the New York nor the New Jersey constitution defines "civil rights"; that definition is left to the legislature. But whether or not a state's constitution provides that the legislature may define and protect the individual's civil rights, the law-making body has that power. That is one of its primary functions. The only

[36] Art. I, § 5.

limitation on that power under our federal system is that the individual's civil rights may not be defined or protected in such a way as to violate the federal Constitution.

There is no doubt of the constitutionality of state statutes outlawing discrimination by employers, employment agencies, and labor unions, under the police power of the state.[37] In the only case in which the United States Supreme Court was faced with a constitutional challenge of a state statute forbidding racial discrimination by labor unions, the Court unanimously held that such a state civil rights law offends neither the due process clause nor the equal protection clause of the Fourteenth Amendment.[38]

Fair employment practices laws do not force an employer to hire employees or a labor union to accept members because they belong to minority racial or religious groups; such laws merely require that the same criteria for employment or union membership be applied to all applicants, regardless of their race, color, or religion. Selection based on discriminatory factors is outlawed because the state legislature finds such selection unreasonable, a threat to the rights and proper privileges of the inhabitants of the state and a danger to "the institutions and foundations of a free democratic society." [39]

The charge was raised against the National Labor Relations Act that it forced employers to hire or retain certain individuals. The United States Supreme Court pointed out that the act left an employer free to hire or discharge "for any cause which seems to it proper" except the specific cause condemned by the act.[40] Instead of forcing unqualified employees or union members on

[37] *Hearings on S. 101 and S. 459, Fair Employment Practice Act,* 79th Cong., 1st Sess. 184 (1945), where cases are cited; James v. Marinship Corp., 25 Cal. 2d 721, 155 P.2d 329 (1944); Dublierer, *Legislation Outlawing Racial Discrimination in Employment,* 5 LAW. GUILD REV. 101 (1945); Hunt, *The Proposed Fair Employment Practices Act—Facts and Fallacies,* 32 VA. L. REV. 1 (1949); Waite, *Constitutionality of the Proposed Minnesota Fair Employment Practices Act,* 32 MINN. L. REV. 349 (1949); Mittenthal, *The Michigan Fair Employment Practices Act,* 35 MICH. ST. BAR J. 41 (1956).

[38] Railway Mail Ass'n v. Corsi, 326 U.S. 88 (1945).

[39] N.Y. EXECUTIVE LAW § 290.

[40] Associated Press v. N.L.R.B., 301 U.S. 103 (1937).

employers or unions, FEP laws are intended to increase the likelihood that job-seekers will be judged solely on the basis of their qualifications.

Nor do FEP laws unconstitutionally interfere with freedom of contract or freedom of association. The right of the state, in the exercise of its police power, to establish reasonable regulations to protect the health, safety, morals, and welfare of its people has been upheld by the United States Supreme Court against the argument that the due process clause of the Fourteenth Amendment proscribes any attempt to limit freedom of contract.[41]

State and Municipal Conflicts

Over forty municipalities enacted local fair employment practices ordinances between 1948 and 1960.[42] In a number of states, notably California, Michigan, Minnesota, Ohio, and Pennsylvania, one or more municipalities had passed local FEP ordinances before the legislature acted to outlaw discrimination in employment on a state-wide basis. While such local ordinances vary widely, they all declare discrimination in employment to be illegal and authorize the city or district attorney to enforce the law by a criminal proceeding against employers, employment agencies, or labor unions that refuse to comply with cease and desist orders of the local board or commission established to receive and act on complaints.

In 1955, the attorney general of Minnesota handed down an opinion, in response to a question asked by the city attorney of

[41] Nebbia v. New York, 291 U.S. 502 (1934).

[42] Bakersfield and San Francisco, Calif.; Chicago, Ill.; East Chicago and Gary, Ind.; Des Moines, Iowa; Ecorse, Hamtramck, Pontiac, and River Rouge, Mich.; Duluth, Minneapolis, and St. Paul, Minn.; Campbell, Canton, Cleveland, Girard, Hubbard, Lorain, Lowellville, Niles, Steubenville, Struthers, Toledo, Warren, and Youngstown, Ohio; Braddock, Clairton, Duquesne, Erie, Farrell, Johnstown, Monessen, Philadelphia, Pittsburgh, and Sharon, Pa.; and Milwaukee, Wis. have FEP ordinances prohibiting discrimination in public and private employment. Richmond, Calif.; Sioux City, Iowa; Baltimore, Md.; St. Louis, Mo.; and Cincinnati, Ohio have FEP ordinances limited to "public" employment.

Minneapolis, to the effect that the passage of a state law banning discrimination in employment did not necessarily invalidate municipal ordinances prohibiting the same conduct. In reaching that conclusion, the attorney general considered whether it was the intention of the state legislature to pre-empt the field to the exclusion of all local regulation and, if that were not the legislative intent, whether the differences in enforcement machinery between the state law and the local ordinances rendered the latter invalid.

The opinion placed considerable reliance upon the absence of any express provision in the state FEP statute invalidating municipal ordinances on discrimination in employment. The attorney general noted that the mere passage of a state law did not remove the need for continued local efforts to counteract existing practices of discrimination and that problems of this nature often yield to local compliance machinery which acts as a supplementary sanction to state law. The opinion belittled the differences between the enforcement procedures of the local and state measures, and concluded that it was not necessary that a statute and an ordinance dealing with the same general subject be identical in every respect. If the ordinance is a valid exercise of the home rule powers of the municipality, it need not contain procedures which are precisely coextensive with those set forth in the state statute regulating the same subject, provided the ordinance does not create a different standard of regulation and is not inconsistent with the state law.[43]

In 1958, the attorney general of Michigan came to the contrary conclusion. He ruled that the fair employment practices ordinances of the cities of Ecorse, Hamtramck, Pontiac, and River Rouge were invalidated when the state enacted an FEP statute in 1955.[44]

Of course, a state statute may expressly save municipal ordi-

[43] Letter of Attorney General Miles Lord of Minnesota to Charles A. Sawyer, dated Oct. 20, 1955.
[44] Ops. Mich. Att'y Gen. No. 2880 (May 22, 1958).

nances, as is the case in the Pennsylvania law which provides:

Nothing contained in this act shall be deemed to repeal any of the provisions of any municipal ordinance, municipal charter or of any law of this Commonwealth relating to discrimination because of race, color, religious creed, ancestry, age or national origin, but as to acts declared unlawful by section five of this act the procedure herein provided shall, when invoked, be exclusive and the final determination therein shall exclude any other action, civil or criminal, based on the same grievance of the complainant concerned.[45]

Provision is also made in that section for the eventuality of a conflict between the interpretation of a provision of the state law and a similar provision of any municipal ordinance. In such case, the interpretation of the state statute is declared to prevail and to apply to the municipal ordinance.

A state statute may also expressly repeal and overrule all municipal FEP ordinances, as is the case in the California law which provides:

Nothing contained in this act shall be deemed to repeal or affect the provisions of any ordinance relating to such discrimination in effect in any city, city and county, or county at the time this act becomes effective, insofar as proceedings theretofore commenced under such ordinance or ordinances remain pending and undetermined. The respective administrative bodies then vested with the power and authority to enforce such ordinance or ordinances shall continue to have such power and authority, with no ouster or impairment of jurisdiction, until such pending proceedings are completed, but in no event beyond one year after the effective date of this act.[46]

Effectiveness of State Fair Employment Practices Laws

Probably the most authoritative evaluation of the effectiveness of state fair employment practices laws is to be found in the responses of the staffs of the twelve state commissions to the 1957

[45] PA. STAT. ANN. (Purdon Supp. 1958) tit. 43, § 962.
[46] 1959 Stat., ch. 121, § 1431.

questionnaire prepared and circulated by the New York State Commission Against Discrimination.[47]

The responses to the questionnaire did not allow a state-by-state comparison of the complaint statistics, since some returns submitted total figures from the inception of the agency, while others made reports for individual years or biennial periods. Moreover, some states included complaints of discrimination in fields other than employment in their totals. Finally, the definition of a complaint varied markedly among the states. Nonetheless, several generalizations were possible.

The number of complaints received by state commissions depends on several interrelated factors. One of these is the extent of discriminatory practices throughout the state. Another factor is the vigor of the state's total antidiscriminatory activity. There seems to have been a yearly rise in the number of complaints in each of the states reporting. No easy conclusions are to be drawn from this rise, however, since one complaint may open an entire plant for employment of minority group members. An educational field visit, without a complaint, may have a similar effect. It may also be assumed that with the passage of time and increased activity on behalf of minority groups, their awareness of their rights under FEP laws will grow.

New York reported the greatest volume of complaints in the field of employment: 4,213 from 1945 to 1957; next was New Jersey: 1,664 from 1945 to 1957; and Connecticut: 715 from 1947 to 1957.

In most states, race and color constituted by far the most frequent basis for complaint. Thus, Connecticut, Michigan, Oregon, Washington, and Wisconsin reported about 95 percent of employment complaints entered on these grounds; Rhode Island, 88 percent; Minnesota, 80 percent; Massachusetts, 76 per-

[47] *Supra* note 35. See also, Bamberger & Lewin, *The Right to Equal Treatment: Administrative Enforcement of Antidiscrimination Legislation,* 74 HARV. L. REV. 526 (1961).

cent; Pennsylvania, 71 percent; New York, 68 percent; and Colorado, 59 percent.

The disposition of employment complaints showed that the great majority of cases were either conciliated where discrimination was found or dismissed on a finding of no probable cause. Only a small number of cases were withdrawn, dismissed for lack of jurisdiction, or prosecuted to the public hearing stage.

The study concludes:

It is difficult in this factual summary to convey the sense of progress which emerges from a close reading of the questionnaire responses and accompanying documents submitted by the 12 states. They cite case after case in which major discriminatory barriers were broken by the activities of the commissions. Many note that the very passage of the law has signified more than simply an expression of a democratic climate of opinion; the existence of this anti-discrimination legislation, coupled with a respect for law and the educational and regulatory work of the commissions, has effected deep-rooted changes in public opinion. These are not abstract changes; they can be measured in new opportunities now available to minorities.

Less measurable, but perhaps of even greater significance in the long run, is the impact of the laws upon the attitudes of minority groups themselves. By protecting the civil rights of all citizens, these laws have helped create among members of minority groups a new sense of confidence and optimism. This is an immediate gain, for which the commissions are in part responsible. And there is promise of even greater achievement in the year ahead.

Chapter 8

FAIR EDUCATIONAL PRACTICES

Just as New York State was the first to create a commission to
handle discrimination in employment based on racial, religious,
or ethnic factors, so this state was also the first to extend the
technique of dealing with discrimination through a specialized
administrative agency to a field other than employment. In 1948
the Education Law was amended to declare "that the American
ideal of equality of opportunity requires that students, otherwise
qualified, be admitted to educational institutions without regard
to race, color, religion, creed or national origin." [1] Educational
institutions are defined as "post-secondary grade" schools, colleges, and universities subject to visitation by the state board of
regents or the state commissioner of education. The statute de-
clares it to be an "unfair educational practice . . . to exclude or
limit or otherwise discriminate" against any person seeking admission as a student because of his race, color, religion, creed,
or national origin, or to penalize any person because he initiated
or participated in a proceeding under the statute. Gratuitously,
the act provides that it shall *not* be an unfair practice for an educational institution "to use criteria other than race, religion,
creed, color or national origin in the admission of students." Provision is made for an educational institution operated or controlled by a religious organization to certify that fact in writing
to the commissioner with a statement that it elects "to be considered" a religious or denominational educational institution for
the purposes of the act. Upon such certification, a college or uni-

[1] EDUCATION LAW § 313; Laws of 1948. ch. 753.

versity would have the right "to select its students exclusively or primarily from members of such religion or denomination," to give them preference, or to make any selection of its students that promotes "the religious principles for which it is established or maintained."

An applicant for admission who believes himself aggrieved by an unfair educational practice may file a verified complaint with the commissioner of education setting forth the particulars of his grievance. Thereupon, the commissioner is required to make an investigation. If he finds probable cause to credit the charge of discrimination, he must attempt "by informal methods of persuasion, conciliation or mediation" to eliminate the grievance. If the informal methods fail, the commissioner refers the matter to the board of regents which may issue a complaint against the educational institution and fix the time and place for a public hearing upon the charge of unfair educational practice. If the evidence adduced at the hearing convinces the regents that the school practiced discrimination as defined in the law, the board issues a cease and desist order, which is reviewable and enforceable by the state courts. Finally, the regents are empowered to promulgate rules and regulations to effectuate the purposes and provisions of the statute.

In 1951 "business and trade schools" were added to the educational institutions covered;[2] and in 1953 the section was amended to make it an unfair educational practice for any educational institution "to accept any endowment or gift of money or property conditioned upon teaching the doctrine of supremacy of any particular race."[3]

The influence of the earlier employment laws is apparent in the total design of the first fair educational practices act. One provision, however, absent from the New York Law Against Discrimination, is present in the 1948 educational practices law because it was deemed vital by proponents of equality of op-

[2] Laws of 1951, ch. 208.   [3] Laws of 1953, ch. 356.

portunity in education. It is the section authorizing the commissioner of education to initiate an investigation on his own motion whenever he "has reason to believe" that discrimination has been practiced against an applicant or against applicants as a group. It was predicted, and experience under the law validated the prediction, that complaints of discrimination by applicants for admission to colleges and universities would be rare. Hence, it was deemed essential to vest the administrative agency with authority to initiate enforcement proceedings whenever there was reason to believe that an unfair educational practice had been committed. Virtually all the progress made under the law in eliminating quotas, discriminatory questions on application forms, and other discriminatory admissions practices at educational institutions is attributable to the self-initiated activities of the associate commissioner of education assigned by the board of regents to enforce the educational practices act.

The educational practices act was limited to "post-secondary" schools for one tactical and two substantive reasons. First, the law of New York already contained a section prohibiting discrimination on the grounds of race, creed, color, or national origin in all public schools.[4] Second, there was no evidence that racial or religious discrimination was practiced at public elementary or secondary schools, which were always available to students who might be rejected by private schools. Tactically, it was considered unwise to evoke the opposition of a group of private secondary schools whose ability to influence the state legislature might be out of all proportion to their ability to influence educational opportunity within the state.

New Jersey again followed hard on the heels of New York. In 1949 this state amended its 1945 law against discrimination to make the experience-tested procedure of the fair employment practices act available also to people who believed that they had been victims of racial, religious, or ethnic discrimination in

[4] EDUCATION LAW § 3201.

"places of public accommodation." [5] "A place of public accommodation" was expressly defined to include "any kindergarten, primary and secondary school, trade or business school, high school, academy, college and university, or any educational institution under the supervision of the State Board of Education, or the Commissioner of Education of the State of New Jersey." An exception was made for an educational facility operated or maintained by a "bona fide religious or sectarian institution," and the right of a natural parent "or one in *loco parentis*" to direct the education of his child was expressly "affirmed." The influence of the New York educational practices act was also obvious in the added (and wholly unnecessary) caution that nothing in the statute should "be construed to bar any private secondary or post-secondary school from using in good faith criteria other than race, creed, color, national origin or ancestry, in the admission of students."

One major difference between the New York and New Jersey statutes should be noted, however. New Jersey vested jurisdiction over discrimination in educational institutions in its already existing Division Against Discrimination, which, as we have noted, was created in 1945 in the Department of Education to handle charges of discrimination in employment. New York, on the other hand, instead of vesting jurisdiction over bias in educational institutions in its established State Commission Against Discrimination, created a new administrative agency within the state Department of Education for this purpose. The difference in treatment of discrimination in educational institutions was a result of the difference between the types of agencies originally created in the two states in 1945 to have jurisdiction over discrimination in employment. Since the New Jersey Division Against Discrimination was a part of the state Department of Education, it was logical to vest the new authority over educational institutions in the existing agency, while the New York

[5] Laws of 1949, ch. 11. See also p. 180 *supra*.

State Commission Against Discrimination was an independent agency, separate and distinct from the Department of Education. Hence, to preserve the traditional, exclusive jurisdiction of the New York Department of Education over all educational matters, a new administrative agency had to be created within the department with authority over discrimination in this field.

Massachusetts, the third state to enact a fair educational practices law, handled the matter somewhat differently. The original act, also passed in 1949, followed the New York pattern and created a new agency in the state Board of Education.[6] In 1956, however, jurisdiction over discrimination in educational institutions was transferred to the independent Massachusetts Commission Against Discrimination.[7] The Massachusetts act follows the New York statute in declaring that "the American ideal of equality of opportunity requires that students otherwise qualified, be admitted to educational institutions without regard to race, color, religion, creed or national origin." Religious or denominational educational institutions are also forbidden to discriminate against qualified students "because of race, color, or national origin." It is declared to be an "unfair educational practice" for an educational institution to exclude or otherwise discriminate against any "United States citizen or citizens seeking admission as students" or to make any "written or oral inquiry concerning the race, religion, color or national origin of a person seeking admission." Religious institutions are expressly authorized to inquire about the religious or denominational affiliations of applicants.

Oregon passed a law in 1951 prohibiting vocational, professional, and trade schools, chartered or licensed under any state statute, from discriminating against any qualified person on account of race, color, religion, or national origin.[8] In 1957 the legislature provided for license suspension or revocation upon

[6] Stat. 1949, ch. 726.   [7] Stat. 1956, ch. 334.
[8] ORE. REV. STATS. §§ 345.240 & 345.250.

proof of violation, and jurisdiction over this area of discrimination was assigned to the Bureau of Labor, which had been given authority over fair employment practices in 1949.[9]

Washington and Pennsylvania followed the New Jersey model by including educational institutions in the definition of "places of public resort, accommodation, assemblage or amusement" at which discrimination was prohibited.[10] In 1957 jurisdiction over charges of discrimination in places of public accommodation, including "any educational institutions, or schools of special instruction" was vested in the Washington State Board Against Discrimination, which theretofore had handled unfair employment practices.[11] Of course, an exception was provided for "any educational facility operated or maintained by a bona fide religious or sectarian institution." Pennsylvania followed in 1961.

Many of the states outside of the South provide in their constitutions or statutes that there shall be no discrimination or segregation in public education. Thus, Colorado, Idaho, New Jersey, and Washington have specific constitutional prohibitions against racial discrimination; while Connecticut, Illinois, Indiana, Massachusetts, Michigan, Minnesota, New York, Pennsylvania, Rhode Island, Washington, and Wisconsin have statutory prohibitions.[12] Only six states to date—Massachusetts, New Jersey, New York, Oregon, Pennsylvania, and Washington—have enacted fair educational laws which provide for protection of the right to equality of opportunity by an administrative agency.

Although there have been no judicial interpretations of the state fair educational laws, there have been several administrative proceedings and investigations which illustrate how these statutes operate.

A group of Negro parents in Englewood, New Jersey, charged the local board of education with establishing school districts

[9] Laws of 1957, ch. 724.
[11] Laws of 1957, ch. 37.
[10] WASH. REV. CODE § 9.91.010.
[12] GREENBERG, RACE RELATIONS AND AMERICAN LAW 388–89 (1959).

in such a way as to exclude Negroes from particular schools and to confine them to segregated schools. A complaint was filed in 1954 with the Division Against Discrimination. After an investigation and a finding of probable cause, attempts at conciliation proved fruitless. Thereupon, the commissioner of education held a public hearing at which testimony and arguments were heard. The local board of education denied any intent, in establishing the school boundary lines, to bring about or perpetuate racial segregation in the public schools. It claimed that recent changes in zoning were motivated solely by a desire to prevent overcrowding in any of the schools.

In May, 1955, the commissioner of education found that the transfers made by the board of education, allegedly to relieve overcrowding, did not meet the standard that the students selected for transfer should be those required to travel the least additional distance between their homes and schools. The board was therefore directed to redraw the boundary lines between the two schools involved in the complaint, so as to take into consideration the distances to be traveled by the children transferred from one school to the other. The new zoning requirements were to be reported to the commissioner by July 1, 1955.

The decision of the commissioner of education then turned to a discussion of the Englewood junior high schools. Testimony at the hearing had disclosed that over a period of years the local board had permitted the development of a junior high school in a Negro neighborhood with an enrollment of fewer than two hundred students, practically all of them Negroes. At the same time, junior high school students from the other four attendance areas in the city went to the main junior high school whose enrollment was predominantly white. The commissioner concluded that maintenance of a small separate junior high school in the Negro district could not be justified on any sound principle of school organization or administration. The board was directed to eliminate the segregated junior high school in the Negro neighborhood and to absorb the Negro students into the large "white" junior high school.[13]

The first complaint filed with the Massachusetts Commission Against Discrimination after it was given jurisdiction over unfair educational practices in 1956 was brought by a New Jersey complainant who charged that his daughter had been rejected by a Massachusetts junior college because she was Jewish. The facts offered in support of the complaint were as follows: The girl had written to the college, using her own name, which was recognizably Jewish. The college advised her that its "quota from New York and New Jersey" had been filled and did not send her an application blank. Three weeks later, however, when the girl's mother wrote to the college (using her maiden name, which was not distinctively Jewish), the college sent an application blank and made no reference to any geographical quota in its reply. The complainant argued that religious discrimination had been practiced against his daughter and that the reference to a geographical quota was solely to conceal the discriminatory practice.

When the college registrar was visited by a representative of the Commission Against Discrimination, the college produced its complete enrollment data. Lists were presented to show that a large number of Jewish students, between 20 and 25 percent, attended the college. It was explained that after June 1, which fell between the two letters of inquiry, vacancies appeared as a result of cancellations by accepted applicants who decided to attend other colleges. The college agreed to write to the complainant, furnishing a full explanation and tendering an application blank. The father accepted the college's explanation, but his daughter was no longer interested in a Massachusetts college since she had enrolled elsewhere.

[13] Walker v. Board of Educ. of the Borough of Englewood, Dep't of Education, Division Against Discrimination, State of New Jersey, No. M-1268, May 19, 1955, 1 RACE REL. L. REP. 255 (1956).

The commission advised the college to avoid the use of the word "quota" in correspondence relating to admissions and to send application blanks in reply to any inquiry, even when an accompanying letter advised the applicant that enrollment had been completed as of that date.[14]

In another case, the chairman of the Massachusetts Commission Against Discrimination asked the state attorney general whether in his opinion the commission was justified in prohibiting colleges from requesting photographs from applicants for admission. The attorney general ruled that such requests were unfair educational practices, notwithstanding the fact that the statute was silent on the specific question. He cited the provision prohibiting "any written or oral inquiry concerning the race, religion, color or national origin of a person seeking admission," and reasoned that the legislature intended to outlaw the request for "any form of information from which an educational institution might determine the race, creed, color or national origin of a student applicant." A photograph, he said, could help the college determine the race or color of the prospective student, and hence came within the prohibition. Significantly, he pointed out that if the language of the statute were ambiguous with respect to the specific question, the interpretation placed on such language by the administrative agency charged with enforcement of the statute would be considered "strong evidence of its meaning." [15]

There is a significant case involving educational institutions which should be discussed here even though it did not arise as a result of the action of a state commission against discrimination. In October, 1953, the Board of Trustees of the State University of New York adopted a resolution banning from the various State University campuses all social organizations which have a "direct or indirect affiliation or connection with any na-

[14] Case No. EDI-1-RC, 2 RACE REL. L. REP. 734, 738 (1956).
[15] Opinion dated December 20, 1957, 3 RACE REL L. REP. 797 (1957).

tional or other organization outside the particular" campus. The resolution, aimed at national fraternities and sororities, also provided that no social organization permitted on any of the campuses of the State University of New York might in policy or practice "operate under any rule which bars students on account of race, color, religion, national origin or other artificial criteria."

A group of national fraternities and sororities commenced an action in the federal district court to restrain the enforcement of the board's resolution. The plaintiffs claimed that the action of the board was an unconstitutional encroachment on their freedom of assembly, denied them equal protection of the laws, and impaired the obligation of existing contracts. Although the plaintiffs introduced evidence to show the value of national affiliations for fraternities and sororities and the absence of discriminatory clauses in their constitutions, the three-judge statutory court dismissed the plaintiffs' cause of action. Circuit Judge Augustus N. Hand, for a unanimous court, said:

We find little merit in the numerous contentions made by the plaintiffs as it is clear that the constitutionality of the action taken here cannot be questioned. A state may adopt such measures, including the outlawing of certain social organizations, as it deems necessary to its duty of supervision and control of its educational institutions. . . . Moreover, the incidental effect of any action or policy adopted upon individuals and organizations outside the university is not a basis for attack.[16]

The court held that an administrative body did not violate due process when, operating under a valid delegation of power from the legislature, it adopted a prospective resolution without giving notice and an opportunity for a hearing to those who might be affected by it. The court also held that the board of trustees acted within its supervisory powers when it decided that social organizations, other than those of a local character and thus completely subject to control by the university authorities,

[16] Webb v. State Univ. of N.Y., 125 F. Supp. 910, 912 (N.D.N.Y. 1954).

were detrimental to the educational objectives and environment at the various branches of the State University. The appeal to the United States Supreme Court was dismissed "for want of a substantial Federal question." [17]

The case is important because its reaffirms the plenary authority of the appropriate administrative board over the educational institutions which make up the state university system. It is also persuasive legal authority for the action of the numerous university boards which in recent years have adopted resolutions ousting fraternities and sororities which do not, by a specified date, abandon discriminatory charter provisions and admissions practices.

[17] Webb v. State Univ. of N.Y., 348 U.S. 867 (1954).

Chapter 9

FAIR HOUSING PRACTICES

Residential housing, despite its importance and its impact upon discrimination in other areas of community life, such as schools, recreational facilities, health and welfare service, and even employment opportunities, appears to be the last of the major areas of discrimination that the states have been willing to attack. Thus, although several states had laws on their books before 1949 prohibiting discrimination in public housing projects, no really effective remedy was available to the person victimized by such discrimination until Connecticut extended the jurisdiction of its Civil Rights Commission in 1949 to include complaints involving public housing.

It will be recalled that in that year Connecticut amended its public accommodations statute to broaden the duties of its Civil Rights Commission. The same amendment added the words "all public housing projects" to the list of place of public accommodation in which discrimination was prohibited.[1] This created a new civil right under state law and provided an administrative remedy. The civil right was the right of "all persons within the jurisdiction" of the state to full and equal consideration for public housing projects without discrimination based on race, creed, or color. The administrative remedy was the time-tested procedure established several years earlier as part of the FEP Law. In 1953 the legislature of Connecticut again amended its public accommodations statute. This time the specific listing of places

[1] Public Act of July 13, 1949.

included within the term "place of public accommodation" was dropped and general language substituted. The term was defined as

any establishment, including, but not limited to, public housing projects *and all other forms of publicly assisted housing,* which caters or offers its services or facilities or goods to the general public (italics added).[2]

Thus, publicly assisted housing, as well as public housing, was brought within the concept of "public accommodations" in Connecticut. The procedures section was strengthened in 1955 by authorizing the Civil Rights Commission to initiate complaints on its own motion, whenever it had "reason to believe" that the law was being violated.[3] By 1957 Colorado, Massachusetts, New Jersey, New York, Oregon, Rhode Island, and Washington had followed the lead of Connecticut in banning discrimination in public and publicly assisted housing and in giving their state commissions jurisdiction over complaints of discrimination in such housing.

In 1955, New York became the first state to ban discrimination in certain types of housing which receive mortgage repayment guarantees from the Federal Housing Administration, the Veterans Administration, or any other governmental agency. The types of housing covered were limited to multiple dwellings containing three or more apartments and to housing projects controlled by one person and containing ten or more contiguous units.[4] One year later the state Commission Against Discrimination was given jurisdiction over complaints charging violation of the 1955 law. California, Colorado, Connecticut, Massachusetts, New Jersey, Oregon, and Washington followed New York in extending their laws to so-called FHA and VA housing.

Finally, four states—Colorado, Connecticut, Massachusetts, and Oregon—passed laws in 1959 prohibiting discrimination in

[2] Public Act of October 1, 1953.
[3] CONN. GEN. STATS. § 3268d (Supp. 1955).   [4] Laws of 1955, ch. 341.

private housing, the first such laws enacted at the state level. (New York City in 1957 and Pittsburgh in 1958 had adopted local ordinances banning discrimination in private housing.) [5] Pennsylvania enacted a fair housing law in 1961 prohibiting discrimination in private housing.

The Colorado Fair Housing Act of 1959 [6] covers all housing, except "premises maintained by the owner or lessee as the household of his family with or without domestic servants and not more than four boarders or lodgers." Thus, the owner of a one-family house who lives in it with his family is free to dispose of his property by sale or lease without being subject to the ban on discriminatory transfers.

The act forbids owners of housing accommodations to refuse to transfer, rent, or lease them to any person because of race, creed, color, sex, national origin, or ancestry. It forbids owners to discriminate in the terms, conditions, or privileges pertaining to housing or in the furnishing of facilities or services. Finally, it bars owners from making any written or oral inquiry or record concerning the race, creed, color, sex, national origin, or ancestry of a person seeking to purchase, rent, or lease. Printing or publishing notices or advertisements relating to the transfer, rental, or lease of housing which indicates discriminatory preference or limitation is also banned. Banks and mortgage institutions are forbidden to make discriminatory inquiries about persons seeking financial assistance for housing, or to discriminate in the terms, conditions, or privileges of such assistance. Massachusetts (1960), New Jersey (1955), Pennsylvania (1961), and Washington (1957) have similar provisions covering banks and other lending institutions.

The Colorado act provides for a limited exception for religious or denominational institutions and organizations operating or controlling housing accommodations. Another exception permits the leasing of premises to members of one sex only, e.g.,

[5] N.Y.C. ADMINISTRATIVE CODE § W41-1.0 (1957); Pittsburgh ordinance, Dec. 8, 1958, supplementing Ordinance No. 237.

[6] Colo. Laws of 1959, ch. 148, § 5.

YMCA and YWCA rooms. Enforcement of the act is entrusted to the Colorado Anti-Discrimination Commission, established in 1955 to administer the state laws against discrimination in employment.

Massachusetts became the second state to enact legislation barring discrimination in private housing.[7] The law applies to "multiple dwellings" and to "contiguously located housing." Multiple dwellings are defined as dwellings occupied as the residences of three or more families living independently of each other. Contiguously located housing is defined as housing offered for sale, lease, or rental by a person who owns or controls ten or more housing accommodations located on land that is contiguous (exclusive of public streets). The measure therefore applies to apartment houses with three or more apartments, and to one- or two-family houses if they are part of a development consisting of at least ten housing units. The new housing law is enforced by the Massachusetts Commission Against Discrimination, together with the state's other laws prohibiting discrimination in employment; places of public accommodation, resort, or amusement; educational institutions; and public, publicly aided, and redevelopment housing.

Connecticut was the third state to enact legislation against discrimination in private housing.[8] The new law covers any housing accommodation offered for sale or rent that is one of five or more housing accommodations, all of which are located on a single parcel of land or on parcels of land that are contiguous (without regard to roads or streets) and owned or controlled by any one person.

The Connecticut law is narrower than the Massachusetts statute, for it covers multiple dwellings only when such dwellings consist of at least five apartments. It is broader as regards one- and two-family housing developments, since it applies to groups of as few as five such units. As in Colorado and Massachusetts,

[7] Mass. Acts of 1959, ch. 239.
[8] Conn. Laws of 1959, Substitute Bill No. 2484, amending CONN. GEN. STATS. § 53-35.

enforcement of the new housing statute is vested in the state agency—here, the Connecticut Civil Rights Commission—responsible for enforcing the state's other laws against discrimination.

Oregon was the fourth state to prohibit discrimination in the sale or occupancy of private housing.[9] The law enacted in this state, however, differed radically from the three earlier state laws.

The first of two new laws amended the Oregon Law Against Discrimination by adding to the definition section, the term "person engaged in the business of selling real property" and defining the term as including anyone selling, leasing, or renting real property as a "business enterprise" or "as an incident to his business enterprise." [10] The new law prohibits all persons "engaged in the business of selling real property" from refusing to sell or rent real property solely because of the race, color, religion, or national origin of the would-be purchaser or lessee. Persons engaged in the business of selling real property are also prohibited from making any other distinctions or restrictions because of race, color, religion, or national origin "in the price, terms, conditions or privileges" in connection with the sale, lease, or occupancy of real property. The publication or display of any advertisement indicating a preference, limitation, or discrimination based on race, color, religion, or national origin is prohibited. Real estate brokers and salesmen are expressly barred from accepting or retaining "a listing of real property . . . with an understanding that a purchaser [or lessee] may be discriminated against . . . solely because of race, color, religion or national origin." Finally, there are the conventional prohibitions against aiding, inciting, or coercing others to violate the law. However, the sale or rental of a house by an owner not in the business of selling or renting houses is not covered by the new

[9] Ore. Laws of 1959, ch. 584.
[10] Ore. Rev. Stats. § 659.033.

law, unless the owner retains a real estate broker, agent, or salesman to find a buyer or lessee or to negotiate the sale or lease. Since the new statute is an amendment to the existing law against discrimination, it is enforced by the existing administrative agency and procedures.

The second new law adds a ground for the revocation or suspension of the license of real estate brokers or salesmen, namely, violation of the Oregon Law Against Discrimination, as amended in 1959.[11]

On the basis of very limited experience in applying and interpreting the state and local fair housing measures enacted to date, it can be seen that a sound fair housing law, in addition to providing for administrative enforcement, should:

1. Prohibit discrimination or segregation in public, publicly aided, redevelopment, urban renewal, and private housing, as well as in housing financed by loans, the repayment of which is guaranteed by any governmental agency;

2. Cover vacant land and parcels of real property intended for the construction of homes or residences;

3. Prohibit oral or written inquiries or records of the race, religion, or ethnic origin of persons seeking to rent or purchase housing and the printing or circulation of advertisements which express any discrimination based on race, religion, or ethnic origin;

4. Reach the activities and listings of real estate brokers, salesmen, and agents who are in the business of selling and renting housing accommodations;

5. Reach the activities of banks, mortgage-lending and insurance companies, and other institutions which provide financial assistance to persons seeking to purchase or improve housing accommodations;

6. Make it unlawful for any person to plan or carry out a program of public or publicly assisted housing, urban redevelop-

[11] ORE. REV. STATS. § 696.300.

ment, or tenant relocation, in such a way as to create, within the program area or elsewhere, discrimination or segregation in housing.

This last provision would attempt to reach the type of discrimination that is sometimes effected by public planning and zoning boards which deliberately create areas of racial or ethnic concentration by determining where and when to locate public or low-cost housing, how to use vacant land, where to undertake slum clearance, where to offer relocation housing to those displaced by public projects, slum clearance, or rezoning and overall urban redevelopment. Prohibiting discrimination in the planning stage would, at least, give a state commission justification for insisting upon an early examination of housing programs with an eye to determining what effect they are likely to have on racial and ethnic concentrations in the total community and for objecting to those which may tend to increase segregation in housing.

An additional sanction available for the enforcement of fair housing laws would be a provision authorizing the appropriate state or local authority responsible for granting licenses to real estate brokers, salesmen, and agents to suspend or revoke the license of any person found, after hearing, to have violated the state law against discrimination. This would be a serious deterrent to discrimination for those in the business of selling and renting real property.

Court Decisions on Fair Housing Laws

While there have been relatively few court challenges to the constitutionality of fair employment practices laws and none to the constitutionality of the educational practices acts or the modern public accommodations statutes, the fair housing measures were promptly challenged. Although the United States Supreme Court has not yet spoken, there are several significant decisions by state courts, including one by the highest court of New Jersey, involving the constitutionality of fair housing laws.

The first case to consider the constitutionality of a fair housing law arose in New York as a consequence of a complaint filed with the State Commission Against Discrimination by a Negro, who charged the Pelham Hall Apartments in New Rochelle, New York, with refusing to lease him an apartment because of his race. The commission investigated the complaint, found probable cause to credit the charges, and sought to adjust the matter through conference, conciliation, and persuasion. When these efforts failed, a public hearing was held. The respondent did not deny the discrimination, but challenged the constitutionality of the statute and argued that its housing accommodations were not within the definition of publicly assisted housing because the commitment to secure the mortgage loan was made by the Federal Housing Administration one day before the effective date of the law barring discrimination in FHA or VA housing. The commission rejected the constitutional attack on the sound theory that it must assume the validity of the law under which it operates. Constitutionality of the statute is appropriately a matter for the courts, not the commission, although this issue should be raised by a respondent in the administrative proceeding if it intends to argue constitutionality in the courts. The commission also rejected the defense that the apartment was not covered by the law, on the ground that the commitment to insure the mortgage loan was not equivalent to the issuance of the loan, which occurred after the effective date of the statute. A cease and desist order was thereupon issued directing the Pelham Hall Apartments to end its discriminatory practice.

Eventually, the commission commenced an action in the New York Supreme Court, County of Westchester, for an order enforcing its determination. The respondent again raised the statutory and constitutional defenses. Justice Samuel W. Eager held that the 1955 amendment, which extended the New York Law Against Discrimination to FHA and VA housing, covered the respondent's apartment house.[12] The court pointed out that although the commitment for FHA mortgage insurance was made before the effective date of the amendment, the actual financing and its insurance by the federal housing agency occurred after that date.

Pelham Hall argued that legislation banning discrimination in housing violated the constitutionally protected right of property owners to choose the persons to whom their property should be sold or leased.

Justice Eager started his discussion of the constitutional issue with the following statement:

The private ownership of private property, free of unreasonable restriction upon the control thereof, is truly a part of our way of life, but, on the other hand, we, as a people do hold firmly to the philosophy that all men are created equal. Indeed, discrimination against any individual here on account of race, color or religion is antagonistic to fundamental tenets of our form of government and of the God in whom we place our trust.[13]

He added that in cases of conflict between the rights of private property owners and the power of the state to regulate its use and enjoyment in the interest of the public welfare, the power of the state, when reasonably exercised, is supreme. In this connection, the court stated that legislation against racial or religious discrimination constitutes an exercise of the state's police power to protect the welfare, health, and peace of the people. It is firmly settled that private property rights are subject to the exercise of the police power in the interest of the public welfare. In determining what legislation the public welfare requires, broad discretion resides in the legislature. Enactments based on the state's police power could be stricken only if they were clearly arbi-

---

[12] Matter of N.Y. State Comm'n Against Discrimination v. Pelham Hall Apartments, 10 Misc. 2d 334, 170 N.Y.S.2d 750 (1958).

[13] 170 N.Y.S.2d at 757.

trary, discriminatory, and without any reasonable basis. The court held that the New York Law Against Discrimination in publicly assisted housing was not the type of statute that the court would be justified in striking down as unconstitutional. It concluded, therefore, that the legislature had acted within the bounds of the police power in enacting measures against racial and religious discrimination in publicly assisted housing.

One specific argument made by Pelham Hall against the constitutionality of the statute in question was that the law violated the equal protection clause of the Fourteenth Amendment because it was limited to publicly assisted housing receiving assistance after July 1, 1955. Pelham Hall argued that owners of housing covered by the law were discriminated against in favor of owners of other housing.

The court disposed of this argument by stating that it was settled law that the state may, without denying equal protection, resort to classification for purposes of legislation so long as the classification "rests upon some reasonable basis, bearing in mind the subject matter and the object of the legislation." In determining whether there was a reasonable basis for limiting the coverage of the law against housing discrimination to specific types of housing, the court "may take into consideration the fact that civil rights and anti-discrimination legislation in this state, and on the federal basis for that matter, has been and is a step-by-step proposition."

A proceeding step-by-step by legislative bodies to eliminate the practice of racial discrimination in affairs closely connected with the lives of our citizens is not only a reasonable, but in view of changing times and circumstances, a required method of procedure in the interest of public welfare.[14]

Hence, the legislature was authorized to proceed as it did in imposing a ban on discrimination in housing "by gradual steps, beginning with provisions applicable to various classes of pub-

[14] *Id*. at 760.

licly owned and managed housing and over a period of time extending the provisions to specified classes of private housing projects inaugurated or carried out with governmental assistance."

Similarly, the legislature was within its rights when it limited the applicability of the law to housing receiving public assistance after July 1, 1955, the date when the particular law went into effect. This did not constitute a discrimination against housing which had received such assistance previously. The Constitution did not, the court added, forbid statutes and statutory changes to have a beginning and thus to differentiate between the rights prior and subsequent to their enactment.

In conclusion, the court stated that "the advisability and wisdom of the statutory provisions against practice of discrimination in publicly assisted housing accommodations was a legislative problem."

The state had the right to leave abstention from racial or religious discrimination in such housing accommodations to the conscience of the individuals. On the other hand, it had the right "to put its authority behind one of the cherished aims of American feeling by forbidding indulgence in racial or religious prejudice" in such accommodations. . . . The Legislature having acted within the limits of its power, the laws are valid.[15]

Hence, the statute was constitutional and SCAD's application to enforce its order against the Pelham Hall Apartments was granted. Although the respondent originally announced its intention to appeal, no appeal was taken from the supreme court decision.

The highest court of New Jersey likewise upheld the constitutionality of that state's law against discrimination in FHA and VA housing. The case arose in the following way: Three Negroes who were rejected as would-be purchasers of homes built by Levitt & Sons, in Levittown, New Jersey, and by Green Fields

[15] *Id.* at 761.

Farm filed complaints with the New Jersey Division Against Discrimination, charging violation of the Law Against Discrimination which, as we have seen, bans discrimination in "publicly-assisted housing accommodations." After the DAD found probable cause to credit charges of discrimination (which had been admitted publicly), efforts to settle the matter by persuasion and conciliation failed. Levitt and Green Fields thereupon brought an action for an injunction to restrain the DAD from proceeding further with the matter on the grounds that it had no jurisdiction over their housing projects and that the Law Against Discrimination was unconstitutional.

The appellate division dismissed the petitions of Levitt and Green Fields, upholding the constitutionality of the statute and the jurisdiction of DAD.[16] An appeal was taken to the Supreme Court of New Jersey, which unanimously affirmed the appellate division and remanded the matter to the Division Against Discrimination for final disposition.[17]

The New Jersey Supreme Court described in detail the extensive federal assistance received by the housing projects to enable them to advertise that FHA financing was available for their purchasers. The court held that the projects came within the term "publicly-assisted housing accommodations" as used in the statute giving the Division Against Discrimination jurisdiction over complaints. The court cited "the clear and positive policy of our State against discrimination as embodied in the New Jersey Constitution, Article I, paragraph 5. Effectuation of that mandate calls for liberal interpretation of any legislative enactment designed to implement it."

Although the petitioners did not raise constitutional objections to the statute on the ground that it violated due process of law, the court said that "freedom with regard to property is not

[16] Levitt v. Division Against Discrimination, 56 N.J. Super. 542, 153 A.2d 700 (1959).
[17] Levitt v. Division Against Discrimination, 31 N.J. 514, 158 A.2d 177 (1960).

inviolable; it is subject to the reasonable exercise of the legislature's police power." The court then rejected the argument that by including only publicly assisted housing, the Law Against Discrimination created an unreasonable and arbitrary classification which violated the Fourteenth Amendment. The court found that, "considering the circumstances which led to the enactment of the statute," it presented no constitutional difficulties with respect to the types of housing selected for coverage. The classification was held reasonable.

Finally, the court held that the prohibition against discrimination in publicly assisted housing did not invade a field of regulation pre-empted by Congress, nor did such prohibition conflict with the supremacy clause of the federal Constitution.

In view of these conclusions, the housing projects of Levitt & Sons and Green Fields Farm were held subject to the Law Against Discrimination, and the Division Against Discrimination had jurisdiction to entertain complaints charging violations of that law. The matter was remanded to the DAD for final disposition. The United States Supreme Court dismissed the appeal "for want of a substantial federal question." [18]

Levitt and Green Fields had signed a stipulation agreeing to cease and desist from discriminating in the sale of their houses if the New Jersey Supreme Court dismissed their petition. That stipulation, among other things, required the developers to sign contracts for homes with the Negro complainants if they still wished to purchase homes in the developments. In addition, the cease and desist agreement was required to be posted where it could be seen by all employees and by would-be purchasers of houses.

A third state court decision deserves mention here.[19] In *Ming*

[18] Levitt v. Division Against Discrimination, 363 U.S. 418 (1960).

[19] We have deliberately omitted any discussion of *O'Meara v. Washington State Bd. Against Discrimination*, No. 535996 (King Co., Wash. Super. Ct., July 31, 1959), because Judge Hodson's decision in that case, holding the Washington housing law unconstitutional, is predicated upon an unsound theory and should be reversed on appeal. See Saks & Rabkin, *Racial and Re-*

v. Horgan, the superior court in Sacramento, California, held that racial discrimination in FHA-insured housing was prohibited, even in the absence of a state statute.[20] The plaintiff in that action charged that he was denied an opportunity to purchase a new home in "one after another of FHA- and GI-insured subdivisions in the Sacramento area," and that such exclusion by the various developers, builders, real estate agents, and others acting in concert with them, was predicated solely upon the fact that he was a Negro. He brought an action for declaratory relief, for damages, and for an injunction.

The evidence at the trial established that the experience of the plaintiff was typical of that suffered by other qualified Negro applicants for new housing located in various developments which advertised that they had FHA or VA "commitments" for terms, conditions, financing, and standards, and that there appeared to be a concert of action among the various contributing segments of the home-building industry to exclude Negroes from original sales of "tract homes in the area." It was clear that there was no economic or financial reason to deny eligibility to Negro families as such.

The defendants contended that as private owners, building and real estate dealers, they have "a perfect right to sell to whomever they chose; that they are at liberty to decline to sell to any person they choose [and] that this is a fundamental right enjoyed by all citizens." Much of the testimony at the trial described the various techniques used by the real estate industry to discourage Negro purchasers from acquiring new homes in areas built for white occupancy. All of the defendants denied any "personal desire" to reject any Negro home-seeker, but contended that responsibility, in each case, to provide homes for minority group occupancy, rested with "the other fellow."

---

ligious Discrimination in Housing—A Report on Legal Progress, 45 Iowa L. Rev. 488, 519–21 (1960).

[20] Ming v. Horgan, 3 Race Rel. L. Rep. 693 (Sacramento Co., Cal. Super. Ct. 1958).

In establishing the terms and conditions for FHA and VA financing, the court said, the federal agencies undertook to approve plans, layouts, utility services, construction standards, and "ultimately mortgage guarantees of loans," in order to encourage an increase in the supply of housing available "to all citizens who can meet minimum requirements of financial responsibility."

The court reasoned that when the federal government entered the field of housing to stimulate construction and make more and better homes available, it was prohibited by "the fundamental law" from differentiating between races, and whether the statute

expresses that limitation in so many words or not, those who operate under that law and seek and gain the advantage it confers are as much bound thereby as the administrative agencies of the government which have functions to perform in connection therewith. Congress must have intended the supply of housing for all citizens, not just Caucasians—and on an equal, not a segregated basis.[21]

Real Estate Offices as Places of Public Accommodation

One other recent development deserves mention in connection with fair housing laws. In 1956, the Connecticut Commission on Civil Rights, responding to an inquiry from the counsel for the New Haven Real Estate Board, ruled that it regarded a real estate agent as operating an establishment which offers its services to the general public and, hence, a place of public accommodation subject to the Law Against Discrimination. Real estate agents and their employees, by that interpretation, were prohibited from refusing their services to any person because of race, creed, or

---

[21] *Id.* at 699. But compare Dorsey v. Stuyvesant Town Corp., 299 N.Y. 512 (1949), *cert. denied,* 339 U.S. 981 (1950), in which the New York Court of Appeals held in a four-to-three decision that the use of eminent domain to condemn property necessary for the housing project and tax exemption for an extended period of years did not constitute such "state action" as would serve to bring the housing project within the equal protection clause of the Fourteenth Amendment. The *Stuyvesant Town* case would probably be decided differently now on the authority of Pennsylvania v. Board of Directors of City Trusts of Philadelphia, 353 U.S. 230 (1957).

color. Subsequently, the attorneys general of California, Massachusetts, and Oregon also ruled that real estate offices were places of public accommodation under their civil rights laws. These interpretations have not been tested in any court. However, they should survive judicial scrutiny if the modern public accommodations statutes are accepted by the courts as remedial legislation to be liberally construed to effectuate the public policy of the state that there be no discrimination on the basis of race, color, or religion with respect to facilities, services, and goods offered to the general public.

CONCLUSION

Chapter 10

STAND OUT OF MY SUNSHINE

In the six years immediately following *Brown v. Topeka,* President Eisenhower, by his statements and by the things he left unsaid, reflected the views and sentiments of large sections of the American people who were inclined to question the efficacy of law as an instrument of social control and advancement in the field of race relations. Persons with this point of view tended to condemn both those who resorted to legal measures to vindicate and implement the desegregation decision and those who resorted to force, demagoguery, and knavery to defeat that decision. To Eisenhower, both parties were "extremists." He urged "moderation," waiting for an inner change, a change within the heart that would bear fruit in peaceful and constructive actions—on the eve of the centenary of the Civil War.

At a news conference in 1959 Eisenhower declared racial segregation morally wrong when it stands in the way of equality of opportunity in *economic* and *political* fields. By failing to mention, in the context, equality of opportunity in *education,* the statement implied that desegregation in the schools was not a moral imperative. He took this line in his solemn Christmas message of 1960, in which he said:

Too often we discern an apathy towards violations of laws and standards of public and private integrity. When, through bitter prejudice and because of differences in skin pigmentation, individuals cannot enjoy equality of political and economic opportunity we see another of these imperfections, one that is equally plain to those living beyond our borders.

The omission of any reference to equality of educational opportunity could not but suggest that "he who is silent is understood to consent."

In the same Christmas message Eisenhower again made the point that law will be ineffective if it is more advanced than morals. On this occasion he stated the argument as follows:

Though we boast that ours is a government of laws, completeness in this work [of living by our national ideals] cannot be achieved by laws alone, necessary though these be. Law, to be truly effective, must command the respect and earnest support of public opinion, both generally and locally. And each of us helps form public opinion.[1]

It is true, of course, that each American in some measure "helps form public opinion," but, obviously, the power of the President to do this is immeasurably greater than that of any other citizen or official. From the record it is clear that Eisenhower did *not* help form a public opinion to support the school desegregation decision, and by his failure to help the forces of law, he gave a measure of respectability to those who believe that the Supreme Court demanded too much too soon. Eisenhower not only failed to support *Brown v. Topeka;* he went beyond moral and legal neutrality by arguing, time and again, that the law must fail when it is in advance of morals.[2] This line of thought did not state but strongly intimated that the Supreme Court had gone too far or had moved too fast and that its decree was, therefore, morally insupportable.

Eisenhower also expressed a theory of federal-state relations that was reminiscent of the views of Andrew Johnson. His statements suggested that perhaps the "Southern manifesto," issued in 1956 by fifteen United States Senators and eighty-one members of the House of Representatives,[3] was not altogether unwarranted

[1] Text of message in N.Y. Times, Dec. 24, 1960, p. 13.
[2] See transcripts of news conferences, as reported on the immediately following days in the N.Y. Times of Sept. 4, 1956; Sept. 3, 1957; also Nov. 23, 1954; March 14, Aug. 18, Sept. 11, 1956; July 17 and Oct. 3, 1957; July 3, Aug. 6, Aug. 20, 1958; Jan. 4, Jan. 21, May 13, July 8, 1959.
[3] Issued March 12, 1956. The exceptions were Senators Lyndon Johnson of

when it called the Supreme Court decision "a clear abuse of judicial power" and an encroachment upon states' rights, and when it blamed the Court for "destroying the amicable relations between the white and Negro races."

Let us examine some of these propositions. We shall find—to borrow a phrase from T. S. Eliot—that "their words have often a network of tentacular roots reaching down to the deepest terrors and desires." [4]

Opposition to *Brown v. Topeka* often takes the form of an assertion that racial adjustments must be left to voluntary conduct. They must flow from the heart or conviction. Any attempt to coerce adjustments in the direction of wider equality, it is said, is bound to fail.

Often, however, a distinction is made between equality in some relations and equality in other relations. President Eisenhower, as we have noted, believed that the law may be used to achieve for the Negro political and economic equality, but he refused to assert that the law may also be used to achieve desegregation in the schools—although if the question concerned "separate but equal" schools, it may be assumed that he would have said that the law may be used to compel the states to provide "equal" schools for the Negro race.

In his widely reprinted public letter to the President, [5] Carleton Putnam made the following distinction:

I would emphatically support improvement of education in Negro schools, if and where it is inferior. Equality of opportunity and equality before the law, when not strained to cover other situations, are

Texas, Estes Kefauver and Albert Gore of Tennessee, and Speaker Sam Rayburn of Texas. COLLIER'S ENCYCLOPEDIA YEARBOOK COVERING THE YEAR 1956, at 507 (1957).
[4] Quoted in MASON, HUMANISM AND POETRY IN THE EARLY TUDOR PERIOD 264 (1959).
[5] This letter was printed in many newspapers as a paid advertisement. See, *e.g.,* N.Y. Times, Jan. 5, 1959, p. 19. The Putnam Letter Committee solicited funds to pay for the insertion of the letter especially in Northern publications.

acceptable ideals because they provide the chance to earn and to progress—and consequently should be enforced by legal fiat as far as is humanly possible. But equality of association, which desegregation in Southern schools involves, pre-supposes a status which in the South the average Negro has not earned. To force it upon the Southern white will, I think, meet with as much opposition as the prohibition amendment encountered in the wet states.

Most white Southerners would not even concede that equality of economic and political opportunity may be implemented by legal process. The Southern states have not adopted fair employment practices acts, and they have consistently opposed any bill in Congress that would outlaw racial discrimination in employment. The votes in Congress on the Civil Rights Acts of 1957 and 1960—acts that have a bearing on the right of suffrage—clearly showed Southern opposition to legal guarantees of political equality. When it comes to equality of educational opportunity, the record of cases in the courts before 1954 shows that the South had interpreted the "separate but equal" doctrine as permission to deny to the Negro the educational equality that the Constitution commands.[6]

It is difficult to see by virtue of what principle it is possible to distinguish legal coercion in favor of economic and political equality from legal coercion in favor of educational equality, for their interdependence is obvious. In the absence of educational equality, it is hard to see how the Negro can hope to achieve equality in economic and political life. "Today," as Chief Justice Warren said for the unanimous Court,

education is perhaps the most important function of state and local governments. Compulsory school attendance laws and the great expenditures for education both demonstrate our recogniton of the importance of education to our democratic society. It is required in the performance of our most basic public responsibilities, even service

[6] See, *e.g.*, the teachers' salary cases typified by Alston v. School Bd. of Norfolk, 112 F.2d 992 (4th Cir. 1940), *cert. denied*, 311 U.S. 693 (1940). See also Sweatt v. Painter, 339 U.S. 629 (1950); McLaurin v. Oklahoma State Regents, 339 U.S. 637 (1950).

in the armed forces. It is the very foundation of good citizenship. Today it is a principal instrument in awakening the child to cultural values, in preparing him for later professional training, and in helping him to adjust normally to his environment. In these days, it is doubtful that any child may reasonably be expected to succeed in life if he is denied the opportunity to an education. Such an opportunity, where the state has undertaken to provide it, is a right which must be made available to all on equal terms.[7]

Segregation, said the Court, denotes the inferiority of the Negro race, and a sense of inferiority affects the motivation to learn, retards the development of the Negro children, and deprives them of benefits they would receive in a nonsegregated school.

This deprivation must carry over to later economic and political opportunities.

The argument that racial equality must be left to voluntary conduct, exempt from legal sanctions, has some respectable backing. Hegel maintained that a constitution cannot be thought out overnight, for it is "the work of centuries, the idea and the consciousness of what is rational, in so far as it is developed in a people." It is, said Hegel,

nothing but a modern folly to try to alter a corrupt moral organization by altering its political constitution and code of laws without changing the religion [or moral beliefs]—*to make a revolution without having made a reformation,* to suppose that a political constitution opposed to the old religion [or morals] could live in peace and harmony with it and its sanctities, and that stability could be procured for the laws by external guarantees.[8]

This is not the place for a detailed philosophical discussion of the mystic view of history and of the past that is involved in this position; or of the absolutization of whatever *is* and of the subjection of the moral judgment to it, with the consequence that *factuality* becomes the supreme judge of the *normative*—that facts become the norm by which morality and validity are judged.

[7] Brown v. Topeka, 347 U.S. 483 (1954).
[8] HEGEL, SELECTIONS (Lowenberg ed. 1929) 276. Italics added.

We shall make only those points that we consider relevant and consequential for our present discussion.

The Supreme Court did not "impose" its law. It "discovered" the law in the nature of American society and history, in the American consensus. The "revolution" in American constitutional law did not precede but followed a social and moral "reformation." In 1954 racial segregation by law existed in only one third of the states, with a population of approximately 50 million people—less than a third of the total population. The nineteen states that had civil rights acts in 1954 had a population almost twice as large, nearly one hundred million people. By 1960 five more states had adopted civil rights acts; and the nine remaining states that had, in 1960, no civil rights acts—nor, of course, segregation statutes—had a population of only six million people. In characteristically democratic ways, the American people, outside of the South and the border states, had shown that they were opposed to racial segregation—at least to racial segregation enforced by law.

On the federal level—apart from Congress, which was paralyzed by filibustering and other tactics used by Southerners—the government tried to take a stand against racial segregation. President Truman announced a pro-integration policy for the armed forces in 1948. The plan was to end all segregation by 1954. The Korean war hastened the process, so that the armed forces were integrated before *Brown v. Topeka*.[9] In the District of Columbia, as we have seen, following a Supreme Court decision in 1953 rapid progress was made in the establishment of equality of civil rights in places of public accommodation. Starting in 1951, with the formation of the Committee on Government Contract Compliance—succeeded in 1953 by the President's Committee on

[9] PRESIDENT'S COMM. ON EQUALITY OF TREATMENT AND OPPORTUNITY IN THE ARMED FORCES, FREEDOM TO SERVE (1950). See also GREENBERG, RACE RELATIONS AND AMERICAN LAW ch. 11 (1959); NELSON, THE INTEGRATION OF THE NEGRO INTO THE U.S. NAVY (1951); Bogart, *The Army and Its Negro Soldiers*, The Reporter, Dec. 30, 1954; Spore & Cocklin, *Our Negro Soldiers*, The Reporter, Jan. 22, 1952.

Government Contracts—the policy of the federal government was to prohibit discrimination on the part of government contractors and their subcontractors.[10]

One may safely say, then, that at the time the Court announced its unanimous decision in *Brown v. Topeka,* outside of the states where school segregation was enforced by state laws, the official polices of the federal government, and of the governments of states in which some two thirds of the American people lived, were against racial segregation or other forms of discrimination.

The letter of Carleton Putnam drew an analogy between opposition to school desegregation and opposition to the Prohibition Amendment, and Senator Fulbright, when he told the Senate that "legislation to regulate men's mores is doomed to failure," [11] also referred to the American experience with prohibition as a precedent. But the analogy disregards crucial differences. At the time when the states were taking action on the Eighteenth Amendment, saloons were illegal in approximately 90 percent of the area of the nation and nearly two thirds of the population were living in dry territory. When the amendment was ratified, thirty of the forty-eight states had prohibition statutes or constitutional amendments. By 1933, when prohibition was repealed, the overwhelming majority of the people had changed their position. The reasons for this reversal of public opinion are many but not relevant here, except that one point may be made: neither Congress nor the states provided adequate machinery for the enforcement of prohibition, and the local police forces "were either indifferent to the prohibition law or became the allies and protectors of the [racketeering liquor] industry." [12]

With respect to *Brown v. Topeka,* on the other hand, the opposition is not national but regional. The American people in general have not found the experiment with equality unsatisfac-

[10] Pasley, *The Non-Discrimination Clause in Government Contracts,* 43 VA. L. REV. 837 (1957).

[11] 106 CONG. REC. 7185 (daily ed. April 8, 1960).

[12] Warburton, *Prohibition,* in 12 ENCYC. SOC. SCI. 499 (1933).

tory. There is no national movement for the repeal of the Four-teenth Amendment. Even in the Deep South—witness Little Rock and St. Louis—school desegregation would have a good chance of success if the demagogic politicians would give the citizens an opportunity to try it. But the rabble-rousing politicians would sooner see their states become a Congolese-like battleground, where law and order were subverted and neighbor lifted sword against neighbor, than let school desegregation be tried even at a snail's pace.

It is odd, to say the least, to hear Southerners argue in favor of "voluntarism." For the record is clear that the people in the South have not practiced voluntarism in race relations. They have always used the full power of the law to compel all persons, with-out regard to their own thoughts or feelings, to practice racial segregation. They have not left the matter of race relations to education, discussion, and similar methods that are used to reach the mind or heart of a person. They have relied on the power of the law to achieve their ends.

Let us consider an incident that may be taken as typifying the Southern record of action.

In 1855, through the efforts of John G. Fee, a Kentucky ab-olitionist minister who was disinherited by his slave-holding par-ents for his antislavery views, Berea College was founded as a coeducational, nonsectarian institution of practical and liberal education. Work was suspended in 1859 and resumed in 1865. Berea was located in Kentucky for the benefit mainly of the peo-ple of the mountains of the eastern part of the state, and was the only college in Kentucky that admitted both white and Negro students.

In 1904 Berea College had an enrollment of 174 Negro and 753 white students. In that year the Kentucky legislature enacted a statute that made it unlawful to maintain any college or school "where persons of the white and Negro races are both received as pupils for instruction." The penalty for maintaining such a college or school was a fine of $1,000, and an additional fine of $500 for each day the institution was operated after conviction. Any white or Negro student attending such school was subject to a fine of $50 for each day he attended. The law provided that a college could operate a branch for the other race "in a different locality, not less than twenty-five miles distant."

The officers and trustees of Berea College—the only institution affected by the law—protested, but to no avail. When the college opened for the academic year 1904–1905, the Negroes were not admitted but placed by the administration in Negro colleges. The white students addressed to the Negro students the following document [13] that deserves to be widely known:

Friends and Fellow-Students: As we meet for the first time under new conditions to enjoy the great privileges of Berea College, we think at once of you who are now deprived of these privileges. Our sense of justice shows us that others have the same rights as ourselves, and the teaching of Christ leads us to "remember them that are in bonds as bound with them."

We realize that you are excluded from the class rooms of Berea College, which we so highly prize, by no fault of your own, and that this hardship is a part of a long line of deprivations under which you live. Because you were born in a race long oppressed and largely untaught and undeveloped, heartless people feel more free to do you wrong, and thoughtless people meet your attempts at self-improvement with indifference or scorn. Even good people sometimes fear to recognize your worth, or take your part in a neighborly way because of the violences and prejudices around us.

We are glad that we have known you, or known about you, and that we know you are rising above all discouragements, and showing a capacity and a character that give promise for your people. . . . And you will always have our friendship, and the friendship of the best people throughout the world. We hope never to be afraid or ashamed to show our approval of any colored person who has the character and worth of most of the colored students of Berea. We are glad that the college is providing funds to assist you in continuing

[13] STEPHENSON, RACE RELATIONS IN AMERICAN LAW 156–57 (1910).

your education, and we are sure the institution will find ways in which to do its full duty by the colored race.

Berea challenged the constitutionality of the statute, but the United States Supreme Court [14] upheld the act on the narrow ground that the college was a Kentucky corporation, and the state had the reserved power to amend, alter, or repeal corporate charters. The first Justice Harlan wrote a strong dissenting opinion. He argued, first, that the statute was not directed at corporations: the legislature sought to prohibit the teaching of the two races in the same college, no matter whether the college was conducted by a corporation or by an individual. "It was the teaching of pupils of the two races *together,* or in the same school, no matter by whom or under whose authority, which the legislature sought to prevent. The manifest purpose was to prevent the association of white and colored persons in the same school."

Harlan then said that the Court should "directly meet and decide the broad question presented by the statute," namely, whether the legislature may make it a crime for a private college to give instruction to both white and Negro students. His opinion was that the statute was an arbitrary invasion of the rights of liberty and property guaranteed by the Fourteenth Amendment. The following passage from Harlan's opinion was especially significant:

If pupils, of whatever race,—certainly, if they be citizens,—choose, with the consent of their parents, or voluntarily, to sit together in a private institution of learning while receiving instruction which is not in its nature harmful or dangerous to the public, no government, whether Federal or state, can legally forbid their coming together, or being together temporarily, for such an innocent purpose. If the commonwealth of Kentucky can make it a crime to teach white and colored children together at the same time, in a private institution of learning, it is difficult to perceive why it may not forbid the assembling of white and colored children in the same Sabbath school, for the purpose of being instructed in the Word of God, although such teach-

[14] Berea College v. Kentucky, 211 U.S. 45 (1908).

ing may be done under the authority of the church to which the school is attached as well as with the consent of the parents of the children. So, if the state court be right, white and colored children may even be forbidden to sit together in a house of worship or at a communion table in the same Christian church. In the cases supposed there would be the same association of white and colored persons as would occur when pupils of the two races sit together in a private institution of learning for the purpose of receiving instruction in purely secular matters. Will it be said that the cases supposed and the case here in hand are different, in that no government, in this country, can lay unholy hands on the religious faith of the people? The answer to this suggestion is that, in the eye of the law, the right to enjoy one's religious belief, unmolested by any human power, is no more sacred nor more fully or distinctly recognized than is the right to impart and receive instruction not harmful to the public. The denial of either right would be an infringement of the liberty inherent in the freedom secured by the fundamental law. Again, if the views of the highest court of Kentucky be sound, that commonwealth may, without infringing the Constitution of the United States, forbid the association in the same private school of pupils of the Anglo-Saxon and Latin races respectively, or pupils of the Christian and Jewish faiths, respectively. Have we become so inoculated with prejudice of race that an American government, professedly based on the principles of freedom, and charged with the protection of all citizens alike, can make distinction between such citizens in the matter of their voluntary meeting for innocent purposes, simply because of their respective races? Further, if the lower court be right, then a state may make it a crime for white and colored persons to frequent the same market places at the same time, or appear in an assemblage of citizens convened to consider questions of a public or political nature, in which all citizens, without regard to race, are equally interested. Many other illustrations might be given to show the mischievous, not to say cruel, character of the statute in question, and how inconsistent such legislation is with the great principle of the equality of citizens before the law.

The racism of the South left little to the free will of the citizens. Segregation was required by law at circuses and tent shows; at theaters and public halls; in parks, playgrounds, and at beaches; at race tracks; in billiard and pool rooms. Members of the two races were prohibited from forming fraternal benefit associations together. A Negro minister could not perform the marriage ceremony for a white couple.[15] There were scores of laws that made it *impossible* for persons to use their own judgment as to whether to associate or not associate with members of the other race.

But all this is conveniently forgotten when a court issues a desegregation decree or when Congress considers a civil rights law, for then the cry is heard that Americans are losing their liberty, that the government is invading the private lives of its citizens. Were the Black Codes and the Jim Crow laws attempts at implementing the Declaration of Independence?

What happened in 1904 at Berea College was repeated in 1960 at the University of Cape Town in the Union of South Africa. Until then the university accepted any properly qualified student regardless of color, and five hundred nonwhite students were enrolled. Then the Nationalist government passed a bill to prohibit nonwhite students from attending. The faculty and the university council protested furiously, but to no avail. Following is a report by Dr. Cornelis de Kiewiet, president of the University of Rochester, of a ceremony at the University of Cape Town to mark the end of voluntarism and liberty:

We gathered together in academic robes on the sunlit campus. . . . At the head of the procession a slim co-ed bore the flaming torch of academic freedom. Behind her two flaming redheads, twins, carried the university standards. We followed into the auditorium, with every seat and square foot of standing room packed.

The torch burned while I spoke. My address was the T. B. Davie memorial lecture in honor of the vice chancellor of the university who almost literally killed himself fighting against the closing of his university to non-whites.

After the lecture, the audience sat in deepest silence while the torch of academic liberty was extinguished. Solemnly the chancellor, the vice chancellor, and the red-robed professors marched to the library.

[15] Konvitz, The Constitution and Civil Rights 134–35 (1947).

There half a dozen of us stood like an honor guard at a funeral before a bronze tablet let into the library wall.

In Latin is carried the inscription, "This bronze memorial dedicated by the chancellor records the taking away of our academic freedom which departed in the year 1960 and returned in the year _____." There was an empty space for the year of resurrection.

Down the steps and past the tablet slowly moved an entire unsmiling academic community.[16]

The memorial of the white students at Berea College also in effect marked the end of academic freedom in 1904, a freedom that was restored, by a decree of the Supreme Court, a half century later.

Another example of Southern dedication to the philosophy of voluntarism and to freedom of association—which are at the heart of Carleton Putnam's protest against the desegregation decree—may be seen in the all-out attack on the National Association for the Advancement of Colored People (N.A.A.C.P.) in some of the Southern states.[17] In a society in which citizens and public officials are zealously devoted to the maximization of personal freedom, people have the right to join associations for educational, charitable, mutual aid, civil liberties, and other purposes. But Southern practices contradict Southern protestations. Let us examine briefly several Supreme Court decisions in which the Southern practice stands out in total nakedness.

In *N.A.A.C.P. v. Alabama*,[18] decided in 1958, the attorney general of Alabama sought an injunction in the state courts to oust the association from the state. He ordered the association to produce records and papers, including names and addresses of all of the association's members and agents in the state. The association produced all the records except the membership lists. As to those lists, the association contended that the state could not

[16] Ithaca Journal, Sept. 6, 1960.
[17] AMERICAN JEWISH CONGRESS, ASSAULT UPON FREEDOM OF ASSOCIATION (1957); also *Freedom of Association*, 4 RACE REL. L. REV. 207 (1959).
[18] N.A.A.C.P. v. Alabama, 357 U.S. 449 (1958).

compel disclosure without violation of freedom of association.

Unanimously reversing the state courts that had upheld the action of the attorney general of Alabama, the United States Supreme Court, in an opinion by Justice Harlan, said that the association had the right to protect its membership lists on behalf of the right of the members to associate freely with others in the pursuit of their private interests. This right of the members—citizens of the state of Alabama—is protected by the constitutional liberty to engage in association for the advancement of beliefs and ideas pertaining to political, economic, religious, or cultural matters. The attorney general's order to produce the membership lists, supported by the coercive power of the state courts, must be regarded, said Justice Harlan,

as entailing the likelihood of a substantial restraint upon the exercise by petitioner's members of their right to freedom of association. Petitioner has made an uncontroverted showing that on past occasions revelation of the identity of its rank-and-file members has exposed these members to economic reprisals, loss of employment, threat of physical coercion and other manifestations of public hostility. . . .

We hold that the immunity from state scrutiny of membership lists which the Association claims on behalf of its members is here so related to the right of the members to pursue their lawful private interests privately and to associate freely with others in so doing as to come within the protection of the Fourteenth Amendment.

In another case,[19] in which two Arkansas cities sought from the N.A.A.C.P. its list of members and contributors, the Supreme Court said:

On this record it sufficiently appears that compulsory disclosure of the membership lists of the local branches of the National Association for the Advancement of Colored People would work a significant interference with the freedom of association of their members. There was substantial uncontroverted evidence that public identification of

[19] Bates v. Little Rock, 361 U.S. 516 (1960). See also Shelton v. Tucker, 81 S. Ct. 247 (1960).

persons in the community as members of the organizations had been followed by harassment and threats of bodily harm. There was also evidence that fear of community hostility and economic reprisals that would follow public disclosure of the membership lists had discouraged new members from joining the organizations and induced former members to withdraw. This repressive effect, while in part the result of private attitudes and pressures, was brought to bear only after the exercise of governmental power had threatened to force disclosure of the members' names. . . . Thus, the threat of substantial government encroachment upon important and traditional aspects of individual freedom is neither speculative nor remote.

Before the Civil War the South was willing to repress and stifle the civil rights and liberties of all citizens in order to maintain slavery;[20] today, much of the same antilibertarian atmosphere persists in an effort to maintain "freedom of association," by which is meant, of course, compulsory segregation of the races. The Aesopian language of the South and its protagonists often tends to create the impression that the South is, in fact, fighting for the fundamental liberties of Americans to live as they please, to associate as they please, that the struggle is to give effect to the ideal of "Live and let live!", although the record of the Southern states shows that, when it has been a question of race relations, they have not been willing to let this question be decided by each person for himself. Instead, the force of the states has interposed itself between man and man, just as today some of the Southern states attempt to interpose themselves between the citizen and the Constitution.

A statement against civil rights laws and fair employment practices acts concludes on the following deep and pious note:

When one's fellow men interpose force and compulsion between him and the Source of his being—whether by the device of government or otherwise—it amounts to interrupting his self-improvement, in conflict with what seems to be the Divine design. Man must be left free to discriminate and to exercise his freedom of choice. This free-

[20] NYE, FETTERED FREEDOM (1949).

dom is a virtue and not a vice. And freedom of choice sows the seeds of peace rather than of conflict.[21]

No mention is made of the Jim Crow laws and customs, of the Black Codes, of the private reprisals, of the economic sanctions that the South has used to deny "freedom of choice."

Nor does the South see that by encouraging flouting of the Constitution in the name of voluntarism, freedom of association, and freedom to discriminate, it is sowing the dragon's teeth of criminality and anarchy; for when children see that their parents have no respect for fundamental law, they cannot help but draw the inference that man lives by might and not by right, that an ounce of force may be worth more than a pound of constitutional law. Enforcement of law in itself is an instrument that aids voluntarism, for when it is certain that "every one who breaks the law will be dealt with by the law, the less will the power of coercion be felt. The more that resistance is seen to be hopeless, the more can the use of force remain latent." [22]

Often, when these arguments are made against the South, the point is made that there is also racial discrimination in the North, and the inference is drawn that the struggle is not really over civil rights but is rather a sectional feud. Of course there is discrimination in the North, but the orders of magnitude are altogether different. While in the North one needs to look for discrimination —and if one looks for it, he will find it—in the South one needs to look for instances of nondiscrimination—and if one looks for such instances, he will find them.

A recent book contains the following statement: "Not long ago there was a great-to-do about the Russian censorship of Pasternak's *Dr. Zhivago*. The editorials and the rhetoric of organized friends of culture kept repeating freedom of speech, freedom of culture. (You would think that we did not have our own means of

---

[21] Harper, Blessings of Discrimination 15 (pamphlet of Foundation for Economic Education, 1951).
[22] Brunner, The Divine Imperative 453 (1957).

censoring, by commercial selection and by swamping.)" [23] In the early years of the Second World War, before Germany declared war on the USSR, when one attacked the Nazi treatment of Jews, fellow-travelers would say: "Look at the U.S.A. Don't we lynch Negroes?" This kind of fallacious reasoning is known in logic as the irrelevant conclusion, the classic example of which is the advice given to an attorney: "You have no case; therefore, abuse the other party's attorney."

In the long run, however, the bad logic and the demagoguery, the incitement to force and violence and mob action will give way to the realization that Burke was right, just, and prudent when he said:

The question with me is, not whether you have a right to render your people miserable, but whether it is not your interest to make them happy. It is not what a lawyer tells me I *may* do, but what humanity, reason, and justice tell me I ought to do. Is a politic act the worse for being a generous one? Is no concession proper, but that which is made from your want of right to keep what you grant? Or does it lessen the grace or dignity of relaxing in the exercise of an odious claim, because you have your evidence-room full of titles, and your magazines staffed with arms to enforce them? [24]

✗ The American people—through Congress, through the Supreme Court, through states' civil rights and fair employment practices acts, through executive action affecting the military and civilian population, and through a Civil War that was the bloodiest and costliest war in American history—have rejected the slavery arguments for the inherent inferiority of the Negro race. With the ending of slavery, a hundred years ago, there should have come an end to the incidents and badges of slavery, concretized in racial segregation enforced by state law and custom. For these badges and incidents of slavery were based on an immoral opinion of what human nature is. Now Americans must

[23] GOODMAN, GROWING UP ABSURD 101 (1960).
[24] BURKE, SECOND SPEECH ON CONCILIATION WITH AMERICA (1775).

still teach one another what it means to be a human being. The choice is not between law as a means and education as a means; for the law is itself a teaching device and education is itself an enforcing device. The disagreements are only superficially over the means. The real disagreements are over the ends—the inclusion of the Negro race in the community of citizens and in the communion of human beings. But in this instance, end and means are inextricably intertwined; for the Constitution, which is a law, demands that the school shall itself be a means and an end: that it be a demonstration of the ideal of equality, and that it contribute to the establishment of a society in which equality is a working ideal. The question that *Ecclesiasticus* asks about one's self can be asked also of a nation: "Who will justify him that sinneth against his own soul? and who will glorify him that dishonoreth his own life?" As the Negro struggles for freedom from dishonor and freedom from indignity,[25] he struggles, too, to free America from dishonor and from indignity. The demand that the Negro makes today is as reasonable as that which Diogenes made of Alexander: "Stand out of my sunshine!"

[25] *Racial Equality*, 27 SOCIAL ACTION, No. 5, 13 (1961).

TABLE OF CASES

TABLE OF STATUTES

FEDERAL STATUTES

STATE STATUTES

INDEX

Abolition, 4-5, 10; *see also* Emancipation; Slavery

Academic freedom, 7

Advertising, barring of discriminatory, 168-71, 188-89

A.F.L., 205; *see also* Labor unions

Africa: transportation of freedmen to, 18-19; effect of winning national independence on U.S. Negroes, 73

Aged, homes for the, discrimination in, 191

Agricultural colleges, 124

Airlines, discrimination in employment practices, 214-15

Alabama: prohibition of manumission, 18; one of Confederate states, 42; and Fourteenth Amendment, 52-55 *passim;* rejection of Thirteenth Amendment, 55*n*; votes against Civil Rights Act of 1870, in House, 60*n*; votes in Senate against Civil Rights Bill of *1957,* 74*n*; denial of right to vote to Negroes, 78-79; school integration issue in, 130; Jim Crowism in transportation in, 132-33; *NAACP* case in, 267-68

Alaska: state civil rights laws in, 157; fair employment practices law, 202

Alcidamus, 24

American Anti-Slavery Society, 130

American Colonization Society, 18-19

American Jewish Committee, 205, 215

Amnesty bill, 92

Anti-Defamation League of B'nai B'rith, 205

Antidiscrimination legislation, effect of, 224

Antilynching act, 71

Antislavery doctrine, spread of, 7

Antislavery societies, 130

Apprenticeships for Negroes, 15, 196; studies on, 216

Argentina, abolition of slavery in, 28*n*

Aristotle, cited, 9*n*, 23-24

Arkansas: no Black Code in, 14*n*; prohibition of manumission, 18; one of Confederate states, 42; and Fourteenth Amendment, 52-55 *passim;* votes against Civil Rights Act of 1870, in House, 60*n*; votes in Senate against Civil Rights Bill of *1957,* 74*n*; Eisenhower's use of federal forces in, 76*n*; school integration issue in, 128, 131; *NAACP* case in, 268-69

Armed forces: freedmen received into, 42; use of, to enforce civil rights statutes, 59, 76; education for children of members of, 85; announcement of pro-integration policy for, by Truman, 260

Attorneys General: duties *re* voting rights, 76, 77, 85-87; civil rights divisions in offices of, 192-93

Baltimore, racial segregation in public parks, 133-34

Battle, John S., member of Commission on Civil Rights, 78*n*, 80*n*

Berea College case, 262-67; dissenting opinion in, 264-65

Berle, Adolf A., Jr., quoted, 139-40

Bethune, Mary McLeod, 194

Bijur, Nathan, 166

Black Codes: passage of, 11, 12-17, 36, 43; Fourteenth and Fifteenth

Index

Latin America, slavery in, 26-35 *passim*

Law: contribution to abolition of slavery, 4-5; attitude toward testimony of Negroes, 17; cost of lawsuits, 179; importance of enforcement of, 270

Learning, institutions of, *see* Education; Public places

Legal rights, protection of, 62-63, 66-68, 85; *see also* Courts; Discrimination

Levitt & Sons and Green Fields Farm case, 246-48

Liberator, 6

Lincoln, Abraham, Emancipation Proclamation, 12, 41, 42

Literacy and literary tests, and voting rights, 81

Lloyd, Arthur Y., quoted, 9-10

Locke, John, 4

Louisiana: early attitude toward slavery in, 6; attitude toward freedmen, 18; one of Confederate states, 42; and Fourteenth Amendment, 52-55 *passim;* votes in Senate against Civil Rights Bill of *1957,* 74n; denial of right to vote to Negroes, 78-79; school integration issue in, 128, 130

Lunch counters, racial segregation at, 134-52 *passim; see also* Sit-ins

Lynch, John, quoted, 94-96

Lynching, 71

"Lynch law," 7

McNamara, Patrick V., quoted, 89n

McPherson, Edward, 45n

Macy, Jesse M., quoted, 17

Maine: state civil rights laws in, 157; discriminatory advertising barred in, 169

Manumission, 17, 18, 21-37

Maryland: a Union slave state, 41; and Fourteenth Amendment, 51n, 53-54, 55-56; rejects Fifteenth Amendment, 57n; votes against Civil Rights Act of 1870 in Congress, 59, 60n; vote on Civil Rights Act of *1960,* 84n; school integration issue in, 131; racial segregation in public parks, 133-34

Massachusetts: on school segregation, 125-30; first state law on discrimination, 155-56; first case in United States under state civil rights statute, 158; discriminatory advertising barred in, 169; Commission Against Discrimination, 182-83, 229, 232-33, 239; civil rights division in office of attorney general, 192; Fair Employment Practices Commission, 201, 215-18; posting of notices, 210-11; racial discrimination as most frequent basis of complaint under FEP laws, 223-24; fair educational practices law, 229, 230; laws against discrimination in public and private housing, 237-42 *passim;* ruling on real estate offices as places of public accommodation, 251

Master race idea, 15

Michigan: state action in, 142-43; civil rights statutes in, 157, 168, 174; discriminatory advertising barred in, 169; civil rights division in office of attorney general, 192; fair employment practices laws, 201, 215-18, 223-24; posting of notices, 210-11; local fair employment practices ordinances in, 220-22 *passim;* prohibitions against discrimination and segregation in schools, 230

Minnesota: state civil rights laws in, 157; fair employment practices laws, 201, 215-18, 220-24 *passim;* prohibitions against discrimination and segregation in schools, 230

Minority: concern with establishment of fundamental rights for, 60-63; *see also specific groups,* e.g., Negroes; *and specific rights,* e.g., Employment

Miscegenation, 50

Mississippi: Black Code adopted in *1865,* 13-14, 15-17, 43; vagrancy law adopted by, 14; prohibition of manumission, 18; one of Confederate states, 42; and Fourteenth Amendment, 52-55 *passim;* rejection of Thirteenth Amendment, 55n; votes in Senate against Civil Rights Bill of *1957,* 74n; school integration issue in, 131

Niebuhr, Reinhold, quoted, 35

Nixon, Richard M., 74

North Carolina: Black Codes of, 15; attitude toward freedmen, 18; one of Confederate states, 42; votes against Civil Rights Act of 1870, in House, 60n; votes in Senate against Civil Rights Bill of *1957,* 74n; and Fourteenth Amendment, 52-55 *passim;* school integration issue in, 131; sit-in demonstrations in, 136; lunch-counter desegregation in, 138

North Dakota, public accommodations statute, 157

Nye, Russell B., 6n; quoted, 7

Office-holding, right to, 50

Office of Production Management, 194

Ohio: anti-Negro elements in, 19; rejection of Fourteenth Amendment, 51n; votes against Civil Rights Act of 1870 in Senate, 59n; state civil rights laws in, 157; fair employment practices laws, 201; posting of notices, 210-11; local fair employment practices ordinances in, 220-22 *passim*

Oklahoma: votes against Civil Rights Act of *1960,* 83n; school integration issue in, 131; sit-in demonstrations in, 136

Onesicritus, 24

Oregon: rejection of Fourteenth Amendment, 51n; state civil rights laws in, 157; discriminatory advertising barred in, 169; fair employment practices in, 183, 215-18, 223-24; Bureau of Labor, 201, 230; fair educational practices law, 229-30; laws against discrimination in public housing, 237-42 *passim;* ruling on real estate offices as places of public accommodation, 251

Paraguay, abolition of slavery in, 28n

Pelham Hall Apartments case, 243-46

Pennsylvania; anti-Negro elements in, 19; reaction to Fugitive Slave Law, 109; state civil rights laws in, 157, 168, 183; discriminatory advertising barred in, 169; fair employment practices laws, 201, 215-18, 223-24; local fair employment practices ordinances in, 220-22 *passim;* prohibitions against discrimination and segregation in schools, 230; fair housing law, 238

Peonage, established by Black Codes, 15

Peru, abolition of slavery in, 28n

Phelps, Wm. W., 99

Philemon, 24

Phillips, Ulrich B., 99; cited, 18

Philosophy, contribution to abolition of slavery, 4-5

Photographs, request for, as part of application to colleges, 233

Pierson, Donald, quoted, 29, 30

Pittsburgh, local ordinances banning discrimination in private housing, 238

Plato, cited, 9

Plessy v. Ferguson case, 128-30, 133, 139

Police power of the state, use of: to enforce "custom" of racial discrimination, 71, 159; to enforce civil rights laws, 147-48, 176, 177, 199, 219, 220, 244-45

Political rights, 14, 66-68, 258; *see also* Voting rights

Poll tax, 14, 85

Portuguese law, influence in Latin America, 32

President's Committee on Civil Rights (1947), recommendations of, 70-72

President's Committee on Government Contracts, 260-61

Primary schools, 228

Private action, distinction between state action and, 136

Private club subterfuge, 183-85, 188-90

Private rights, 147-48

Private schools, 125

Prohibition, similarities and differences between school desegregation and, 261-62

Property rights, 65-68

Public accommodations: state legislation on, 155-93; criteria to deter-